Virtue in Media

This work establishes a contemporary profile of virtue in professional media practice. Author Patrick Lee Plaisance examines the experiences, perspectives, moral stances, and demographic data of two dozen professional exemplars in journalism and public relations. Plaisance conducted extensive personal "life story" interviews and collected survey data to assess the exemplars' personality traits, ethical ideologies, moral reasoning skills and perceived workplace climate.

The chosen professionals span the geographic United States, and include Pulitzer Prize winners and trendsetting PR corporate executives, ranging from rising stars to established veterans. Their thoughts, opinions, and experiences provide readers with an insider's perspective on the thought process of decision makers in media.

The unique observations in this volume will be stimulating reading for practitioners, researchers, and students in journalism and public relations. *Virtue in Media* establishes a key benchmark, and sets an agenda for future research into the moral psychology of media professionals.

Patrick Lee Plaisance is Professor of journalism and media communication at Colorado State University. His research focuses on media ethics theory, moral psychology, journalism values, and media sociology, and he teaches media ethics, reporting and communication theory. Prior to his academic career, he worked for nearly 15 years as a journalist at numerous American newspapers.

Virtue in Media

The Moral Psychology of Excellence
in News and Public Relations

Patrick Lee Plaisance

Routledge
Taylor & Francis Group

NEW YORK AND LONDON

First published 2015
by Routledge
711 Third Avenue, New York, NY 10017

and by Routledge
2 Park Square, Milton Park, Abingdon, Oxon, OX14 4RN

Routledge is an imprint of the Taylor & Francis Group, an informa business

© 2015 Taylor & Francis

Library of Congress Cataloging-in-Publication Data

Plaisance, Patrick Lee.
  Virtue in media : the moral psychology of excellence in news & PR / Patrick Lee Plaisance.
     pages cm.
  Includes bibliographical references and index.
  1. Mass media—Moral and ethical aspects. 2. Journalism—Objectivity. 3. Journalists—Interviews. I. Title.
  P94.P555 2015
  175—dc23
  2014000002

ISBN: 978-0-415-70743-5 (hbk)
ISBN: 978-0-415-70744-2 (pbk)
ISBN: 978-1-315-88676-3 (ebk)

Typeset in Sabon
by Apex CoVantage, LLC

To Atisaya, as always, and to my son Carter

CONTENTS

This book project argues that we have much to gain by looking closely at some of the most successful and ethically admirable media practitioners to better understand what makes them tick. It presents original research conducted over the past six years with a selected group of "exemplars" in journalism and public relations—Pulitzer Prize-winning writers and editors, executives of trendsetting PR firms, veterans and young stars known for their ethical leadership. Their experiences and personal and professional narratives detailed in themed chapters are instructive and inspiring to media ethics scholars and students alike. Their key narrative themes are combined with a quantitative analysis of the exemplars' personality traits, moral reasoning skills, levels of idealism and other factors to construct a "profile" of ethical motivation among media practitioners—a picture of the moral psychology of excellence in news and PR. In short, the media exemplars participating in this study "cluster" to a remarkable degree on these key moral psychology factors. Based on this profile, this book culminates by providing a model of morally motivated self-identity that is largely shaped by features of 1) individuals' moral development, 2) their ethical ideology, 3) their personality traits and 4) their professional environment, or moral ecology. These components, in turn, emphasize a constellation of morally driven principles that are borne out in both the quantitative data and the qualitative "life story" narratives of the exemplars:

- Moral courage
- Concern for welfare of others
- Social justice
- Affirmative respect

- Anticipation of potential harm
- Collaborative tendencies

More broadly speaking, this book is intended to introduce media ethics scholars to moral psychology research approaches and to suggest that such inductive work is critical if the field is to continue maturing as a discipline. Previous research has made use of single research tools among those used here or focused on isolated psychological features of media practitioners. But this project is unprecedented in its scope, harnessing a range of moral psychology instruments to attempt a more holistic picture of media behavior. The research presented here is a mixed-methods approach, and the book's structure mirrors that of a research journal article, making it easily accessible to both students and researchers in media ethics. Chapter 1 provides an overview of the ferment in moral psychology research and the promise it holds for scholarship in media ethics. Chapter 2 details the design of the study of media exemplars. Chapters 3 and 4 present analysis of the survey-based quantitative data. The four chapters that follow present key themes recurring within the exemplars' "life story" narratives: "Professionalism and Public Service," "Moral Courage," "Humility and Hubris" and "Crucibles of Experience." Readers most interested in the exemplars' life story narratives may focus on the chapters devoted to those themes and gloss over the quantitative chapters, or vice versa.

More importantly, this book project promotes an agenda that is both methodological and theoretical in nature. Regarding method, I feel strongly that the future of media ethics as a field of scholarship rests heavily on the ability to build a solid empirical foundation for the normative claims we may wish to make about what media practitioners should or should not do. It is not the job of media ethics scholars to berate media practitioners into being more ethical. They, like everyone else, are already moral agents. Much work needs to be done to better understand important media sociological and psychological factors that help or hinder moral action. This project is a modest effort in this direction. The moral psychology instruments used in this research are far from exhaustive, and it is hoped their demonstrated usefulness may invite more efforts to increase our understanding of the moral lives of media practitioners. Such moral psychology methods open up exciting new paths of scholarship. As such, this project can be considered an attempted antidote to the deductive normative—and often quasi-theological—theorizing that has long dominated our field, particularly the more recent efforts to assert universal ethical standards for media practitioners in every culture.

Such talk of the need for more empirical work to bolster our normative claims can easily be criticized as suffering from the naturalistic fallacy—the longstanding concern among moral philosophers that we cannot assert what *should be* based on observations of what *is*. Hence, the second theoretical component of this project's agenda. The moral psychology profile that emerges here—indeed, the whole of moral psychology as an approach for inquiry—dovetails with the framework of neo-Aristotelian virtue ethics. Rather than draw on deontological claims that predominate media ethics scholarship, this book project argues that a more fruitful path lies in exploring connections between desirable, pro-social behavior and how individuals grasp (and ultimately can be taught to embrace) notions of virtue. Focusing on the moral lives of individuals using this approach—truly *attending to* myriad individual manifestations of virtue—may better anchor our normative claims in a way that deductive calls for "doing one's duty" do not. This path of inquiry also ushers exciting opportunities to glimpse the universal: Such research offers ways to more formally explore these manifestations across political, economic and cultural environments, to better explain relationships among variables and clarify potentially important distinctions. It is in this spirit, as a small step onto this path, that this book project is offered.

ACKNOWLEDGEMENTS

The number of people who have given encouragement, inspiration, assistance and guidance since this project's inception is too large to list here. As with most worthwhile research, collaboration is part of its soul. Above all, I owe a debt of gratitude to the two dozen professional men and women across the country who agreed to participate in this study. They were asked to devote several hours each, subjecting themselves to lengthy survey questionnaires and probing personal interviews over the last few years. Without their generosity of time, attention and spirit, this sort of research simply would not be possible. Time and again, I was humbled and inspired by you all. My debt to Atisaya, Wife and Executive Editor, is one that will never be fully repaid. My son Carter and daughter Simone have my gratitude for enduring incessant research trips. I thank Chuck Huff of St. Olaf College and his research colleagues for providing the initial inspiration for this project with their work with exemplars in the computer science field. I also drew heavily from Anne Colby and William Damon's landmark book on moral exemplars, *Some Do Care: Contemporary Lives of Moral Commitment.* I am deeply grateful to Clifford Christians for his time, attention and mentorship over the years and to Linda Bathgate for her enduring support of media ethics scholarship. I wish to thank Lee Wilkins for her support and encouragement, and as always, I am lucky to have Elizabeth Skewes as such a congenial partner in research. I also am grateful to my department and to the College of Liberal Arts at Colorado State University for ongoing support of my scholarship.

INTRODUCTION

Virtue in Journalism and Public Relations

The aim of most media ethics books—often explicit, sometimes implied—is to cultivate and/or advocate for better behavior in media. The vast majority do so by dwelling on instances of moral failure, on examples of harm stemming from moments of thoughtlessness, on damage done when the better angels of our professional lives take a back seat to expedience, profit maximization and other less noble motives. This is not one of those books. Instead, the motivational claim here is that we, as media ethics theorists, researchers and educators, have much work to do in building a better empirical knowledge base about the personal, psychological and environmental influences that factor into virtuous behavior. A survey of the media ethics research landscape makes clear that, for all our praise of media work that embodies virtue, our understanding of virtue in professional media work remains both abstract and rudimentary. It is abstract in that the work in media ethics theory so often focuses on broad, normative claims about how journalists and others in media work should think this way or that, yet doing so in a way that does not seriously attempt to account for actual behavior. It remains rudimentary in that the field has not articulated a theory that accounts for the range of influences that encourage or prevent moral action. This book attempts to provide an avenue to do so.

A good way to begin developing such a theory is by systematically studying those who are admired for their high-quality work and the standards they maintain. This is not to say merely that the brightest lights of journalism and public relations should be studied so that more people can try to better emulate them—while that would indeed be a great outcome, as a goal, it is a bit simplistic. The value of research on exemplars is much broader than that. By looking closely at the psychological makeup of those who are among the most admired in their fields, by studying the motivations, passions and features of what makes exemplars tick, we can begin to better understand the composition of professional virtue itself—not as a shimmering, atomistic quality that is either present or absent, but as the product of a constellation of factors that help or hinder one's ability to perform moral action.

Why study media exemplars? This project is rooted in a rich tradition of exemplar research in virtue theory, sociology and psychology. For Confucius and his followers, emulation of models and exemplars was among the most efficient methods of learning and indeed serves as a key structure of the *Analects,* the enduring moral code dating to 500 B.C. As with most any focus on virtuous behavior, it underscores the writings of the ancient Greeks; "What the superior man thinks is good, that is what is *really* good," Aristotle wrote (Maslow, 1971, p. 9). The pretentious air of such a statement notwithstanding, those who are admired for their ability to manifest virtue in their work, to exhibit moral courage, to pursue quality despite obstacles, undoubtedly can help illuminate the virtuous potential of us all. Discerning patterns among traits, values and motivations of exemplars will inevitably strengthen the empirical foundation for our media ethics theorizing and better anchor our normative claims in the narratives of experience. Such work gets us closer to "a generally applicable, empirically adequate account of actual moral functioning," as John Doris and Stephen Stich argued (2006, pp. 15–16). Researchers, by studying exemplars' responses to institutional and professional pressures, also have gained valuable insights about what skills, traits and critical thinking strategies to cultivate in education and professional training programs as a way to lay the groundwork for more exemplary behavior. While definitions vary, exemplars are individuals whose work is perceived as embodying the principles and best potential of their field. They are not saints. But they are respected by their peers, not just for the degree of professional success they have achieved but for a sustained commitment to quality. They also are considered manifestations of *professionalism* in the original sense of the word: They exhibit a professed commitment not to mere craft or advancement but to the idea of maintaining a focus on a bigger picture—of performing duties in the service of something bigger than themselves, of serving the public through the utilization of their skills and talents. Abraham Maslow, the iconoclastic psychologist who devoted much of his life work to studying various types of exemplars, said such people have achieved a state of "self-actualization":

> Self-actualizing people are, without one single exception, involved in a cause outside their own skin, in something outside of themselves.

They are devoted, working at something, something which is very precious to them—some calling or vocation in the old sense, the priestly sense. They are working at something which fate has called them to somehow and which they work at and which they love, so that the work-joy dichotomy in them disappears.

(1971, p. 43)

Moral exemplars, moreover, are "people who have shown long-standing commitment to moral purposes, thus exemplifying good principles and virtues," according to theorists Anne Colby and William Damon (1992, p. 27). Both Colby and Damon are leery of throwing the term "moral exemplar" around loosely and use it with caution, since people's moral values can vary widely, and any such moral heroes inevitably suffer from human imperfection. Indeed, researchers have even suggested that there are multiple types of moral exemplars, with distinctive "virtues" attached to specific kinds of moral excellence (Walker & Hennig, 2004). The term is used only suggestively here as well. Yet, the carefully selected 24 individuals that serve as the basis for this study, while representing nowhere near a comprehensive list, are considered exemplary in many ways. They were selected through a process of professional peer referral, and they include some of the most widely known and respected names in journalism and public relations. The 12 journalism exemplars hold five Pulitzer Prizes among them and are visionaries in the worlds of print and digital news. The 12 PR professionals include top corporate executives who have been credited with shaping professional ethics in PR and also include multiple recipients of the Gold Pick and Silver Anvil awards, the highest honors bestowed by the Public Relations Society of America. All were generous with their time, subjecting themselves to probing "life story" face-to-face interviews that often ran two hours or more and gave their responses to an intensive, 13-page survey assessing everything from their personality traits to their politics. While the lives and experiences of the exemplars focused on here are not intended as representative of a "leadership" group in journalism or public relations, they do span a diverse range of backgrounds, political orientations and demographic makeup. Some are young stars relatively new in their careers; many are established veterans at the peak of their professions. A few have recently retired. They include 12 women and 12 men, Caucasians, African-Americans and Asians, liberals and conservatives, Jews, Christians and resolute agnostics. They hail from 10 states: California, Colorado, Florida, Illinois, Maryland, Massachusetts, Missouri, Nebraska, New York and Virginia. All were interviewed between April 2010 and September 2012. Those willing to be identified include:

- Ron Culp, former managing partner of Ketchum in Chicago and former PR chief of corporations including Sears, Pitney Bowes and Sara Lee.
- Peter Pitts, former managing partner of Porter-Novelli in New York, former communications chief for the U.S. Food and Drug Administration and cofounder of the Center for Medicine in the Public Interest.
- Julie Hall, former executive vice president of Schneider Public Relations in Boston and coauthor of *The New Launch Plan: 152 Tips, Tactics and Trends from the Most Memorable New Products.*
- Felicia Blow, vice president of Paul D. Camp Community College in southeast Virginia.
- Mark Seibel, managing editor of the Washington, D.C. bureau of McClatchy Newspapers and Pulitzer Prize recipient.
- Denis Finley, editor of the Norfolk *Virginian-Pilot.*
- Laura Frank, executive director of the Rocky Mountain News Network and Denver-based veteran investigative journalist.
- Margaret Freivogel, editor of the *St. Louis Beacon* and Missouri Medal recipient.
- Ellyn Angelotti, digital trends and social media faculty member at the Poynter Institute for Media Studies in St. Petersburg, Florida.
- David Donald, data and computer-assisted reporting editor for the Center for Public Integrity in Washington, D.C.
- Lane DeGregory, staff writer for the *Tampa Bay Times* and Pulitzer Prize recipient.
- Jim Brady, editor of Digital First Media and president of the board of directors of the Online News Association.

(In all subsequent chapters, pseudonyms will be used for all quotes and anecdotes to maintain guarantees of confidentiality, except for specific instances in which exemplars agree to have their names attached.) While they were not chosen based on any presumption that they were morally superior, as a group, they produced moral reasoning scores that were above the average moral-development levels of journalists and PR professionals who were studied in earlier research (Coleman & Wilkins, 2009; Wilkins & Coleman, 2005). In considering themes of their personal and professional histories, together with their extensive survey responses, some exciting patterns begin to emerge: a shared notion of reformative justice, a personal ethos of humility that nonetheless features patterns of moral courage and significant hubris, a sense of moral development forged by pivotal experiences. Some significant quantitative patterns, too, emerge in the relationships among the exemplars' moral reasoning skills, personal outlooks and traits and their ethical ideologies.

Such focus on the exemplary among us is humbling, inspiring and theoretically instructive. Maslow called such research focusing on the nature of exemplars and their manifestations of virtuous work "growing-tip" research. "[I]t is at the growing tip of a plant that the greatest genetic action takes place. As the youngsters say, 'That's where the action is'" (1971, p. 7). John F. Kennedy didn't call the dozen politicians he wrote about in *Profiles of Courage* "exemplars," but he treated them as models of political courage and presented their life stories as instructive in the same vein: "the ideals they lived for and the principles they fought for, their virtues and their sins, their dreams and their disillusionments, the praise they earned and the abuse they endured" (1961, p. 21). Maslow (1971) argued that if we wanted to learn about the possibilities of human potential, we must study the most effective and enlightened among us. His development of concepts such as self-actualization and peak experience has helped form the foundation of humanistic psychology research, which focuses on the value and meanings of human experience:

> If we want to answer the question how tall can the human species grow, then obviously it is well to pick out the ones who are already tallest and study them. If we want to know how fast a human being can run, then it is no use to average out the speed of a "good sample" of the population; it is far better to collect Olympic gold medal winners and see how well they can do. If we want to know the possibilities for spiritual growth, or moral development in human beings, then I maintain that we can learn most by studying our most moral, ethical or saintly people.
>
> (1971, p. 7)

In their landmark study, Colby and Damon (1992) identified a constellation of traits and attitudes driving moral exemplars. The researchers concluded that exemplars devote a significant amount of their resources to fulfill their perceived moral commitments. They also exhibit a strong commitment to public service, often inspiring others to do the same. Samuel Oliner and Pearl Oliner (1988) studied the motivations and characteristics of Europeans who risked their lives to rescue Jews during World War II. Lawrence Walker (1999) found meaningful differences in personality traits among selected moral, religious and spiritual exemplars. Daniel Hart and Suzanne Fegley (1995) found that adolescents nominated as community leaders described themselves in terms of moral personality traits and yet were no more advanced in their moral reasoning skills than "average" youths. Researchers also have studied selected exemplars to better grasp the dynamics of altruism (e.g., Hoehn, 1983; Lee, Kang, Lee & Park, 2005; Mastain, 2007). Researcher Chuck Huff and colleagues discerned important patterns of values, work habits and personality traits among a selected group of exemplars in the computer science field (Huff & Barnard, 2009; Huff, Barnard, & Frey, 2008a, 2008b). Arguing compellingly for a multidimensional understanding of virtuous action, their work is based on a four-component model that suggests the ability to perform virtuous work is rooted in personality traits, internalization of morality, moral ecology, moral skills and knowledge. This study also can be considered an answer, in its own small way, to the call for a better understanding of what we mean by "expertise," including moral expertise. Experts, no matter from what field, tap their vast knowledge in unique ways and have honed a gift for seeing not only the bigger picture but how to maximize their potential within it, Darcia Narvaez and Daniel Lapsley (2005) argued:

> Experts in morality, like experts of all kinds, can be expected to perceive and act upon the world in a markedly different way than do moral novices. For example, experts in moral sensitivity are able to more easily pick up on the morally relevant affordances in the environment (e.g., What is my role in this situation? What should I do? What am I capable of doing? What does the context allow?). . . . Indeed, to study how far humans can develop in skill and knowledge in any domain, we must study experts. This should be as true for moral psychology as for any other domain.
>
> (2005, pp. 151–152)

Focus on exemplars is not without precedent in media ethics, though other works take a more normative, abstract angle. In their 2009 volume featuring two dozen "moral mentors" from Jesus to Confucius, Clifford Christians and John Merrill compellingly argued that these figures illustrated the "diversity of means to the universal ends of personal and social betterment" (p. 1). Similarly, Sharon Bracci and Clifford Christians showcased a dozen theorists who offer diverse ethical frameworks for further work in communication ethics (2002).

To write about the dispositions, motives and achievements of media exemplars, and to leave it at that, is merely interesting. But the aim here is much more substantial. These exemplars provide the connective tissue for a virtue ethics framework that has power to energize both media ethics theory and media practice. In his 2010 essay, "Media Ethics: Towards a Framework for Media Producers and Media Consumers," ethicist Nick Couldry made a compelling argument that the nature and reach of our contemporary global media system requires a serious retooling of our normative ethics that accounts more fully for our interactivity and audience participation in media content. He suggested the superiority of a neo-Aristotelian virtue ethics over a focus on duty and sketched the outlines of such a framework for a global media ethic:

> In Aristotle's original virtue ethics, the reference point was a view of "human nature" that very few if anyone would now accept because of its offensive features (women as "naturally" inferior to men, "barbarian" others as naturally inferior, slaves as "naturally" second-class humans); clearly such features must be discarded from any workable neo-Aristotelianism today. But, unless we deny that there is such a thing as human nature, Aristotle's questions remain a useful starting point even if they may not yield all we need to know about how to act in particular media-related situations. . . . Aristotelian virtue ethics (by contrast with other types of virtue ethics) takes as its reference point the degree to which virtuous dispositions will contribute to "human flourishing," that is, a good life individually and together.
>
> (2010, pp. 65–66)

Couldry's reference to "human flourishing" here echoes the virtue ethics of Philippa Foot, which is central to the normative claims of this book. Citing the limits of an ethical theory based on a Kantian notion of practical reason, Foot returned virtue ethics to a central place in moral philosophy with her landmark 2001 book, *Natural Goodness*. Virtuous behavior, she said, is that which contributes to human flourishing, just as a good root system is critical for the health of an oak tree. "No one can act with full practical rationality in the pursuit of a bad end," she noted (p. 14). Drawing on Foot's work, this project aims, among other things, to bring virtue ethics to the forefront of media ethics theorizing, using the profiles and lessons of these exemplars to do so.

Some will inevitably argue that the approach suggested here is not sufficiently normative, or even that it unsuccessfully tries to skirt the naturalistic fallacy—that is, it implies or outright posits *ought* statements through mere descriptions of what *is*. But dismissing the value of research in moral psychology and the experiential focus of researchers in humanistic psychology as merely descriptive would be erroneous and based on an incomplete account of virtue ethics. Both bodies of work open up avenues for exciting projects in an interpretive ethics that can only lend added heft to the normative, universalist claims we might ultimately embrace. Both essential dimensions of our work as media ethicists—our philosophical theorizing and our harnessing of social science modes of inquiry—cannot represent a zero-sum game. The relationship between the two should be discursive rather than mutually exclusive. Far from setting aside the tenets of classical and contemporary philosophy, the moral psychology research approach presented here opens new opportunities to understand, engage and influence the conditions of virtuous behavior in media practice so that they might more clearly reflect our ethical (and universal) principles. Kirk Schneider and colleagues counter recent assaults on the emergent field of humanistic psychology and the premium it places on human experience: "[C]onsider what the personal dimension (the intimate and resonant) could bring to psychology's various components—to the statistical mindset of methodology, the standardization mentality of psychotherapy, the group consciousness of multiculturalism, the nihilism of poststructuralism" (2001, p. xxiv). Similarly, media ethics can only grow as a field with more such interdisciplinary, empirical and interpretive efforts. Too often moral philosophers and ethicists arguably have relied upon normative claims without an adequate grounding in, and even shunning, the social science fields—a state that has hindered ethics theorizing, Doris and Stich argued:

> The thought that moral philosophy can proceed unencumbered by facts seems to us an unlikely one: there are just too many places where answers to important ethical questions require—and very often presuppose—answers to empirical questions. . . . [T]hese literatures are often deeply relevant to important debates, and it is therefore intellectually irresponsible to ignore them.
>
> (2005, pp. 115–116)

At the very least, we must recognize the implicit challenge of moral psychology to the trend in media ethics theorizing of championing the universal:

> Thinking of normative ethical knowledge as something to be gleaned from thinking about human good relative to particular

ecological niches will make it easier for us to see that there are forces of many kinds, operating at many levels, as humans seek their good; that individual human good can compete with the good of human groups and nonhuman systems; and finally, that only some ethical knowledge is global—most is local, and appropriately so.

(Flanagan, Sarkissian & Wong, 2008, p. 19)

Focus on the individual experiences of the many opens portals through which we might glimpse the universal. Such inductive inquiry is by nature local, contextual—and parsimonious. But it is simultaneously suggestive, interpretive—and ultimately discursive with universalist claims and assumptions, enabling us to clarify the validity and legitimacy of our normative notions.

The immediate value of such a study should be apparent. By methodically constructing a profile of media exemplars, this study adds something to the media ethics field that it does not yet have. Such a documentation of themes, patterns and relationships among factors that influence exemplars' abilities to perform the virtuous and admired work that they do provides an unprecedented window into the nature of "moral functioning." Yet, beyond this profile of virtue in media, the broader intent of this project is twofold. The first is theoretical. The essence of any worthwhile theory-building in social science depends largely on the discursive quality produced by a combination of effective deductive and inductive efforts. Close study of subjects in the media trenches, aimed at fully understanding their motivations, contextual pressures and their levels of self-actualization, serves to increase the authority of our prescriptions for a more ethical media system. It will also be argued later that the profile of virtue in media presented here provides compelling justification for a media ethic of "pluralistic universalism" promoted by many prominent theorists—that we can articulate a credible set of "core" ethical principles (such as integrity, responsibility, public service) that ought to drive the behavior of all media professionals while also acknowledging that the manifestations of those principles necessarily depend on social, cultural and professional contexts. The second intent here is methodological. It is hoped that the dual-method approach used in this study demonstrates the value and enormous potential of a more systematic application of well-established research instruments and methods drawn from social and moral psychology. As media ethics scholars, we must make more use of empirical strategies because doing so gives us a more solid foundation for identifying structural weaknesses in our media systems and for prescribing grounded normative claims. The phenomenological analysis used here to uncover themes and sense-making in the life story interviews also can open up new possibilities of theorizing about motivations and behavior.

As a field, media ethics arguably enjoys an overabundance of normative claims. Too often, media ethics research appears to have put the normative cart in front of the empirical horse. The need now is for more systematic efforts to interpret and assess actual practices and motivations of those working in media—to build theory by more effectively completing the discursive cycle between abstract norms and motivated behavior. As the field of media ethics grows, it will not be enough to simply become more eloquent in espousing this or that normative philosophical framework for media practice. The maturation of media ethics theory also hinges on our ability to develop stronger interdisciplinary skills, to draw upon and harness established social science theories and methodologies. And in our radically transforming media landscape, the need to do so has never been more urgent. Ultimately, it will be the quality of the discursive blend of our dual-approach research that will lend the greatest power—and authenticity—to our call for a universalist ethic in media.

Chapter 1 (Moral Psychology: The Grand Convergence) provides an overview of moral psychology as a field that focuses on the intersection of human sciences and moral deliberation. Interested as it is in the interaction between behavior and moral claims, the field emphasizes virtue ethics rather than the "rightness" of specific actions. This chapter provides a brief survey of key claims and conclusions of recent moral psychology research, thereby suggesting the enormous potential of applications of moral psychology to media research and providing context for the aims of this study. Chapter 2 (Design of an Exemplar Study) lays out the mixed-method design of this study. The five-component survey instrument is in reality four surveys in one, using established tools to measure personality traits, ethical ideologies, perceived ethical workplace climate and moral reasoning skills—all combined with a wide range of demographic data. This empirical approach is complemented by the use of a well-known "life story" interview format, the transcripts of which are then analyzed using a more qualitative, phenomenological method to closely examine the meanings of personal and professional experiences of the exemplar subjects. Chapter 3 (A Profile of Media Exemplars by the Numbers) is the first of two chapters that present results of quantitative analysis of the survey data, focusing on descriptive statistics derived from demographic information and the various survey components. Chapter 4 (Patterns That Point to Virtue) continues the quantitative analysis with inferential statistics that examine the relationships among personality traits, moral reasoning, ethical ideologies and other factors. It also will explore ways in which these relationships point to key themes in the exemplars' life story interviews. Chapter 5 (Professionalism and Public Service) is the first of four chapters that examine prominent, recurring themes discerned from the life story interview transcripts. Uniformly, the journalism and PR exemplars articulated a driving sense of public service in their work and emphasized how central this was to their professional satisfaction. Chapter 6 (Moral Courage) explores the notion of moral courage, or perseverance, in the face of personal and professional adversity, challenges and criticism. Far from expressing pride or boastfulness, the exemplars often articulated this idea of moral courage through examples of "trials by fire," which served to define and refine their motivations and professional outlooks. Chapter 7 (Humility and Hubris) explores the apparent twinned dynamic of exemplary achievement—while their anecdotes and narratives regularly showcased a high degree of modesty by emphasizing team efforts, help received and opportunities offered, exemplars also often exhibited some of the more egoistic features often associated with high achievement, such as elitism, entitlement and exceptionalism. Chapter 8 (Crucibles of Experience) discusses how exemplars perceive the powerful effects of key moments in their personal and professional lives, from childhood traumas to career triumphs, to which they attribute their ambitions, passions and motivations. The Conclusion (Lessons for Media Ethics Theory) provides a synthesis of the key findings based on survey and interview data and suggests how it all contributes to a profile of virtue in media, culminating in a proposed "model of the morally motivated self." It also will lay out an avenue for further applications of moral psychology research to build media ethics theory.

REFERENCES

Bracci, S.L., & Christians, C.G. (2002). *Moral engagement in public life: Theorists for contemporary ethics.* New York: Peter Lang.

Christians, C.G., & Merrill, J.C. (2009). *Ethical communication: Moral stances in human dialogue.* Columbia: University of Missouri Press.

Colby, A., & Damon, W. (1992). *Some do care: Contemporary lives of moral commitment.* New York: Free Press.

Coleman, R., & Wilkins, L. (2009). The moral development of public relations practitioners: A comparison with other professions and influences on higher quality ethical reasoning. *Journal of Public Relations Research 21* (3), 318–340.

Couldry, N. (2010). Media ethics: Towards a framework for media producers and media consumers. In *Media ethics beyond borders: A global perspective* (S.J.A. Ward & H. Wasserman, Eds.), 59–72. New York: Routledge.

Doris, J.M., & Stich, S.P. (2005). As a matter of fact: Empirical perspectives on ethics. In *The Oxford handbook of contemporary philosophy* (F. Jackson & M. Smith, Eds.), 114–152. Oxford: Oxford University Press.

Doris, J.M., & Stich, S.P. (2006). Moral psychology: Empirical approaches. In *Stanford Encyclopedia of Philosophy*. Available: http://plato.stanford.edu/entries/moral-psych-emp/. Retrieved 3 February 2012.

Flanagan, O., Sarkissian, H., & Wong, D. (2008). Naturalizing ethics. In *Moral psychology (Vol. 1: The Evolution of morality: Adaptations and innateness)* (W. Sinnott-Armstrong, Ed.), 1–25. Cambridge, MA: MIT Press.

Foot, P. (2001). *Natural goodness*. Oxford: Oxford University Press.

Hart, D., & Fegley, S. (1995). Prosocial behavior and caring in adolescence: Relations to self-understanding and social judgment. *Child Development 66*, 1346–1359.

Hoehn, R.A. (1983). *Up from apathy: A study of moral awareness and social involvement*. Nashville, TN: Abingdon Press.

Huff, C.W., & Barnard, L. (2009, Fall). Moral exemplars in the computing profession. *IEEE Technology and Society Magazine*, 49–54.

Huff, C.W., Barnard, L., & Frey, W. (2008a). Good computing: A pedagogically focused model of virtue in the practice of computing (part 1). *Journal of Information, Communication and Ethics in Society 6* (3), 246–278.

Huff, C.W., Barnard, L., & Frey, W. (2008b). Good computing: A pedagogically focused model of virtue in the practice of computing (part 2). *Journal of Information, Communication and Ethics in Society 6* (4), 284–316.

Kennedy, J.F. (1961). *Profiles in courage*. New York: Harper and Brothers.

Lee, D.Y., Kang, C.H., Lee, J.Y., & Park, S.H. (2005). Characteristics of exemplary altruists. *Journal of Humanistic Psychology 45* (2), 146–155.

Maslow, A. (1971). *The farther reaches of human nature*. New York: Viking Press.

Mastain, L. (2007). A phenomenological investigation of altruism as experienced by moral exemplars. *Journal of Phenomenological Psychology 38*, 62–99.

Narvaez, D., & Lapsley, D.K. (2005). The psychological foundations of everyday morality and moral expertise. In *Character psychology and character education* (D.K. Lapsley & F.C. Power, Eds.), 140–165. South Bend, IN: University of Notre Dame Press.

Oliner, S.P., & Oliner, P.M. (1988). *The altruistic personality: Rescuers of Jews in Nazi Europe*. New York: Free Press.

Schneider, K.J., Bugental, J.F.T., & Pierson, J.F. (Eds.) (2001). *The handbook of humanistic psychology: Leading edges in theory, research and practice*. Thousand Oaks, CA: SAGE.

Walker, L.J. (1999). The perceived personality of moral exemplars. *Journal of Moral Education 28* (2), 145–162.

Walker, L.J., & Hennig, K.H. (2004). Differing conceptions of moral exemplarity: Just, brave, and caring. *Journal of Personality and Social Psychology 86* (4), 629–647.

Wilkins, L., & Coleman, R. (2005). *The moral media: How journalists reason about ethics*. Mahwah, NJ: Lawrence Erlbaum Associates.

CHAPTER 1

Moral Psychology: The Grand Convergence

Imagine that you are the driver of a municipal trolley. While serving your route and coasting down an incline, you realize that the trolley's brakes have failed. Panic-stricken, you look ahead and see, working on the track, a group of five men. You are unable to warn them to jump out of the way; on your present course, your trolley will surely run them down and kill them. However, you also see a small rail spur in front of the spot where the men are working. You have the ability to switch your trolley to the spur and thus avoid a catastrophe. But just as you realize this, you see a sixth worker dutifully working alone on the rail spur, and again, you have no way of warning him. What do you do? How might you morally justify your actions? How might you explain that switching to the spur and killing the single worker is more defensible than not acting at all and killing the five? Then consider this: While you are frantically trying to contemplate your impossible choices, also up ahead is a footbridge over the trolley tracks. Standing on the bridge, watching your trolley, is a man named George. George instantly realizes that your trolley is out of control, and he is familiar enough with trolleys to know that the only way to stop it would be to drop a very heavy weight in its path. But the only available, sufficiently heavy weight is a fat man next to him on the bridge. George, too, then, also has a dilemma: He can either shove the fat man down onto the track, thereby killing him, or he could refrain from doing this, and thus let the workers die. What might be George's most defensible course of action, and why?

The scenario above was first proposed by moral philosopher Philippa Foot in 1967 and later expanded upon by Judith Jarvis Thomson in 1976. While it is just one of many such dilemma scenarios that have preoccupied philosophers for centuries, the "Trolley Problem," as Foot's came to be called, is among the more famous. Foot's point was to make us think about the moral weight we assign to our intentions and to the various duties we have to others. Since our duty to avoid harming others is paramount, usually trumping other "positive" duties such as giving aid, more harm is avoided by switching to the rail spur, she concludes. But what about a surgeon who could also save five lives by killing a patient and distributing her organs to five other people who would otherwise die? The math is the same, but Foot says the moral equation is quite different: Unlike the trolley driver, who confronts the conflict between the two "negative" duties of avoiding harm to one or to five, the surgeon must weigh a negative duty against the "positive" duty of rendering aid. In such cases, both Foot and Jarvis argued, our duty to refrain from inflicting harm on others trumps our duty to provide aid to others. Thus, George, watching the trolley from the footbridge, must opt for "letting die" and refrain from "killing":

> Here is something bad, up for distribution, a speeding trolley. If nothing is done, five will get it, and one will not; so five will die and one will live. It strikes us that it would be better for five to live and one die than for one to live and five die, and therefore that a better distribution of the bad thing would be for the one to get it, and the five not to. If the one has no more claim against the bad thing than any of the five has, he cannot complain if we do something to *it* in order to bring about that it is better distributed: i.e., it is permissible for [the driver] to turn [the trolley]. But even if the one has no more claim against the bad thing than any of the five has, he can complain if we do something to *him* in order to bring about that the bad thing is better distributed: i.e., it is not permissible for George to shove his fat man off the bridge into the path of the trolley [author's emphasis].
>
> (1976, p. 215)

The Trolley Problem gets us into the realm of moral psychology, or the study of the intersection of behavior, motivations and questions about our moral agency. The Trolley Problem and its variants have engaged not only moral philosophers but neuroscientists, economists and evolutionary psychologists. It also has spawned a huge body of work, research and commentary known as "trolleyology," which "makes the Talmud look like CliffsNotes," joked one philosopher (Appiah, 2008). Such moral psychology dilemma exercises have engaged a wide range of philosophers and scientists, not necessarily because they illuminate how we might act in the most moral fashion when faced with a crisis, but because they suggest how we might better understand moral functioning itself. Philosophers and ethicists are most concerned with exploring our reasons for embracing certain principles, such as avoidance of harm and courage, and with articulating justifications for using those principles to guide actions in a given situation. Psychologists, neuroscientists and cognitive researchers are interested in all the various forces that shape our behavior—personality traits, dispositions, motivations, social contexts, cultural environments. Moral psychology, then, is a valuable, transdisciplinary arena of theory and research that brings all these concerns together, encouraging us to construct a more holistic view of human behavior and moral deliberation. We don't make judgments in vacuums. We are neither creatures of abstraction, who blindly follow our moral beliefs whatever situation we find ourselves in, nor are we simply a collection of nerve endings that respond impulsively to any external stimuli. Two researchers, Daniel Cervone and Ritu Tripathi, hinted at the daunting complexity facing psychologists interested in studying the nature of the moral life:

> The components of moral functioning that are identified [in decades
> of research on moral reasoning] encompass psychological functions
> that are diverse: interpreting situations, formulating courses of
> action, contemplating and selecting among alternative values
> that bear on a given circumstance, executing courses of action.
> If one considers also the psychological structures and processes
> (declarative and procedural knowledge, affective systems, cognitive
> appraisal processes, etc.) that may come into play as individuals
> execute each of these four functions (interpreting, formulating,
> selecting, executing), the resulting set of psychological systems is
> so diverse that it becomes difficult to identify systems that are *not*
> involved in moral reasoning or action [authors' emphasis].
>
> (2009, p. 30)

Moral psychology theorists argue that moral philosophers and social scientists must learn from each other and join forces to cultivate a more comprehensive understanding of human moral agency. Philosopher and cognitive theorist Owen Flanagan and his colleagues described the need for this sort of synthesis that explores the interconnectedness of moral theory with theories of our social and psychological lives:

> Moral imperatives and judgments can guide action and motivate
> individuals not because of anything internal to their syntax,
> semantics, or logical structure, still less because our biology makes

us think that they refer to something objective, but rather because of how they relate to vital human needs, desires, interests, such as a need for safety, security, friendship, reciprocity, and a sense of belonging. . . . Without these contingent facts about the species *Homo sapiens,* morality would be inert.

(Flanagan, Sarkissian & Wong, 2008, p. 47)

This chapter provides a brief survey of the field of moral psychology as the basis for this study of exemplars in journalism and public relations. It will summarize key claims of the field, review the issues that have been emphasized in recent research and outline major debates among moral psychology theorists. It will then review central implications of moral psychology research regarding moral development, education and normative claims. Finally, it will discuss the value of and need for media ethics researchers to draw on moral psychology methods and theory, toward which this study of media exemplars is but a rudimentary step, to strengthen and mature the field.

OVERVIEW OF MORAL PSYCHOLOGY

"Ethics must not—indeed cannot—*be* psychology, but it does not follow that ethics should *ignore* psychology" [authors' emphasis] (Doris & Stich, 2005, p. 115). This challenge by two prominent moral psychology theorists, John Doris and Stephen Stich, could be considered the galvanizing slogan for the field. For much of the twentieth century, philosophy and science went their separate ways. Moral philosophers had little use for the empirical sciences, fearful of what is known as the naturalistic fallacy, or committing illogical leaps from the descriptive to the normative—that is, asserting claims about what we *should* do based on mere descriptions of the way things *are.* Such "ought" statements can never be justified by stating what is, and the naturalistic fallacy rightly remains a concern in moral philosophy. An unfortunate result, however, was that "too many moral philosophers and commentators on moral philosophy . . . have been content to invent their psychology or anthropology from scratch" (Darwall, Gibbard & Railton, 1997, pp. 34–35). Social scientists, conversely, had little use for the abstract and largely unquantifiable claims of philosophy, fearful of resting "hard science" on deceptively simple and often muddled assumptions behind the nature of values and other "squishy" concepts. Consequently, the mutual exclusivity of the two realms has "discouraged investigators in the biological, behavioral and social sciences from undertaking philosophically informed research on ethical issues" (Doris & Stich, 2005, p. 115). As a result, the field of moral philosophy developed largely ignorant of developments in biology and psychology, and empirical researchers studying human behavior kept bumping up against broader, moral implications of the personal and social dynamics that their "scientific" language was hard-pressed to incorporate. But since the 1990s, however, many philosophers have drawn on recent advances in cognitive psychology, brain science and evolutionary psychology to inform their work. And many scientists in those fields have recognized the potential explanatory power of incorporating the language of moral philosophy.

As a discipline, moral psychology concerns itself with the intersection of human sciences and moral deliberation. It is a central focus of researchers in philosophy, psychology, neuroscience and even anthropology and economics. As such, the field touches on both the profound and the prosaic. By studying tragically brain-damaged individuals, researchers have gained insight in the workings of our brains when we make moral decisions. Other research seeks to tease out the nature of norms and values that appear to be universal, in contrast to culturally bound concepts. For example, the field has something to say about the persistence of clashing conservative and liberal ideologies. Psychologist Jonathan Haidt (2001, 2007) has developed what he and others call five "foundational" moral principles that, more or less, most rational people embrace as important:

- Harm/care. It is wrong to hurt people; it is good to relieve suffering.
- Fairness/reciprocity. Justice and fairness are good; people have certain rights that need to be upheld in social interactions.
- In-group loyalty. People should be true to their group and be wary of threats from the outside. Allegiance, loyalty and patriotism are virtues; betrayal is bad.
- Authority/respect. People should respect social hierarchy; social order is necessary for human life.
- Purity/sanctity. The body and certain aspects of life are sacred. Cleanliness and health, as well as their derivatives of chastity and piety, are all good. Pollution, contamination and the associated character traits of lust and greed are all bad.

Haidt's research shows that liberals feel strongly about the first two principles, preventing harm and ensuring fairness but only minimally embrace the other three. In contrast, conservatives place greater value on loyalty, authority and purity, which often strike liberals as backward or outdated. Conservatives, too, embrace the value of harm prevention and fairness, but not with the zeal of liberals. Political writer Will Wilkinson described this dichotomy:

> While the five foundations are universal, cultures build upon each to varying degrees. Imagine five adjustable slides on a stereo equalizer that can be turned up or down to produce different balances of sound. An equalizer preset like "Show Tunes" will turn down the bass and "Hip Hop" will turn it up, but neither turns it off. Similarly, societies modulate the dimension of moral emotions differently, creating a distinctive cultural profile of moral feeling, judgment and justification. If you're a sharia devotee ready to stone adulterers and slaughter infidels, you have purity and in-group pushed up to 11. PETA members, who vibrate to the pain of other species, have turned in-group way down and harm way up.
>
> (Jacobs, 2009, pp. 50–51)

PSYCHOLOGY, REASONING AND MORAL EXEMPLARS

More broadly, moral psychology research represents a valuable effort to provide a strong empirical foundation for normative ethics theorizing by suggesting connections between the theories and methodologies of psychology and the values and principles of moral philosophy. The link between virtue theory and moral psychology, in fact, was made as early as 1958, when Anscombe sought to shift the focus of the philosophy of ethics away from systems analysis to the concept of virtue. Most recently, Appiah (2008) articulated the relationship between moral psychology and virtue ethics, which, according to Doris and Stich, typically left the notion of "character" unanalyzed beyond a simplistic disposition to act in a certain way (Doris and Stich, 2005, pp. 116–123). Virtuous action, as more applied ethics research is suggesting, is not contingent on character *or* context but on the complex interchange between character *and* context. As Robert Solomon, a contemporary philosopher, noted, "circumstances and character cannot be pried apart and should not be used competitively as alternative explanations of virtuous or vicious behavior" (2005, p. 654). Moral psychology is less concerned with justifying the rightness of specific *actions*, as is the case with Kantianism, utilitarianism and other frameworks, and aligns itself instead with virtue ethics and the concern of what constitutes notable *character*. Consequently, in addition to drawing on hugely expensive and sophisticated neurology and brain-scan technology, research in moral psychology also utilizes more straightforward, paper-based psychological survey instruments that effectively measure individuals' personality traits, values systems, ethical ideologies and moral reasoning skills. With these instruments, empirical researchers have been able to "operationalize" or quantify important philosophical and ethical concepts such as moral development, empathy and people's relative emphasis placed on concerns about pursuing justice and avoiding harm. Moral psychology "investigates human functioning in moral contexts, and asks how these results may impact debate in ethical theory," according to Doris and Stich (2006, p. 1).

This is not to say that such rigorous, empirical approaches should replace important qualitative ways of knowing. All human activity is interpretive, and much of what is accepted as knowledge defies the empiricist framework. Clifford Christians, James Carey (1981) and others have eloquently described the power and essential nature of nonquantitative modes of research. In its multidisciplinary approaches, moral psychology is aimed at augmenting both the rich conceptualizing power of more qualitative approaches and the deductive, normative claims we so often make about moral agency. "[I]t is a matter of empirical facts and not of metaphysical speculation that we touch life in terms of patterns, connections and relationships which constitute for us the meaning of our experiences and indeed our lives," said theorist Hans Peter Rickman (1961, p. 30). Rather than provide merely a descriptive ethics, moral psychology provides a basis to develop an interpretive analysis of those connections and relationships. In their adaptation of Jonathan Haidt's model of moral intuition and social influence for a science engineering education context, psychology researcher Chuck Huff and colleagues studied a group of computer science "exemplars." They found important patterns of values, work habits and personality traits among their computer science exemplars. Two distinct exemplar types emerged: the "craftperson" and the "reformer." The craftperson tended to focus on clients and users, perceived themselves as quality service providers and drew primarily on existing professional values (user focus, customer need, software quality). Reformers, in contrast, appeared concerned with perceived injustices in the social system and sought to use their expertise to influence organizational, professional and social values to address them (Huff & Barnard, 2009).

MORAL REASONING, HARM AND CULTURE

A predominant trend in the field has been a focus on documenting neurologically based commonalities among moral perceptions and what key individual factors might determine moral decision making and moral judgments (see Doris & Stich, 2006). Researchers are realizing that "all moral judgments reflect the complex output of numerous psychological processes—controlled cognition, mental-state reasoning, emotional responding—and that individual and cultural differences emerge at every level" (Young & Saxe, 2011, p. 323). Moral psychology research also is aimed at clarifying important distinctions of broad moral concepts. Take the concept of harm, for example. The nature of harm and the relative weight of various types of harm (e.g., acts that directly result in harm compared with harm caused by omission) have been worked over extensively by moral philosophers. When asked to assess scenarios that parallel the Trolley Problem (cause harm to one and thus spare more people, for example), researchers found striking differences in the ability of people to articulate reasons, or principles, for their moral judgments. In other words, some people showed conscious reasoning about their judgments—harm caused by direct action was worse than harm cause by omission—while others appeared to act solely on their hunches, or intuitions, when it came to rejecting harm intended as a means to a goal rather than accepting harm caused as a side effect of a goal (Cushman, Young & Hauser, 2006). What this means is that we most likely make moral judgments in multiple ways—sometimes really thinking about why something is good or bad and sometimes just relying on our intuitions, *depending on the type of potential harm we might be contemplating.* Other work in moral psychology seeks to pinpoint what exactly makes something "moral" or not and thus when and why a perception or claim motivates moral judgment. Take, for example, the concept of disgust. Disgust often has nothing to do with any moral judgment, such as the disgust one feels when stepping in dog poop. (One might be driven to seek out the dog's owner and heap moral opprobrium on him or her, but that's another matter.) But disgust also comes in a "moralized" form, such as one's disgust at concentration camps. What exactly defines the difference? In his study on disgust norms, Shaun Nichols argued that "normative claims that are 'affect-backed,' i.e., that prohibit an action that is emotionally upsetting, will be better remembered than non-affect-backed normative claims" (2002, p. 243). For example, research has found that people are not as offended by "affectively neutral normative violations," such as a dinner guest drinking tomato soup out of a bowl, as they are when confronted with "affectively charged normative violations," such as a dinner guest spitting into a water glass before drinking from it—even when the host says such behavior is OK. Nichols, in his analysis of sixteenth-century etiquette norms that are preserved in contemporary norms, concluded that the overwhelming number of norms that survive are ones tied to emotional responses on disgust—such as "contemporary manners that continue to frown upon groping one's crotch, ear picking, retching, and projectile spitting" (2002, p. 251). "[I]t might well be that some of our moral norms gained an edge in cultural fitness by prohibiting actions that are likely to elicit negative affect," Nichols concluded (pp. 251–252). While disgust likely has evolutionary roots, it is mainly a cultural product: Young children will put almost anything into their mouths and will not develop "contamination sensitivity" until age 5 to 7 (Rozin, Hammer, Oster, Horowitz & Marmora, 1986). Haidt and colleagues argued that, based on their cross-cultural research, people base disgust responses on a set of "embodied schemata," or "patterns of experience that are based on bodily knowledge or sensation," that rests on a sense of "core disgust" but that results in wide cultural variations (Haidt, Rozin, McCauley & Imada, 1997, p. 122). They conclude: "socio-moral disgust is not a quirk of the English language. People in all cultures have bodies which provide them with rich sets of embodied schemata. Each culture draws from these schemata to spin its own particular 'webs of significance,' upon which its social and moral life is based" (p. 128).

MORAL JUDGMENT AND BRAIN SCIENCE

The field of moral psychology also encompasses an exciting and burgeoning body of neuroethics research that has explored how different parts of the brain "light up" or exhibit increased blood flow when subjects are presented with different types of ethical dilemmas using magnetic imaging techniques such as fMRI (e.g., Fehr & Camerer, 2007; Greene, Nystrom, Engell, Darley & Cohen, 2004; McGuire, Langdon, Coltheart & Mackenzie, 2009; Moll & de Oliveira-Souza, 2007; Spitzer, Fischbacker, Herrnberger, Grön & Fehr, 2007). Researchers are concluding that "there is no specifically moral part of the brain" (Greene & Haidt, 2002, p. 522) but rather that many different parts of the brain play a role depending on the type of dilemma we are struggling with and the emotional resonance of the issue. In one of these efforts, the researchers concluded that "neural activity in classically 'cognitive' brain regions predicts a particular type of moral judgment behavior, thus providing strong support for the view that both 'cognitive' and emotional processes play crucial and sometimes mutually competitive roles" (Greene et al., 2004, pp. 396–397). In another, researchers found that damage to the ventromedial prefrontal cortex "increases 'utilitarian' choices in moral dilemmas (i.e., judgments favoring the aggregate welfare over the welfare of fewer individuals), strongly supporting the notion that normal moral judgments spring from a complex interaction of cognitive and emotional mechanism relying on specific neural structures" (Moll & de Oliviera-Souza, 2007, p. 319). Researchers also have been able to manipulate individuals' moral judgments by magnetically stimulating key areas of the brain, such as the right temporo-parietal junction (RTPJ). As Liane Young and Rebecca Saxe described:

> Participants with a high RTPJ response weigh beliefs and intentions more heavily when judging accidental harms, assigning less blame for the unintended bad outcome; participants with low response blame more on the basis of outcome alone. Temporarily disrupting RTPJ activity using transcranial magnetic stimulation also result in more outcome-based moral judgments.
>
> (2011, p. 324)

This groundbreaking work challenges assumptions in ethics theory about the nature of moral development, the function of free will, the homogeneity of ethical dilemmas, the usefulness of using scenarios to gauge ethical decision making and even the deliberative nature of how people respond to ethical dilemmas. Such neuroscience work also appears to be settling longstanding debate over whether moral judgments are the result of emotional and nonrational processes or of reasoning. As Joshua Greene and Jonathan Haidt concluded, "findings from several areas of cognitive neuroscience have begun to converge on an answer: emotions and reasoning both matter, but automatic emotional processes tend to dominate" (2002, p. 517).

MERGING FACTS AND VALUES: PHILIPPA FOOT

Among the intellectual forebears of moral psychology was an unassuming Oxford professor who spent 40 years building her case challenging the orthodoxy of moral philosophy, which held that values were entirely different in nature from facts: We could not "prove" or verify them, and therefore their objective existence was always suspect. While her Trolley Problem made her famous, it only occupied a few brief lines out of a large body of philosophical essays. More importantly, Philippa Foot, who was the granddaughter of Grover Cleveland and who died in 2010, was among the most prominent contemporary philosophers who effectively argued that our "facts" and our moral interpretations are connected and that virtues such as courage and wisdom are indispensable to human life. The orthodoxy of moral philosophy beforehand had always been that facts and values are logically independent: In nature, we can see objective "facts" through science; values, in contrast, were considered only "attitudes" in our heads that we project onto the world as we like. But through the 1950s, 1960s, 1970s and 1980s, Foot developed her argument that we can clearly see "objective" reasons for acting morally if we focus on virtues and vices (temperance, avarice) rather than on more difficult, abstract concepts such as the nature of goodness and duty. In her landmark 2001 book, *Natural Goodness*, she argued that vice is a defect in people the same way that poor roots are a defect in a tree or poor vision a defect in an owl: The two "natural" cases have clear normative implications (what "ought" to be) yet are also entirely factual. Foot in essence compellingly argued that, yes, even from a scientific view, you could identify good and evil in the world. This, ultimately, helped open the door between philosophy and science to begin talking to each other in a new, exciting and productive way.

OUR EMOTIONS DRIVE OUR REASONS: JONATHAN HAIDT

This chapter began with Foot's provocative runaway trolley scenario; here is another one—not from a philosopher but from someone from the other side of the Atlantic and of the empirical divide: a Virginia psychologist.

> Julie and Mark are brother and sister. They are traveling together in France on summer vacation from college. One night they are staying alone in a cabin near the beach. They decide that it would be interesting and fun if they tried making love. At the very least it would be a new experience for each of them. Julie was already taking birth control pills, but Mark uses a condom too, just to be safe. They both enjoy making love, but they decide not to do it again. They keep that night as a special secret, which makes them feel even closer to each other. What do you think about that? Was it OK for them to make love? (Haidt, 2001, p. 814)

With this what-if case, Jonathan Haidt challenged the long-standing assumptions about how we make moral judgments. Rather than drawing on our capacity for reason and carefully deliberating the ways in which Julie and Mark might be considered not guilty of any moral transgression or morally blameworthy for violating a legitimate social taboo, Haidt argued that we instead tend to make quick evaluative judgments driven more by the importance of social and cultural factors. His landmark 2001 article, "The Emotional Dog and its Rational Tail," argued that cognitive and social science research has effectively revolutionized our understanding of moral deliberation. Our moral judgments, Haidt said, should be studied "as an interpersonal process" (p. 814). The typical moral condemnation with which we are likely to greet Julie and Mark's story, Haidt says, can be best described as follows:

> In the social intuitionist model, one feels a quick flash of revulsion at the thought of incest and one knows intuitively that something is wrong. Then, when faced with a social demand for a verbal justification, one becomes a lawyer trying to build a case rather than a judge searching for the truth. One puts forth argument after argument, never wavering in the conviction that Julie and Mark were wrong, even after one's last argument has been shot down. In the social intuitionist model it becomes plausible to say, "I don't know, I can't explain it, I just know it's wrong."
>
> (2001, p. 814)

This approach, Haidt argued, is more consistent with research in a wide range of empirical fields such as social and cultural psychology and anthropology. Just as cognitive processing and bias-perception research strongly suggests that systematic reasoning rarely supersedes existing attitudes, Haidt suggested that "moral reasoning" doesn't deserve the starring role it's been given in the ethical deliberations that people supposedly perform. Instead, Haidt's "social intuitionist" model of morality says people really only use actual reasoning skills to make moral judgments when the judgment might affect other people. Otherwise, he argued, people instantly draw on their preconceived judgments, and they "rarely override their initial intuitive judgments just by reasoning privately to themselves because reasoning is rarely used to question one's own attitudes or beliefs" (2001, p. 819). Haidt's influential argument is a direct descendant of David Hume's famous assault on the assumed primacy of reason: "We speak not strictly and philosophically when we talk of the combat of passion and of reason," Hume wrote. "Reason is, and ought only to be the slave of the passions, and can never pretend to any other office than to serve and obey them" (1739–1740/1969, p. 462). Haidt concluded that breakthroughs in neurology and cognitive science have indeed brought us full circle:

> Rationalist models made sense in the 1960s and 1970s. The cognitive revolution had opened up new ways of thinking about morality and

moral development, and it was surely an advance to think about moral judgment as a form of information processing. But times have changed. Now we know (again) that most of cognition occurs automatically and outside of consciousness . . . and that people cannot tell us how they really reached a judgment. . . . Now we know that the brain is a connectionist system that tunes up slowly but is then able to evaluate complex situations quickly. . . . Now we know that emotions are not as irrational[,] . . . that reasoning is not as reliable[,] . . . and that animals are not as amoral . . . as we thought in the 1970s. The time may be right, therefore, to take another look at Hume's perverse thesis: that moral emotions and intuitions drive moral reasoning, just as surely as a dog wags its tail.

(2001, p. 830)

Taken together, the work of a British woman who recast moral philosophy and the work of an American man who applies the power of empiricism to theories of moral judgment, illustrates the grand convergence, in all its disruption and excitement, that is the field of moral psychology research.

DEBATES IN THE FIELD

There are many points on which moral psychology theorists have reached wide agreement. One is the fundamentally multidimensional nature of our moral lives. We are "pluralistic" in the values that we hold, prioritizing them differently based on specific factors of a given situation. We are neither mere bundles of emotional impulses nor are we automatons who adopt a moral framework and proceed to apply it uniformly in every dilemma. Researchers also have embraced a range of well-tested psychological tools that are used to measure factors that influence moral cognition: personality traits, value systems, moral reasoning skills and also more technologically sophisticated tools: brain scans such as magnetic resonance imaging and psychometric instruments. But moral psychology also is a field of great ferment. High-stakes debates are frequent and robust. Theorists continue to struggle with how best to explain the neurological processing involved in our moral judgments. There is continuing heated debate among moral psychology researchers regarding how we might say with confidence that behavior is consistently governed by robust psychological traits (the "globalist" position) despite how outside factors so often seem to dictate the likelihood that people act on, or fail to act on, traits such as courage and generosity (the "situationist" argument) (see Kamtekar, 2004; Ross & Nisbett, 1991). Also, the "nativist" debate rages: whether or not, or to what extent, we humans are "hard-wired" with a set of ideas about what is "moral" and what isn't. Are our moral norms largely evolutionary adaptations? Some say they are (Ruse & Wilson, 1986); others say they are not (Ayala, 1987, 1995). Eighteenth-century Scottish philosopher Francis Hutcheson claimed that "the Author of Nature has determin'd us to receive . . . a Moral Sense, to direct our Actions, and to give us still nobler Pleasures" (1725/1994, p. 75), and his view still carries weight with evolutionary and developmental psychologists. In their extensive body of research, for instance, Leda Cosmides and John Tooby argued that the brain apparently does have some sort of innate component of moral functioning:

> Our ancestors have been members of social groups and engaging in social interactions for millions and probably tens of millions of years. To behave adaptively, they not only needed to construct a special map of the objects disclosed to them by their retinas, but a social map of persons, relationships, motives, interactions, emotions, and intentions that made up their social world. . . . [T]he evolved architecture of the human mind contains functionally specialized, content-dependent cognitive adaptations for social exchange.
>
> (1992, pp. 163, 220)

Others, however, strongly oppose such views, arguing they rest on shaky assumptions and wishful thinking. "All this talk of [moral] modules and mechanism may make some shudder, especially if they recall that eugenics emerged out of an effort to find the biological sources of evil," researcher Jesse Prinz argued. "Morality, like all human capacities, depends on having particular biological predispositions, but none of these, I submit, deserves to be called a 'moral faculty' " (2008, pp. 367–368).

REASON AND EMOTION IN MORAL JUDGMENTS

The nativist debate is closely tied to the one over how best to explain the relationship between rationality and emotion in our moral judgments. The pioneering developmental psychologist Lawrence Kohlberg insisted that reason played a central role in our moral judgments with his cognitive development theory and rejected "irrational emotive theories" (1971, p. 188). He regularly insisted on a rationalist and even Platonic model in which "affect" may be taken into account by reason but in which reason ultimately calls the shots—"moral reasoning is the conscious process of using ordinary moral language," he said (Kohlberg, Levine & Hewer, 1983, p. 69). Others, such as Haidt, have rejected this idea, arguing instead that any "reasoning" that goes on in our judgments is post hoc—we're being lawyers arguing our point of view after we've made our decisions, not judges seeking the truth. We are hard-wired so that our emotional triggers, or "affective" responses, have a key, and perhaps at times a primary, role in the structure of our moral decision making:

> When we engage in moral reasoning, we are using relatively new cognitive machinery that was shaped by the adaptive pressures of life in a reputation-obsessed community. We are capable of using this machinery dispassionately, such as when we consider abstract problems with no personal ramifications. But the machinery itself was "designed" to work with affect, not free of it, and in daily life the environment usually obliges by triggering some affective response.
>
> (Haidt, 2007, p. 1000)

Moral psychology researchers continue to try to refine the relationship between rationality and intuition—a sense that something's "just the right thing to do," or that an act "is just wrong." Emotions play a "critical role" in most all of our moral judgments, Nichols argued (2004). Greene and colleagues (2004) proposed a two-system model for moral judgment in which one system is characterized by the engagement of cognitive systems—we actually weigh justifications for doing or not doing something—and another system is characterized by the engagement of affective systems, where we rely on our gut reaction. Other theorists have found further support for this view (Cushman et al., 2006).

But there are still other ways to think about the dynamic of moral judgments. One is an "epidemiological" theory about moral norms first developed by Dan Sperber (1996). This approach seeks to identify and isolate features of human psychology that are universal (e.g., we all have an ability to reason about physics), combined with a claim that certain ideas and norms, within specific cultural environments, are more likely to survive than others. In other words, certain ideas may emerge as more attractive and psychologically resonant in different cultural contexts and thus will be preserved and handed down through generations. The flexibility of this epidemiological approach, psychologists say, can account for the wide range of ways that "harm" is understood across cultures—why the Yanomamo tribesmen award any captured women as wives to warriors, but only after she is raped by all the raiders (Chagnon, 1992, p. 190), or why Hopi Indian children routinely captured birds to torture and starve them even though Hopi culture acknowledges the creatures as sentient beings (Brandt, 1959, p. 102). This idea of "cultural fitness" is the focus of much attention. Nichols argued further that emotional systems also constitute yet another factor in shaping what norms get adopted in a culture and which do not. "[T]he epidemiological approach is entirely consistent with rich normative diversity," argued Nichols (2002, p. 240). "The epidemiological approach merely tries to explain which norms, once they emerge in a culture, will survive better."

One of the valuable results of the interaction of philosophers and empirical scientists in moral psychology research is that each group has forced the other to clarify and refine what exactly they mean when they use terms and concepts. For example, there is a rich line of inquiry into the nature and origins of social taboos such as incest. To what extent are moral objections to incest innate or culturally cultivated? Can we separate out the moral dimension of such a taboo from its evolutionary biological function? In her work on cultural oppositions to incest, Debra Lieberman argued that our moral prohibitions against incest are evolutionary "by-products" of other psychological and social needs (2008). However, others argue that she is mistakenly using the term "moral sentiments" when she isn't talking about morality at all. Richard Joyce argued that Lieberman, in her efforts to place her findings within a larger philosophical framework, misuses the term "moral." We must be more careful, he said, in our distinctions between psychological motivations (i.e., is an aversion to incest a cultural "by-product" or result of more direct pro-social motivations?) and explicitly moral matters (i.e., someone has transgressed a norm and is blameworthy) (Joyce, 2008, pp. 198–199).

IMPLICATIONS FOR EDUCATION AND PEDAGOGY

In the *Republic,* Plato discussed the need to cultivate moral skills in individuals, just as they are taught professional skills or crafts. Similarly, the study of exemplars, expertise and moral judgment making has prompted educators to implement strategies to cultivate moral knowledge, and even help provide the basis for moral intuition in the classroom. Haidt, in promoting his "social intuitionist" model of moral reasoning, said we mistakenly assume our decision making is guided by rationalism and that "a correct understanding of the intuitive basis of moral judgment may therefore be useful in helping decision makers avoid mistakes and in helping educators design programs (and environments) to improve the quality of moral judgment and behavior" (2001, p. 815). Moral psychology research has opened exciting possibilities for cultivating future exemplars by focusing on moral skills and knowledge in the classroom. Indeed, developmental psychologists are directing their own research to explore what kinds of moral-education strategies may be most effective. For example, Darcia Narvaez has proposed a character-development model for schools called Integrative Ethical Education, based on expertise research and on the theory that we develop our "moral sense" through four distinct processes:

- Ethical sensitivity: Our ability to quickly and accurately "read" a situation to determine what role we might play and to generate effective solutions that take possible consequences into account.
- Ethical judgment: Our ability to bring existing mental "schemas," or mental frameworks, to bear on complex problems.
- Ethical motivation: Our ability to place value on an ethical "ideal" and thus define ourselves in terms of moral traits.
- Ethical action: Our ability to focus on both the issue at hand and on ethical principles and follow through on a resolution (Narvaez, 2002).

Chuck Huff and his colleagues take a similarly holistic approach in their call for a more integrated ethics-training component for the engineering professions. Huff and colleagues (2008a, 2008b) drew on a detailed study of selected exemplars in the computer science field specifically to help build a pedagogical model for cultivating moral skills in training programs. They detailed key features in online classes for science and engineering ethics that "exercise the moral imagination and help to produce moral sensitivity" (Huff & Frey, 2005, p. 404). The goal of their research was to help "understand how computer professionals sustain ethical action in their careers, with the aim that this model will help us to think through the pedagogy of professional ethics" (2008a, p. 248). Studying media exemplars offers similar value to journalism and communication programs in general and media ethics curriculum in particular.

APPLICATION TO MEDIA ETHICS

Exposure to ethics theory and extensive exploration of ethical dilemmas do seem to have an effect on media ethics students. This author has used the Forsyth Ethics Position Questionnaire (1980), which provides a reliable assessment of people's levels of idealism and the degree to which they see the world in relativistic terms—key dimensions of one's "ethical ideology." In a study of 106 students enrolled in a media ethics course over 3 years, the author found that both their levels of idealism and their relativistic thinking significantly decreased after taking the course. This suggests that course content resulted in students' recognizing greater complexity in the world and that, as moral agents, our actions are judged largely on the effect they may have on others and not merely on our own self-interested interpretations and justifications (Plaisance, 2007).

While journalists and public relations professionals haven't yet been put into fMRI machines so that researchers might study their brains' blood-flow activity when they're presented with ethical dilemmas, media researchers have begun applying theories and methods of moral psychology. Most notably, researchers have documented the moral-reasoning skills of journalists and PR professionals. Lee Wilkins and Renita Coleman have used the Defining Issues Test (DIT) (Rest, 1973, 1974), which has assessed the moral development of tens of thousands of people, in multiple professional and social populations, over several decades. In their study of 249 journalists around the country, Wilkins and Coleman found that, despite widespread cynicism about the ethics of journalists, their average moral reasoning "P score" was relatively high, at 48.68, suggesting they were at the upper reaches of what moral development theorists call standard, or "conventional" reasoning levels. The journalists ranked just below the average for seminarians, philosophers, medical students and practicing physicians—all of whom generally have much more formal education than most journalists. For comparison, American adults in general have an average P score of 40, and that of high school students is 31 (Wilkins & Coleman, 2005, pp. 37–39). PR professionals scored an average of 46.2 on the DIT—a few notches below that of journalists, dental students and nurses (Coleman & Wilkins, 2009, p. 333).

There have been other moral psychology efforts in media research, many of which make use of the Forsyth Ethics Position Questionnaire (EPQ) instrument rather than the DIT. (This study used the Forsyth measurement and the DIT, both of which are discussed in more detail in Chapter 3). A partial explanation may be the differences in the ease of use of each. Whereas the DIT presents test subjects with up to six scenarios and requires them to spend 20 minutes or more responding to 12 statements for each, the much briefer Forsyth EPQ presents 20 brief statements with which subjects are asked to agree or disagree. Using the EPQ, researchers have found that PR professionals with high idealism and low relativism scores had a greater tendency to make stricter ethical judgments of professional PR standards (Kim & Choi, 2003). Also, marketers who have higher levels of idealism tend to emphasize ethical values and social responsibility more than those with lower levels (Singhapakdi,

Kraft, Vitell & Rallapalli, 1995). Also, consumers' moral judgments on sexual- and fear-based appeals in advertising seems to be tied to their levels of idealistic thinking (Maciejewski, 2004; Treise, Weigold, Conna & Garrison, 1994). Most recently, an ambitious study of journalists in 18 countries drew on the EPQ and concluded that journalists' ethical orientations—the degree to which they embraced values such as honesty and the duty to avoid harm—varied in meaningful ways based on their cultures and their news organizations (Plaisance, Hanitzsch & Skewes, 2012).

While valuable, these efforts are largely fragmentary, applying moral psychology methods and measures piecemeal. Moreover, they only hint at efforts to fully incorporate psychological theories of cognition, motivation and dispositions. Clearly, there is enormous potential to advance media research by bringing moral psychology to bear in a more systematic way. The following chapters elaborate on one modest effort to do so.

REFERENCES

Anscombe, G.E.M. (1958). Modern moral philosophy. In *Collected philosophical papers*. Oxford, UK: Basil Blackwell, 26–42.

Appiah, K.A. (2008). *Experiments in ethics*. Cambridge, MA: Harvard University Press.

Ayala, F. (1987). The biological roots of morality. *Biology & Philosophy 2*, 235–252.

Ayala, F. (1995). The difference of being human: Ethical behavior as an evolutionary by-product. In *Biology, ethics, and the origins of life* (H. Rolston, Ed.), 113–135. Boston: Jones & Bartlett.

Brandt, R. (1959). *Ethical theory*. Englewood Cliffs, NJ: Prentice Hall.

Cervone, D., & Tripathi, R. (2009). The moral functioning of the persona as a whole: On moral psychology and personality science. In *Personality, identity, and character: Explorations in moral psychology* (D. Narvaez & D.K. Lapsley, Eds.), 11–29. New York: Cambridge University Press.

Chagnon, N. (1992). *Yanomamo* (4th ed.). New York: Harcourt Brace Jovanovich.

Christians, C.G., & Carey, J.W. (1981). The logic and aims of qualitative research. In *Research methods in mass communication* (G.H. Stempel & B.H. Westley, Eds.), 342–362. Englewood Cliffs, NJ: Prentice-Hall.

Coleman, R., & Wilkins, L. (2009). The moral development of public relations practitioners: A comparison with other professions and influences on higher quality ethical reasoning. *Journal of Public Relations Research 21* (3), 318–340.

Cosmides, L., & Tooby, J. (1992). Cognitive adaptations for social exchange. In *The adapted mind: Evolutionary psychology and the generation of culture* (J.H. Barkow, L. Cosmides & J. Tooby, Eds.), 163–228. New York: Oxford University Press.

Cushman, F., Young, L., & Hauser, M. (2006). The role of conscious reasoning and intuition in moral judgment. *Psychological Science 17* (12), 1082–1089.

Darwall, S., Gibbard, A., & Railton, P. (Eds.). (1997). *Moral discourse and practice: Some philosophical approaches*. New York: Oxford University Press.

Doris, J.M., & Stich, S.P. (2005). As a matter of fact: Empirical perspectives on ethics. In *The Oxford handbook of contemporary philosophy* (F. Jackson & M. Smith, Eds.), 114–152. Oxford: Oxford University Press.

Doris, J., & Stich, S. (2006). Moral psychology: Empirical approaches. In *Stanford Encyclopedia of Philosophy*. Available: http://plato.stanford.edu/entries/moral-psych-emp/. Retrieved 3 February 2012.

Fehr, E., & Camerer, C.F. (2007). Social neuroeconomics: The neural circuitry of social preferences. *Trends of Cognitive Sciences 11* (10): 319–427.

Flanagan, O., Sarkissian, H., & Wong, D. (2008). What is the nature of morality? A response to Casebeer, Railton and Ruse. In *Moral psychology (Vol. 1: The evolution of morality: Adaptations and innateness)* (W. Sinnott-Armstrong, Ed.), 45–52. Cambridge, MA: MIT Press.

Foot, P. (1967). The problem of abortion and the doctrine of the double effect. *Oxford Review 5*, 5–15.

Foot, P. (2001). *Natural goodness*. Oxford: Oxford University Press.

Forsyth, D.R. (1980). A taxonomy of ethical ideologies. *Journal of Personality and Social Psychology 39* (1), 175–184.

Greene, J., & Haidt, J. (2002). How (and where) does moral judgment work? *Trends in Cognitive Sciences 6* (12), 517–523.

Greene, J.D., Nystrom, L.E., Engell, A.D., Darley, J.M., & Cohen, J.D. (2004). The neural bases of cognitive conflict and control in moral judgment. *Neuron 44*, 389–400.

Haidt, J. (2001). The emotional dog and its rational tail: A social intuitionist approach to moral judgment. *Psychological Review 108* (4), 814–834.

Haidt, J. (2007). The new synthesis in moral psychology. *Science 316*, 998–1002.

Haidt, J., Rozin, P., McCauley, C., & Imada, S. (1997). Body, psyche and culture: The relationship between disgust and morality. *Psychology and Developing Societies 9* (1), 107–131.

Huff, C.W., & Barnard, L. (2009, Fall). Moral exemplars in the computing profession. *IEEE Technology and Society Magazine*, 49–54.

Huff, C.W., Barnard, L., & Frey, W. (2008a). Good computing: A pedagogically focused model of virtue in the practice of computing (part 1). *Journal of Information, Communication and Ethics in Society 6* (3), 246–278.

Huff, C.W., Barnard, L., & Frey, W. (2008b). Good computing: A pedagogically focused model of virtue in the practice of computing (part 2). *Journal of Information, Communication and Ethics in Society 6* (4), 284–316.

Huff, C., & Frey, W. (2005). Moral pedagogy and practical ethics. *Science and Engineering Ethics 11* (3), 389–408.

Hume, D. (1739–1740/1969). *A treatise of human nature*. London: Penguin.

Hutcheson, F. (1725/1994). *An inquiry concerning the original of our ideas of virtue or moral good*. In *Philosophical writings* (R.S. Downie, Ed.), 67–113. London: J.M. Dent.

Jacobs, T. (2009, May-June). Morals authority. *Miller-McCune*, 46–55.

Joyce, R. (2008). Aversions, sentiments, moral judgments, and taboos. In *Moral psychology (Vol. 1: The evolution of morality: Adaptations and innateness)* (W. Sinnott-Armstrong, Ed.), 195–203. Cambridge, MA: MIT Press.

Kamtekar, R. (2004). Situationism and virtue ethics on the content of our character. *Ethics 114*, 458–491.

Kim, Y., & Choi, Y. (2003). Ethical standards appear to change with age and ideology: A survey of practitioners. *Public Relations Review 29* (1), 79–89.

Kohlberg, L. (1971). From is to ought: How to commit the naturalistic fallacy and get away with it in the study of moral development. In *Cognitive development and epistemology* (T. Mischel, Ed.), 151–235. New York: Academic Press.

Kohlberg, L., Levine, C., & Hewer, A. (1983). *Moral stages: A current formulation and a response to critics*. Basel, Switzerland: Karger.

Lieberman, D. (2008). Moral sentiments relating to incest: Discerning adaptations from by-products. In *Moral psychology (Vol. 1: The evolution of morality: Adaptations and innateness)* (W. Sinnott-Armstrong, Ed.), 165–190. Cambridge, MA: MIT Press.

Maciejewski, J.J. (2004). Is the use of sexual and fear appeals ethical? A moral evaluation by Generation Y college students. *Journal of Current Issues and Research in Advertising 26* (2), 97–105.

McGuire, J., Langdon, R., Coltheart, M., & Mackenzie, C. (2009). A reanalysis of the personal/impersonal distinction in moral psychology research. *Journal of Experimental Social Psychology 45*, 577–580.

Moll, J., & de Oliveira-Souza, R. (2007). Moral judgments, emotions and the utilitarian brain. *Trends in Cognitive Sciences 11* (8), 319–321.

Narvaez, D. (2002). Integrative ethical education. In *Handbook of moral development* (M. Killen & J. Smetana, Eds.), 703–732. Mahwah, NJ: Lawrence Erlbaum Associates.

Nichols, S. (2002). On the genealogy of norms: A case for the role of emotion in cultural evolution. *Philosophy of Science 69*, 234–255.

Nichols, S. (2004). *Sentimental rules: On the natural foundations of moral judgment*. New York: Oxford University Press.

Plaisance, P.L. (2007). An assessment of media ethics education: Course content and the values and ethical ideologies of media ethics students. *Journalism & Mass Communication Educator 61* (4), 378–396.

Plaisance, P.L., Hanitzsch, T., & Skewes, E.A. (2012). Ethical orientations of journalists across the globe: Implications from a cross-national survey. *Communication Research*.

Prinz, J.J. (2008). Is morality innate? In *Moral psychology (Vol. 1: The evolution of morality: Adaptations and innateness)* (W. Sinnott-Armstrong, Ed.), 367–406. Cambridge, MA: MIT Press.

Rest, J.R. (1973). Morality. In *Cognitive development* (J. Flavell & E. Markman, Eds.). Manual of Child Psychology, 4th ed., vol. 3, 556–629. New York: John Wiley & Sons.

Rest, J.R. (1974). Manual for the Defining Issues Test (unpublished manuscript), University of Minnesota.

Rickman, H.P. (1961). Introduction. In *Pattern and meaning in history* (W. Dilthey). New York: Harper & Row.

Ross, L. & Nisbett, R.E. (1991). *The person and the situation: Perspectives of social psychology*. Philadelphia, PA: Temple University Press.

Rozin, P., Hammer, L., Oster, H., Horowitz, T., & Marmora, V. (1986). The child's conception of food: Differentiation of categories of rejected substances in the 16 months to 5 year range. *Appetite 7*, 141–151.

Ruse, M., & Wilson, E. (1986). Moral philosophy as applied science. *Philosophy 61*, 173–192.

Singhapakdi, A., Kraft, K.L., Vitell, S.J., & Rallapalli, K.C. (1995). The perceived importance of ethics and social responsibility on organizational effectiveness: A survey of marketers. *Journal of the Academy of Marketing Science 23* (1), 49–56.

Solomon, R.C. (2005, November). What's character got to do with it? *Philosophy and Phenomenological Research 71* (3), 648–655.

Sperber, D. (1996). *Explaining culture*. Cambridge, MA: Blackwell.

Spitzer, M., Fischbacker, U., Herrnberger, B., Grön, G., & Fehr, E. (2007). The neural signature of social norm compliance. *Neuron 56*, 185–196.

Thomson, J.J. (1976). Killing, letting die and the trolley problem. *Monist 59* (2), 204–217.

Treise, D., Weigold, M.F., Conna, J., & Garrison, H. (1994). Ethics in advertising: Ideological correlates of consumer perceptions. *Journal of Advertising 23* (3), 59–69.

Wilkins, L., & Coleman, R. (2005). *The moral media: How journalists reason about ethics*. Mahwah, NJ: Lawrence Erlbaum Associates.

Young, L., & Saxe, R. (2011). Moral universals and individual differences. *Emotion Review 3* (3), 323–324.

CHAPTER 2

Design of an Exemplar Study

Research to better understand the experiences that shape people's beliefs, perspectives and behaviors necessarily falls into two largely distinct domains. There are those who conduct interviews and try to be inconspicuous observers—who engage in the qualitative approach. And others rely on quantitative approaches to measure people's responses to survey questions and experimental situations. There are compelling reasons why these two are often mutually exclusive areas. The method we use, of course, depends on the questions we are asking. And each method requires its own set of skills, expertise and resources—the supply of which is almost always finite. But social science also has a rich history of work using a mix of the two methods. The predictive power of quantitative data can push mere description far beyond interesting yet lightweight anecdote. Qualitative analyses, similarly, brings to life the richness of actual experience that statistics can mask. While much more challenging and difficult to pull off than sticking to a single, "cleaner" approach, a mixed-method approach, when used effectively, can offer unprecedented clarity and depth to the subject at hand. The combination approach used here is the best way to build a full profile of the journalists and PR professionals who are among the most respected and accomplished in their fields. It also maximizes the power available to fully appreciate and interpret their experiences, outlooks and the lessons they have to offer. It is modeled on the moral psychology work of other accomplished researchers, all of whom have produced compelling evidence that moral functioning is best understood as a complex dynamic of factors that include self-narratives, moral reasoning and personality traits. Lawrence Walker and Jeremy Frimer studied dozens of "caring" and "brave" exemplars—recipients of the Caring Canadian Award, recognizing people who have volunteered years of service to provide care for others, and recipients of the Canadian Medal of Bravery, given to people who risked their lives to rescue others (2007, 2009). Chuck Huff and his colleagues emerged with a compelling profile of excellence in computer science by studying exemplars in that field in the United Kingdom and Scandinavia—"people who are successfully integrating ethical concern into their practice of computing" (Huff & Barnard, 2009, p. 48). Huff and his team argued that what they were after in their research, a profile of what made exemplars able to perform virtuous work on a sustained basis, called for a multipronged approach. Any single method was inadequate to capture the range of factors that make up our moral lives. If we consider the complex nature of our moral decision making, this only makes sense: A host of both internal and external factors shape our ability and our motivations to act out on the ethical principles that we embrace. Consequently, an "adequate" approach to moral psychology will integrate variables of individual intuitive assessments, effective persuasion reasoning and personal judgment: "It will treat moral judgment as the product of a dual processing system that mixes affect and cognition in both processes. It will treat moral action as the interaction of situational pressures, personal moral commitments (of various kinds), and the social moral-support system" (Huff & Frey, 2005, pp. 393–394). Huff, Barnard and Frey described their model as informed by contemporary virtue theory and one that documented "moral action in social context":

> The four-component model . . . grounds moral action in relatively stable personality characteristics, guides moral action based on the integration of morality into the self-system, shapes moral action by the context of the surrounding moral ecology, and facilitates moral action with morally relevant skills and knowledge. . . . The model seeks to explain the daily performance of moral action . . . and to illuminate the ways that . . . professionals might be trained to be more active, ethically committed, and ethically effective in their daily performance, across the lifespan of their careers.
>
> (2008a, p. 285)

The design of this study follows their mixed-method approach. Lengthy face-to-face interviews with journalism and PR exemplars captured their formative experiences, perspectives and convictions in their own words. Extensive survey data provide compelling, and more objective, measures of key aspects of their personal and professional lives.

SELECTION OF EXEMPLARS

The group of 24 journalism and public relations professionals featured here is a purposive rather than a representative sample. That is, the individuals were not selected to reflect a cross-section of the industries; as a group, they do not "represent" their fields in a broader sense. This is appropriate, since the goal here is not to be able to derive data from a strict probability sample of media professionals that then can be generalized to them all. Aside from the more systematic work to identify discrete personality traits, such probability sampling is very rare in moral psychology research. In moral development research specifically, there has never been an attempt to generalize to the population, as researchers routinely do with public opinion surveys and electoral polling. Daniel Riffe, Stephen Lacy and Frederick Fico (1998), in their authoritative methods text, described three conditions that justify the use of nonprobability sampling. First, "the material being studied must be difficult to obtain" (p. 85). This is certainly true to efforts to build a moral psychology profile of professional exemplars. In addition to the delicate nature of ethics as a topic, any valid multidimensional profile calls for multiple assessments, which depends upon a considerable time commitment on the part of those asked to participate. The survey instrument for this project covered 13 pages and took roughly 50 minutes to complete. The second condition that justifies a nonprobability sample is limited resources. Personal interaction with selected exemplars across 10 states was required to cultivate the needed level of commitment to the study over the course of more than two years. The third condition is when the study is tackling a "little known" topic that nonetheless is "of importance to the scholarly, professional, or policy making communities" (Riffe et al., 1998, p. 85). While researchers have addressed single aspects of moral reasoning among media professionals, this study is unique in that it attempts to build a more holistic picture of the moral psychology of a selected group.

A study of the factors that allow exemplary professionals to do virtuous work naturally invites a focus on the search for people worthy of the title "moral exemplar." Yet, as the introduction stated, this term is used with extreme wariness. The term is always likely to provoke skepticism, not only because people disagree about the nature of moral standards, but they also often use different evaluative criteria to judge whether someone's behavior embodies those standards. Any work in media ethics that dares to hold someone up as a "moral exemplar" invites heightened scrutiny, expectations of sainthood and more questions than it can likely answer. Rather than burdening its subjects with such an unwieldy term, this study methodically sought successful and well-respected media professionals whose work was judged to be exemplary by their peers and whose reputations featured a motivating concern for professional ethics. This is not to imply that only universally admired folks need apply. Even revered spiritual leaders such as Jesus or Mohammed were reviled by their contemporaries. The journalists and PR practitioners focused on here may well be considered controversial; they may not be "representative" of professional media exemplars (if such a group even exists); and none of them, often by their own admission, should be mistaken for a saint.

The effort here to identify and study exemplars is not a new one. As the introduction noted, researchers from a diverse array of fields have looked closely at the lives and behaviors of noted exemplars, seeking to document what makes them tick. The assumption behind all these is that exemplars have something to teach us all about adversity, integrity and the manifestation of widely accepted ethical principles. For any work involving exemplars, a good place to start is the landmark 1992 social psychology book *Some Do Care: Contemporary Lives of Moral Commitment* by Anne Colby and William Damon. Both authors are prominent researchers who have spent their careers studying human development and how people cultivate moral character. In their book, they present detailed profiles of 23 identified "exemplars"—some prominent and known for their work on behalf of the welfare of others, some quite obscure. Damon and Colby, too, were cautious about using the term moral exemplar and relied on an outside, ideologically diverse "nominator group" to help identify potential subjects. While not perfect, the system helped avoid reliance on arbitrary judgments and minimize the researchers' own biases. They articulated a working definition of what they meant by "exemplar," which this study has adopted:

> In calling someone a moral exemplar, we mean to imply that the individual exemplifies some widely shared ideas of what it means to be a highly moral person (and we do not mean in a neutral sense), but not that the individual is morally perfect or ideal. We were not seeking the occasional saint who lives a pure and unblemished existence, however much we might revere such a person. Rather, we wished to understand the more common life stories of highly dedicated persons who, through their sustained commitment and talents, labor to make the world a better place. Our interest was in people who have shown long-standing commitment to moral purposes, thus exemplifying good principles and virtues. We did not seek or expect perfection from our moral exemplars.
>
> (1992, p. 27)

A more recent study of exemplars also took the lead of Damon and Colby's system. In their extensive work with exemplars in the computer science field, Chuck Huff and his colleagues, with support from the National Science Foundation, also recruited a panel of experts, established criteria modeled on Damon and Colby's work and approached the panel's nominees to ask them to participate as well as to seek their suggestions of other possible subjects (Huff & Barnard, 2009). To identify a pool of exemplars in journalism, this study began by canvassing the members of the board of directors of the American Society of News Editors as well as other prominent names in the field and asking for nominations of individual journalists who were perceived to fit the criteria based on Damon and Colby's description. Similarly, the members of the board of directors of the Public Relations Society of America were also asked for exemplar candidates. All the potential subjects were then approached, presented with an outline of the study and asked to participate. They also were asked if they had colleagues who they thought should also be considered for the study. Special efforts were made to maximize geographic, racial and ethnic diversity among the research subjects. Roughly 50 potential subjects were approached before a pool of 24 subjects agreed to participate. Several particularly attractive potential subjects said they felt the research project was worthwhile but could not commit the required time to participate. The 24 subjects represent 10 states and were interviewed personally between April 2010 and September 2012. The study protocols were reviewed and approved by the Institutional Review Board at Colorado State University, which enforces federal research ethics and standards, and all subjects were guaranteed confidentiality and are referred to using pseudonyms except where explicit permission was given to identify them in specific stories considered extraordinarily compelling or representative in some way.

THE INTERVIEW

Most any questions about the factors that make exemplary professionals tick require, at the very least, some quality time simply listening to them talking about themselves, their work and their values. Storytelling is a common and critical feature of being human. Sociologists and other researchers have long known that we have an instinctive, perhaps even biological, need to tell stories, to use stories to make sense of the world and indeed to know ourselves through our storytelling. Freud, of course, was among the first to systematically use personal narratives as a basis for scientific inquiry into people's motives, fears, values and sense making. The method reached maturation with Erik Erikson's studies of Luther (1958) and Gandhi (1969). Erikson also used the life history to explore how historical moments influenced lives (1975). Dan McAdams, one of the most prominent psychology researchers who have largely defined the contemporary field of "narrative" studies, argued that the psychological and social value of what we include in the stories we tell cannot be underestimated. "The stories people fashion to make meaning out of their lives serve to situate them within the complex social ecology of modern adulthood," he wrote. "It is within the realm of narrative identity, therefore, that personality shows its most important and intricate relations to culture and society. . . . *The self comes to terms with society through narrative identity*" [author's emphasis] (2008, pp. 242, 243). Cognitive psychologist Jerome Bruner (1987, 1991) has demonstrated that personal meaning, and thus individuals' reality, is constructed during the making and telling of one's narrative, and that our own experiences take the form of the narratives we use to tell about them; "stories are our way of organizing, interpreting, and creating meaning from our experiences while maintaining a sense of continuity through it all" (Atkinson, 2007, p. 232). So our stories about ourselves not only describe us, but they can define us. "Invoking William James's famous distinction, the self encompasses a subjective storytelling 'I' whose stories about personal experience become part and parcel of a storied 'me,'" McAdams wrote. "The self is both the storyteller and the stories that are told" (2008, p. 244).

Academics have come up with many different systems to study personal narratives. Some involve highly structured series of interview questions keyed to explore specific psychological concepts. Others involve audio recordings of free-ranging oral histories. And there are as many methods to analyze the resulting narratives. But one widely accepted approach has been a focus on what is called the "life story"—using general questions asking people to recount key experiences in their lives and looking closely at their own descriptions for meaning and patterns. "Life stories," McAdams wrote, "function to make lives make sense by helping to organize the many different roles and features of the individual life into a synthetic whole and by offering causal explanations for how people believe they have come to be who they are" (2008, p. 243). At a more basic level, researcher Robert Coles said, "we owe it to each other to respect our stories and learn from them" (1989, p. 30). Over a career studying people's life stories, McAdams noted that Americans routinely rely on what he called a "narrative of redemption":

> The redemptive self is a life-story prototype that serves to support the generative efforts of midlife men and women. Their redemptive

life narratives tell how generative adults seek to give back to society in gratitude for the early advantages and blessings they feel they have received. . . . Evolving from the Puritans to Emerson to Oprah, the redemptive self has morphed into many different storied forms in the past 300 years as Americans have sought to narrate their lives as redemptive tales of atonement, emancipation, recovery, self-fulfillment, and upward social mobility. The stories speak of heroic individual protagonists—the *chosen people*—whose *manifest destiny* is to make a positive difference in a dangerous world, even when the world does not wish to be redeemed. The stories translate a deep and abiding script of American exceptionalism into the many contemporary narratives of success, recovery, development, liberation, and self-actualization that so pervade American talk, talk shows, therapy sessions, sermons, and commencement speeches [author's emphasis].

(2008, pp. 255–256)

The life story interview format

For decades, the notion of treating people's "life stories" in a scientific way was considered laughable. Stories are "too soft and human lives too big," and "only the most romantic of psychological investigators" spent much time taking them seriously. But that began to change in the 1980s, when researchers became "newly sensitized to the power of societal myths and cultural narratives in shaping human behavior in social contexts" (McAdams, 2001, pp. 100, 101). Using Erikson's notion that we begin developing our "ego identity" through narrative explanation in our adolescent years, McAdams developed the life story interview format to help systematically examine people's self-definitions. The life story, while capturing seemingly irrelevant autobiographical memories and even self-referential embellishment, nonetheless is a way to view one of the three critical "levels" of personality. The first level, dispositional traits, refer to fairly stable features of individual personalities, such as extraversion and nervousness. The second level refers to characteristic adaptations, which are the various ways we cope and adjust to social roles and contexts—our motives, defense mechanisms, values and beliefs. But neither of these levels can adequately explain how we make meaning of our lives and gain a sense of coherence to all our experiences. "A person's identity is not to be found in behavior, nor—important though this is—in the reactions of others, but in the capacity to keep a particular narrative," Anthony Giddens said

(1991, p. 54). If we are to really understand someone, we must have an idea about how she tries to "explain" herself. This is where the value of the life story comes in. McAdams (1985, 1993, 1996) developed the life story interview format to be used as a standardized instrument in a broad range of research and "provide integration and meaning" that complements the study of personality traits and dispositional characteristics (McAdams, 2001, p. 117). It includes coding guidelines to extract themes such as agency, communion and redemption (Foley Center, 2008).

McAdams's life story interview format features seven sections: life chapters, key scenes in the life story, future script, challenges, personal ideology, life theme and reflection (Appendix A). It can take up to three hours, depending on the openness of the interview subject. McAdams acknowledges that no single "story" defines a person and that stories people tell often include irrelevant details, embellishments or even represent an "ideal self" that doesn't actually describe the person doing the talking. But this, too, can reflect the realities of developmental psychology: The stories we tell about ourselves, the true and less-than-truthful, can suggest important things about our motivations, aspirations and even about the culture we live in. McAdams's format also seeks to emphasize the "integrative" nature of stories—that is, it focuses on topics that are most likely to enable subjects to demonstrate how they might weave their experiences into a coherent narrative that says something about the self. Format questions include asking subjects to describe both a positive and a negative childhood memory, what they see as a "turning point" in their lives and an event in which they felt they displayed wisdom. The format is structured yet open-ended; it leaves subjects with the option to choose to discuss either personal or professional moments of importance to them.

While no two life stories, of course, will be the same, there are important commonalities, or truths, about the stories that people tell, all of which hold important clues for careful listeners to fully appreciate a story's value. McAdams outlined six "principles" or themes that emerge again and again in the study of life stories (2008, pp. 244–248):

- *The self is storied.* All autobiographical memories are "highly selective and strategic." Storied recollections of the past are sometimes less important for the details of what is recounted than for their expression of personal meaning. "Life stories . . . are always about both the reconstructed past and the imagined future," McAdams said.

- *Stories integrate lives.* "Stories do many things: They entertain, educate, inspire, motivate, conceal, reveal, organize and disrupt. Among their most important functions, however, is *integration*," McAdams said. "Whether aimed at finding meaning in yesterday's conversation around the water cooler or in a 15-year marriage that ended two decades ago, autobiographical reasoning is an exercise in personal integration—putting things together into a narrative pattern that affirms life meaning and purpose."
- *Stories are told in social relationships.* "[A]ny narrative of the self cannot be understood outside the context of its assumed listener or audience, with respect to which the story is designed to make a point or produce a desired effect," McAdams said. "Autobiographical narrators anticipate what their audiences want to hear, and these anticipations influence what they tell and how they tell it."
- *Stories change over time.* "Autobiographical memory is notoriously unstable . . . [and] contributes to change in the life story over time," McAdams said. "As people's motivations, goals, personal concerns, and social positions change, furthermore, their memories of important events in their lives and the meanings they attribute to those events may also change." In a 3-year longitudinal study that asked college students to recall and describe 10 key scenes in their life stories on three different occasions, only 28 percent of the memories described at Time 1 were repeated 3 months later, and 22 percent of the original memories were chosen and described again 3 years after the original assessment (McAdams et al., 2006).
- *Stories are cultural texts.* Researchers have suggested that "narrative accounts of the life course in modern Western cultures are expected to begin in the family, to involve growth and expansion in the early years, to trace later problems back to earlier conflicts, to incorporate epiphanies and turning points that mark change in the protagonist's quest, and to be couched in the discourse of progress versus decline," McAdams said. Research has documented how the life story narratives of Americans differ in important ways from those of Asian cultures, where individuals are less likely to focus on themselves.
- *Some stories are better than others.* "A life story suggests a moral perspective, in that human characters are intentional, moral agents whose actions can always be construed from the standpoint of what is 'good' and what is 'bad' in a given society," McAdams said.

The life story as research tool

Use of the life story model has resulted in a rich body of work to examine key features and patterns in a wide range of populations. Judith Modell (1992) identified common themes and narrative strategies in the stories that birth parents tell about why they gave up their children for adoption. Barbara Walkover (1992) found that married couples on the edge of parenthood told stories about their future in which they idealized their yet-unborn children, reflecting an irrational belief in the perfectibility of childhood. Ruth Linn (1997) identified several key categories of narrative styles among Israeli soldiers who refused to engage in what they believed to be immoral acts of aggression. Gary Gregg (1996) suggested that young Moroccans used a "hybrid" narrative form mixing traditional Islamic faith and features of modernity to define themselves. Bertram Cohler, Andrew Hostetler and Andrew Boxer (1998) examined the hopes, conflicts and frustrations in the life stories of gay couples. Michele Crossley (2001) explored how HIV patients construct the meaning of home in their life narratives. Psychology researchers have used rigorous qualitative and quantitative analysis to explore the meanings of people's life narratives in a wide range of populations. Janet Landman (2001) and Shadd Maruna (2001) focused on reformed criminals, examining how their narratives featured the subjects of shame, confession and rehabilitation. Bertram Cohler and Phillip Hammack (2006) tracked the life narratives of gay men over time, focusing on their struggles to define themselves at different points in U.S. history. Tova Halbertal and Irit Koren (2006) showed how the life stories of highly religious Jewish gays and lesbians described their lives with "parallel" narrative tracks. Narrative theories of generativity, redemption and adaptation have been validated by a generation of studies involving children and adolescents, mothers of Down Syndrome children, alcoholics and even the architect Frank Lloyd Wright (see de St. Aubin, 1998; King & Hicks, 2006; McLean & Thorne, 2003; Singer, 2005). In their study of moral exemplars among computer science professionals, Huff and colleagues, by coding life story narratives, discerned significant distinctions between identified *craftpersons* focused on how to best serve clients and users and *reformers* more intent on addressing organizational or social injustices (Huff & Barnard, 2009, p. 50; see also Huff & Rogerson, 2005). Researchers have found significant correlations between life narrative themes and core personality traits such as extraversion and openness to experience (McAdams et al., 2004).

Phenomenological analysis

All life story interviews in this study were transcribed, and all exemplars were invited to edit their transcriptions for any passages that they did not want included, even anonymously, in the analysis. Edited transcripts were then analyzed using what researchers call a "phenomenological" approach—the study of experience and perception "from the point of view of the behaving organism itself," as one twentieth-century psychologist described it (Snygg, 1941, p. 406). Exemplars' life stories are read closely for details as well as narrative structure, and recurring themes, narrative emphases and value descriptions are identified and categorized (Giorgi, 1989; Polkinghorne, 1989). Rather than seek to interpret possible causes of subjects' experience or impose judgment on the validity or worth of their stories, research using the phenomenological approach seeks to fully understand the meaning-making processes of lived experience. It is particularly effective in accounting for McAdams's six features of life stories described above. While phenomenology produced a rather dense philosophical system based on the work of Husserl (1962/1977), Merleau-Ponty (1945/1962) and later even psychological "critiques" by Sartre (1939/1962, 1940/1962), the phenomenological method at its most basic is a process that seeks to discern "invariant" experiences among subjects, leading to "grasping the essential pattern of a structure" and thereby illuminate "the universal elements and relationships that constitute experience in general" (Polkinghorne, 1989, pp. 42, 43). At its most basic, the aim of the phenomenological approach is to articulate "the psychological meanings being lived by the participant that reveal the nature of the phenomenon being researched" (Giorgi & Giorgi, 2003, p. 252).

THE SURVEY

The other half of the study design, complementing the qualitative interview material, is based on responses to an extensive 13-page survey provided by all the participating exemplars (Appendix B).[1] In fact, the exemplars were given four survey instruments—distinct assessment tools that measure very different things. In addition to a battery of demographic items, the survey measured subjects' responses in four domains: personality traits, ethical ideologies, perceived workplace ethical climate and moral reasoning skills. The idea of combining several measures was borrowed from the work of Huff and his colleagues, who argued in their work on computer science exemplars that a multidimensional approach is the most compelling way to capture the constellation of factors that enable or hinder professionals from doing virtuous work (see Huff & Barnard, 2009; Huff, Barnard, & Frey, 2008a, 2008b). Specific assessments used here, however, are not identical to those used by Huff and his colleagues. Whereas their four-component model of moral action calls for assessment of subjects' value systems, the instrument to do so was not included in this design due to the limits of integrating its largely nonparametric data with parametric data collected by the other assessment tools. Instead, this design used a questionnaire that measures people's degrees of idealism and relativism, both a key component in their "ethical ideologies."

Personality traits

Personal traits are well-established psychological constructs and have been conceptualized as "dimensions of individual differences in tendencies to show consistent patterns of thoughts, feeling and actions" (McCrae & Costa, 1990, p. 23). A series of empirical analyses over the decades has developed five robust personality traits that theorists trace to evolutionary adaptiveness. A large body of data indicates that these five factors are nearly universal: They manifest themselves in several different types of personality inventory tools across different cultures, language groups, religions, political ideologies and age groups (McCrea & John, 1992; McCrae & Costa, 1997). This is not to say the Five Factor Model (FFM) is universally supported; debate continues over its validity and usefulness. And descriptions of traits cannot be mistaken for comprehensive descriptions of personality. Yet the FFM remains "the most widely accepted model of personality trait structure" (Costa & McCrae, 2009, p. 299). This project relied on the Big Five Inventory-44 (John, Donahue & Kentle, 1991), an easy-to-use questionnaire that asks subjects to rate their agreement to 44 items, each of which is keyed to one of the five traits. The NEO Personality Inventory (NEO-PI) and other condensed versions are widely considered to be reliable measures of what are referred to as the "Big Five" traits:

- *Extraversion*. Sonia Roccas and colleagues (2002) suggested that people who exhibit extravert features prioritize achievement and stimulation over adherence to tradition. This trait is associated with leadership, successful job interviews and higher earnings (Costa & McCrae, 2009, p. 315). Huff and colleagues, by extension, suggested that the trait of extraversion "might help support a particular kind of moral excellence that involves leadership and facilitating change in society" (2008a, p. 256).

- *Neuroticism*. This measure of "negative emotional reactivity" is related to capacity for information acquisition and prevalence of short-sighted decision making. It is also inversely related to job satisfaction and directly related to burnout (Costa & McCrae, 2009). Huff and colleagues found that their computer science moral exemplars scored significantly lower on neuroticism measures than expected, and they speculated that high scorers may also exhibit difficulties in other areas examined with their moral agency model, such as moral imagination and perseverance (Huff et al., 2008a, p. 256).

- *Agreeableness*. While not a nominal indicator of virtue, this trait is tied to the expression of virtue and has variously been called social adaptability, likeability, friendly compliance and love (John & Srivastava, 1999). It is also related to cooperation in work settings (Costa & McCrae, 2009). However, as Owen Flanagan illustrated in his discussion of saints and virtue (1991), agreeableness and saintliness are often not at all correlational.

- *Openness*. This trait is particularly relevant to "learning and to performance in jobs that require creativity or adaptation to change" (Costa & McCrae, 2009, p. 315). While its connection to virtuous action may not be readily apparent, Huff and colleagues noted that different types of professional moral exemplars exhibited contrasting degrees of openness to experiences: So-called craftpersons had higher scores than the reformers. And both are likely to interact with other environmental factors assessed in their model.

- *Conscientiousness*. High scores on this dimension have been tied to success in the workplace and career and other attributes and thus may reflect the premium placed on good work among media professionals—particularly in the present climate of heightened public scrutiny. In a study that analyzed the personality traits present in people's descriptions of moral exemplars, conscientiousness was the most important (Walker, 1999, p. 154).

Ethical ideologies

Measuring individuals' orientation to different moral philosophies has enabled researchers to tie degrees of idealism and degrees of relativistic thinking to proclivities to view ethical questions in certain ways. Idealists generally express greater concern for avoiding harm to others and generally reflect a Kantian sensibility that emphasizes moral obligations, while less idealistic individuals tend to believe that some degree of harm is unavoidable even with the noblest of intentions, reflecting a more utilitarian outlook. Typically, some individuals assume that desirable consequences can, with the "right" action, always be obtained, whereas others are more outcome-oriented, for they admit that harm will sometimes be necessary to produce a greater social good. Relativistic thinking generally rejects the claim that external moral laws should guide behavior and insists that moral judgments are primarily situational. The tensions among the strains of moral thought embodied by these two dimensions stretch back to Socrates and remain the focus of much contemporary moral philosophy (e.g., Audi, 1997; Moore, 1903; Ross, 1930).

Psychologist Donelson Forsyth (1980) developed a useful and accessible tool, the Ethics Position Questionnaire (EPQ), for measuring people's idealism and relativism, and thus identifying their "ethical ideology." Most recently, a meta-analysis of research examining variables influencing ethically questionable business decisions concluded that measures based on Forsyth's idealistic-relativistic typology served as reliable predictors of perceived ethical and unethical conduct. Individuals with an internal, accessible belief prohibiting harming others were found less likely to make unethical choices (Kish-Gephart, Harrison & Treviño, 2010). Based on responses to 20 items on a 9-point likert scale (10 items related to relativistic claims, 10 items related to idealistic claims), the EPQ has been tested widely and shown to be reliable, valid and not correlated with social desirability. It has been used to explain a range of behaviors and beliefs among a wide variety of populations. For example, Forsyth found significant differences across the four ideologies with respect to attitudes toward abortion, euthanasia, homosexuality and human in vitro fertilization (1980). EPQ responses also suggest that people who demonstrate high idealism scores are more likely to judge perceived unethical behavior more harshly and have a greater ethic of caring (Forsyth, Nye & Kelly, 1988). People with high relativism scores tend to show more Machiavellian tendencies (Leary, Knight & Barnes, 1986). Applied extensively in research on business and marketing sectors, the EPQ also has led researchers to claim that potential corporate whistleblowers described as nonrelativistic were more likely to report peer wrongdoing (Barnett,

Bass & Brown, 1996) and that ethical ideology responses reflect employees' abilities to identify verbally sexually harassing behaviors (Keyton and Rhodes, 1997). Researchers also have used the EPQ to establish relationships between ethical orientations and right-wing authoritarianism (McHoskey, 1996), nihilistic tendencies (McHoskey et al., 2000), support for animal experimentation (Wuensch & Poteat, 1998) and discriminatory attitudes (Wilson, 2003).

In a study of public relations professionals using the EPQ, Yungwook Kim and Youjin Choi (2003) found that those with high idealism or low relativism reported a greater tendency to make stricter ethical judgments of professional standards. The EPQ has been used most extensively in research with marketers and to gauge consumer judgments on advertising. Researchers have found that the more idealistic and less relativistic marketers tended to exhibit higher honesty and integrity than the less idealistic and more relativistic marketers (Vitell & Singhapakdi, 1993). Anusorn Singhapakdi and colleagues (2003) found that idealism levels positively influence a marketer's perceptions regarding the importance of ethics and social responsibility in achieving organizational effectiveness and that relativism appears to be negatively related to the same.

Moral reasoning

Just as we grow as physical and intellectual beings, we also develop morally through our lives. Moral development theory attempts to explain how, beginning with the myopic self-interestedness of early childhood, our empathies and scope of concern increases, and broad moral principles of justice, harm prevention and dignity become more salient in our values and decisions. While there is continuing debate over the precise nature of our moral selves and how to weight the influence of factors such as moral emotion and self-identification (see Blasi, 1984, 1995; Eisenberg, 1986), the dominant theory of moral development rests on the work of Lawrence Kohlberg, who argued that we develop as more sophisticated moral beings as our sense of the concept of justice expands through stages. He argued that, as moral reasoning develops, individuals become more likely to draw on moral principles in making judgments in moral situations. Our moral development moves through six hierarchical stages, ranging from self-interest, to conformity to group norms and societal expectations and finally to the application of broader, universal moral principles. At Kohlberg's higher stages of moral reasoning, moral principles and their universal and prescriptive nature become more salient; as a result, individuals feel more compelled to behave consistent with their judgments. The motivation for moral action, then, stems directly from moral understanding (Hardy & Carlo, 2005, p. 233).

Based on this theory, researchers developed a tool to assess moral reasoning skills. This tool, the Defining Issues Test (DIT), has been used in a wide range of populations over the last four decades and has shown to have strong validity in measuring one's moral development. Unlike the BFI-44 personality assessment or the EPQ measuring ethical ideology, the DIT, developed by James Rest (1979), is considerably more demanding of research subjects: It presents up to six brief ethical scenarios, or dilemmas, and asks them to respond to 12 statements for each dilemma. A resulting P score measures the percentage of time that people appear to be applying higher-level, universal principles in their reasoning and responses to the dilemmas. So, a P score of 40 means principles at the highest stages are being used by the individual about 40 percent of the time, with lower-level reasoning being used 60 percent. Rather than "assigning" people to specific stages, the DIT also relies on schema theory, which says that we typically draw on bits of information stored in our long-term memory to process information we're presented with, whether it be a television commercial or an ethical dilemma. So, if a person has acquired a schema reflecting the application of higher-stage principles, statements at that stage will "activate" those schemas. If not, lower-stage schemas are used. Rest and colleagues (1999) theorized that people are primarily in one stage but can use ethical reasoning from lower and higher stages as well; "Rather than a staircase with steps, moral development is seen as a shifting distribution" (Coleman & Wilkins, 2009, p. 320).

The DIT has been administered to more than 30,000 people in more than 500 published studies and books. As Daniel Lapsley says, "few research instruments command as much confirmatory evidence as does the DIT. It has strong psychometric properties. . . . It is sensitive to sequential development. It is not contaminated by cohort or generational effects. It can be discriminated from other variables (e.g., IQ, personality variables, attitudes, other measures of cognitive development)" (1996, p. 100). Studies have found that moral development is influenced by education and a variety of other factors. Religion has been shown to have a negative effect on DIT scores. More fundamental or conservative religious beliefs have been correlated with lower levels of moral development (Lawrence, 1978; Parker, 1990). People who identify as politically liberal also tend to have higher DIT scores than do conservatives (Rest et al., 1999). The DIT design allows for a surprising degree of flexibility; it can accommodate topic-specific ethical dilemmas to be inserted. This study takes advantage of the developments implemented by Lee Wilkins and Renita Coleman (2005; Coleman & Wilkins, 2009) in their studies that incorporated journalism- and public relations-specific scenarios into the DIT instrument.

Ethical workplace climate

A generally accepted idea of "the right thing to do" and an understanding of how ethical issues should be handled can be seen as making up the "ethical climate" of an organization. "[C]orporations, like individuals, have their own sets of ethics that help define their characters. And just as personal ethics guide what an individual will do when faced with moral dilemmas, corporate ethics guide what an organization will do when faced with issues of conflicting values" (Cullen, Victor & Stephens, 2001, p. 50). Drawing on the same moral-development concepts as the DIT, business researchers Bart Victor and John Cullen designed a tool to assess an organization's ethical climate based on employee responses. The Ethical Climate Questionnaire (ECQ) presents 36 statements and asks subjects to respond based on their perceptions of their organizational culture. The ethical climates mapped through the ECQ, they argue, "identify normative systems that guide organizational decision-making and the systemic responses to ethical dilemmas" (1988, p. 123). The ECQ roughly follows the stage groupings that Kohlberg theorized most people go through in their moral development: ego and self-interest, group conformity and utilitarian rule-making and finally, application of broad, universal principles. Each of these three levels also can be keyed to certain "referents" that serve as the source of members' cues regarding what is ethically appropriate. The source could be the employees' self-determined ethical beliefs (individual), the organization's standards and policies (local) or external to the individual and organization, such as a professional organization (cosmopolitan) (Cullen, Victor & Bronson, 1993). Together, the moral-development levels and the levels of referents provide a three-by-three matrix that "maps" an organization's ethical climate. For example, organizations with either a highly "benevolent" (reflecting conventional moral reasoning) or a highly "principled" climate (reflecting higher reasoning stages) might be associated with predominantly ethical employee behavior. Conversely, an organization with a high "egoism" climate (reflecting lower-level reasoning) could be associated with unethical behavior among employees (Peterson, 2002, p. 314). The implications for management and long-term corporate viability could be significant,

Cullen and colleagues argued: "For example, a rules-oriented climate that plays down the importance of the employee's individual judgment could lead to misinterpretation or conflict between various roles and regulations. A climate that is low on caring could create an environment in which employees are treated in callous and potentially illegal ways; such a climate may lower motivation and increase the turnover rate" (Cullen et al., 2001, p. 60). In one study, the relationship between ethical climate dimensions and unethical behavior was stronger for organizations without a code of ethics (Treviño, Butterfield & McCabe, 1998).

COMBINING QUALITATIVE AND QUANTITATIVE DATA

The biographical richness of the life story interviews, together with data from the survey, help build an unprecedented, multidimensional profile of exemplary media professionals. The design allows us to explore the claim that personality, moral reasoning and other factors are interactive and all serve as components of the moral self—and even of the very idea of personality, as McAdams has long argued: "Indeed, personality may be seen as a unique patterning of traits, adaptations and stories. Dispositional traits, such as those presented in the Big Five taxonomy, provide an initial sketch of human individuality: characteristic adaptations, such as motives and developmental tasks, fill in the details; and life stories provide integrations and meaning" (2001, pp. 117–118).

In addition to the immediate goal of working toward a multidimensional picture of moral action in media, this study design has a broader agenda, as mentioned in the introduction. It is hoped that this mixed-method approach suggests a fruitful path for future media ethics research, one that augments the normative philosophical explication that has defined so much of the field. Such systematic, inductive efforts can only strengthen the theoretical claims we make about what media practitioners should do, and it may well suggest pedagogical and professional-development strategies to cultivate the features and perspectives of the exemplars among us in future generations.

NOTE

1. Use of the Defining Issues Test (DIT) requires a license and thus is omitted from the survey instrument for proprietary reasons.

REFERENCES

Atkinson, R. (2007). The life story interview as a bridge in narrative inquiry. In the *Handbook of narrative inquiry: Mapping a methodology* (D.J. Clandinin, Ed.), 224–245. Thousand Oaks, CA: SAGE.

Audi, R. (1997). *Moral knowledge and ethical character.* New York: Oxford University Press.
Barnett, T., Bass, K., & Brown, G. (1996). Religiosity, ethical ideology and intentions to report a peer's wrongdoing. *Journal of Business Ethics 15*, 1164–1174.
Blasi, A. (1984). Moral identity: Its role in moral functioning. In *Morality, moral behavior, and moral development* (W.M. Kurtines & J.L. Gewirtz, Eds.), 129–139. New York: Wiley.
Blasi, A. (1995). Moral understanding and the moral personality: The process of moral integration. In *Moral development: An introduction* (W.M. Kurtines & J.L. Gewirtz, Eds.), 229–253. Needham Heights, MA: Allyn & Bacon.
Bruner, J. (1987). Life as narrative. *Social Research 54* (1), 11–32.
Bruner, J. (1991). The narrative construction of reality. *Critical Inquiry 18*, 1–21.
Cohler, B.J., & Hammack, P.L. (2006). Making a gay identity: Life story and the construction of a coherent self. In *Identity and story: Creating self in narrative* (D.P. McAdams, R. Josselson & A. Lieblich, Eds.), 151–172. Washington, D.C.: American Psychological Association.
Cohler, B.J., Hostetler, A.J., & Boxer, A. (1998). Generativity, social context, and lived experience: Narratives of gay men in middle adulthood. In *Generativity and adult development* (D.P. McAdams & E. de St. Aubin, Eds.), 227–264. Washington, D.C.: American Psychological Association.
Colby, A., & Damon, W. (1992). *Some do care: Contemporary lives of moral commitment.* New York: Free Press.
Coleman, R., & Wilkins, L. (2009). The moral development of public relations practitioners: A comparison with other professions and influences on higher quality ethical reasoning. *Journal of Public Relations Research 21* (3), 318–340.
Coles, R. (1989). *The call of stories: Teaching and the moral imagination.* Boston: Houghton Mifflin.
Costa, P.T., & McCrae, R.R. (2009). The five-factor model and the NEO inventories. In the *Oxford handbook of personality assessment* (J.N. Butcher, Ed.), 299–322. Oxford: Oxford University Press.
Crossley, M. (2001). Sense of place and its import for life transitions: The case of HIV positive individuals. In *Turns in the road: Narrative studies of lives in transition* (D.P. McAdams, R. Josselson, & A. Lieblich, Eds.), 279–296. Washington, D.C.: American Psychological Association.
Cullen, J.B., Victor, B., & Bronson, J.W. (1993). The Ethical Climate Questionnaire: An assessment of its development and validity. *Psychological Reports 73*, 667–674.
Cullen, J.B., Victor, B., & Stephens, C. (2001). An ethical weather report: Assessing the organization's ethical climate. *Organizational Dynamics*, 50–62.
de St. Aubin, E. (1998). Truth against the world: A psychobiographical exploration of generativity in the life of Frank Lloyd Wright. In *Generativity and adult development: How and why we care for the next generation* (D.P. McAdams & E. de St. Aubin, Eds.), 391–428. Washington, D.C.: American Psychological Association.
Eisenberg, N. (1986). *Altruistic emotion, cognition and behavior.* Hillsdale, NJ: Lawrence Erlbaum Associates.
Erikson, E. (1958). *Young man Luther: A study in psychoanalysis and history.* New York: W.W. Norton.
Erikson, E. (1969). *Gandhi's truth: On the origins of militant nonviolence.* New York: W.W. Norton.
Erikson, E. (1975). *Life history and the historical moment.* New York: W.W. Norton.
Flanagan, O. (1991). *Varieties of moral personality: Ethics and psychological realism.* Cambridge, MA: Harvard University Press.
Foley Center for the Study of Lives. (2008). The life story interview. Available: www.sesp.northwestern.edu/foley/instruments/interview/. Retrieved 2 April 2012.
Forsyth, R.D. (1980). A taxonomy of ethical ideologies. *Journal of Personality and Social Psychology 39* (1): 175–184.
Forsyth, R.D., Nye, J.L., & Kelley, K. (1988). Idealism, relativism and the ethic of caring. *Journal of Psychology 122*, 243–248.
Giddens, A. (1991). *Modernity and self-identity: Self and society in the late modern age.* Stanford, CA: Stanford University Press.
Giorgi, A. (1989). One type of analysis of descriptive data: Procedures involved in following a scientific phenomenological method. *Methods 1*, 39–61.

Giorgi, A.P., & Giorgi, B.M. (2003). The descriptive phenomenological psychological method. In *Qualitative Research in Psychology: Expanding perspectives in methodology and design* (P.M. Camic, J.E. Rhodes & L. Yardley, Eds.), 243–273. Washington, D.C.: American Psychological Association.

Gregg, G. (1996). Themes of authority in life-histories of young Moroccans. In *Representations of power in Morocco* (S. Miller & R. Bourgia, Eds.), 215–242. Cambridge, MA: Cambridge University Press.

Halbertal, T.H., & Koren, I. (2006). Between "being" and "doing": Conflict and coherence in the identity formation of gay and lesbian orthodox Jews. In *Identity and story: Creating self in narrative* (D.P. McAdams, R. Josselson & A. Lieblich, Eds.), 37–61. Washington, D.C.: American Psychological Association.

Hardy, S.A., & Carlo, G. (2005). Identity as a source of moral motivation. *Human Development 48,* 232–256.

Huff, C.W., & Barnard, L. (2009, Fall). Moral exemplars in the computing profession. *IEEE Technology and Society Magazine,* 49–54.

Huff, C.W., Barnard, L., & Frey, W. (2008a). Good computing: A pedagogically focused model of virtue in the practice of computing (part 1). *Journal of Information, Communication and Ethics in Society 6* (3), 246–278.

Huff, C.W., Barnard, L., & Frey, W. (2008b). Good computing: A pedagogically focused model of virtue in the practice of computing (part 2). *Journal of Information, Communication and Ethics in Society 6* (4), 284–316.

Huff, C., & Frey, W. (2005). Moral pedagogy and practical ethics. *Science and Engineering Ethics 11,* 389–408.

Huff, C.W., & Rogerson, S. (2005). Craft and reform in moral exemplars in computing. Paper presented at the ETHICOMP205 conference in Linkoping, September.

Husserl, E. (1962/1977). *Phenomenological psychology.* (Trans. J. Scanlon). The Hague: Nijhoff.

John, O.P., Donahue, E.M., & Kentle, R.L. (1991). *The Big Five Inventory – Versions 4a and 54.* Berkeley: University of California at Berkeley, Institute of Personality and Social Research.

John, O.P., & Srivastava, S. (1999). The big five trait taxonomy: History, measurement and theoretical perspectives. In *Handbook of personality: Theory and research* (L.A. Pervin & O. P John, Eds.), 102–138. New York: Guilford.

Keyton, J., & Rhodes, S.C. (1997). Sexual harassment: A matter of individual rights, legal definitions or organizational policy? *Journal of Business Ethics 16,* 129–146.

Kim, Y., & Choi, Y. (2003). Ethical standards appear to change with age and ideology: A survey of practitioners. *Public Relations Review 29,* 79–89.

King, L.A., & Hicks, J.A. (2006). Narrating the self in the past and future: Implications for maturity. *Research in Human Development 3,* 121–138.

Kish-Gephart, J.J., Harrison, D.A., & Treviño, L.K. (2010). Bad apples, bad cases and bad barrels: Meta-analytic evidence about sources of unethical decisions at work. *Journal of Applied Psychology 95* (1), 1–31.

Landman, J. (2001). The crime, punishments and ethical transformation of two radicals: Or how Katherine Power improves on Dostoevsky. In *Turns in the road: Narrative studies of lives in transition* (D.P. McAdams, R. Josselson, & A. Lieblich, Eds.), 35–66. Washington, D.C.: American Psychological Association.

Lapsley, D.K. (1996). *Moral psychology.* Boulder, CO: Westview Press.

Lawrence, J.A. (1978). *The component procedures of moral judgment-making.* Unpublished doctoral dissertation, University of Minnesota. Dissertation Abstracts International, 1979, 40, 896-B. University Microfilms No. 7918360.

Leary, M.R., Knight, P.D., & Barnes, B.D. (1986). Ethical ideologies of the Machiavellian. *Personality and Social Psychology Bulletin 12,* 75–80.

Linn, R. (1997). Soldiers' narrative of selective moral resistance: A separate position of the connected self? In *The narrative study of lives (Vol. 5)* (A. Lieblich & R. Josselson, Eds.), 94–112. Thousand Oaks, CA: SAGE.

Maruna, S. (2001). *Making good: How ex-convicts reform and rebuild their lives.* Washington, D.C.: American Psychological Association.

McAdams, D.P. (1985). *Power, intimacy, and the life story: Personological inquiries into identity.* New York: Guilford Press.

McAdams, D.P. (1993). *The stories we live by: Personal myths and the making of the self.* New York: Morrow.

McAdams, D.P. (1996). Personality, modernity, and the storied self: An contemporary framework for studying persons. *Psychological Inquiry 7,* 295–321.

McAdams, D.P. (2001). The psychology of life stories. *Review of General Psychology 5* (2), 100–122.

McAdams, D.P. (2008). Personal narratives and the life story. In *Handbook of personality: Theory and research* (O.P. John, R.W. Robins & L.A. Pervin, Eds.), 242–262. New York: Guilford Press.

McAdams, D.P., Anyidoho, N.A., Brown, C., Huang, Y.T., Kaplan, B., & Machado, M.A. (2004). Traits and stories: Links between dispositional and narrative features of personality. *Journal of Personality 72* (4), 761–784.

McAdams, D.P., Bauer, J.J., Sakeada, A.R., Anyidoho, N.A., Machado, M.A., Magrino-Failla, K., et al. (2006). Continuity and change in the life story: A longitudinal study of autobiographical memories in emerging adulthood. *Journal of Personality 74,* 1371–1400.

McLean, K.C., & Thorne, A. (2003). Late adolescents' self-defining memories about relationships. *Developmental Psychology 39,* 635–645.

McCrae, R.R., & Costa, P.T. (1990). *Personality in adulthood.* New York: Guilford.

McCrae, R.R., & Costa, P.T. (1997). Personality trait structure as a human universal. *America Psychologist 52,* 509–516.

McCrae, R.R., & John, O.P. (1992). An introduction to the five-factor model and its applications. *Journal of Personality 60,* 175–215.

McHoskey, J.W. (1996). Authoritarianism and ethical ideology. *Journal of Social Psychology 136* (6), 709–717.

McHoskey, J.W., Betris, T., Worzel, W., Szyarto, C., Kelly, K., Eggert, T., . . . Anderson, H. (2000). Relativism, nihilism and quest. *Journal of Social Behavior and Personality 14* (3), 445–462.

Merleau-Ponty, M. (1945/1962). *The phenomenology of perception.* (Trans. C. Smith). New York: Humanities Press.

Modell, J. (1992). "How do you introduce yourself as a childless mother?" Birthparent interpretations of adulthood. In *Storied lives: The cultural politics of self-understanding* (G.C. Rosenwald & R.L. Ochberg, Eds.), 76–94. New Haven, CT: Yale University Press.

Moore, G.E. (1903). *Principia Ethica.* Cambridge: Cambridge University Press.

Parker, R.J. (1990). The relationship between dogmatism, orthodox Christian beliefs, and ethical judgment. *Counseling and Values 34* (3), 213–216.

Peterson, D.K. (2002). The relationship between unethical behavior and the dimensions of the Ethical Climate Questionnaire. *Journal of Business Ethics 41,* 313–326.

Polkinghorne, D.E. (1989). Phenomenological research methods. In *Existential-phenomenological perspectives in psychology: Exploring the breadth of human experience* (R.S. Valle & S. Halling, Eds.), 41–60. Ann Arbor, MI: Plenum Press.

Rest, J.R. (1979). *Development in judging moral issues.* Minneapolis: University of Minnesota Press.

Rest, J.R., Narvaez, D., Bebeau, M.J., & Thoma, S.J. (1999). *Postconventional moral thinking: A neo-Kohlbergian approach.* Mahwah, NJ: Lawrence Erlbaum Associates.

Riffe, D., Lacy, S., & Fico, F.G. (1998). *Analyzing media messages: Using quantitative content analysis in research.* Mahwah, NJ: Lawrence Erlbaum Associates.

Roccas, S., Sagiv, L., Schwartz, S.H., & Knafo, A. (2002). The big five personality factors and personal values. *Personality and Social Psychology Bulletin 28* (6), 789–801.

Ross, W.D. (1930). *The right and the good.* Oxford: Clarendon Press.

Sartre, J-P. (1939/1962). *Sketch for a theory of the emotions.* (Trans. P. Mariet). London: Methuen.

Sartre, J-P. (1940/1962). *The psychology of imagination.* New York: Citadel Press.

Singer, J.A. (2005). *Personality and psychotherapy: Treating the whole person.* New York: Guilford Press.

Singhapakdi, A., Kraft, K.L., Vitell, S.J., & Rallapalli, K.C. (2003). The perceived importance of ethics and social responsibility on organizational effectiveness: A survey of marketers. *Journal of the Academy of Marketing Science 23* (1), 49–56.

Snygg, D. (1941). The need for a phenomenological system of psychology. *Psychological Review 48*, 404–424.

Treviño, L.K., Butterfield, K.D., & McCabe, D.L. (1998). The ethical context of organizations: Influences on employee attitudes and behaviors. *Business Ethics Quarterly 8*, 447–476.

Victor, B., & Cullen, J.B. (1988). The organizational bases of ethical work climates. *Administrative Science Quarterly 33*, 101–125.

Vitell, S., & Singhapakdi, A. (1993). Ethical ideology and its influence on the norms and judgments of marketing practitioners. *Journal of Marketing Management 3*, 1–11.

Walker, L.J. (1999). The perceived personality of moral exemplars. *Journal of Moral Education 28* (2), 154–162.

Walker, L.J., & Frimer, J.A. (2007). Moral personality of brave and caring exemplars. *Journal of Personality and Social Psychology 93*, 845–860.

Walker, L.J., & Frimer, J.A. (2009). Moral personality exemplified. In *Personality, identity and character: Explorations in moral psychology* (D. Narvaez & D.K. Lapsley, Eds.), 232–255. New York: Cambridge University Press.

Walkover, B.C. (1992). The family as an overwrought object of desire. In *Storied lives: The cultural politics of self-understanding* (G.C. Rosenwald & R.L. Ochberg, Eds.), 76–94. New Haven, CT: Yale University Press.

Wilkins, L., & Coleman, R. (2005). *The moral media: How journalists reason about ethics.* Mahwah, NJ: Lawrence Erlbaum Associates.

Wilson, M.S. (2003). Social dominance and ethical ideology: The end justifies the means? *Journal of Social Psychology 143* (5), 549–558.

Wuensch, K.L., & Poteat, G.M. (1998). Evaluating the morality of animal research: Effects of ethical ideology, gender and purpose. *Journal of Social Behavior and Personality 13* (1), 139–150.

CHAPTER 3

A Profile of Media Exemplars by the Numbers

As discussed in the previous chapter, the media exemplars were selected through a process that was designed to identify people who were known for their sustained commitment to quality work. Even so, the resulting demographic profile is useful, particularly when we turn shortly to more detailed data analysis. It is worthwhile to consider the 24 exemplars both as a group and to examine distinctions between the journalists and the public relations professionals. They hail from 10 states: California, Colorado, Florida, Illinois, Maryland, Massachusetts, Missouri, Nebraska, New York and Virginia. All were interviewed between April 2010 and September 2012. Overall, they range in ages from 28 to 66, with an average age of 49.5. They are rooted in their communities, having lived in the same one for more than 13 years on average. They tend to be politically middle-of-the-road, though socially liberal and fiscally conservative (Table 3.1). They constitute a relatively affluent group; more than half reported incomes of more than $110,000. The group is evenly divided by gender, and one quarter of them are non-white (four African-Americans, one Hispanic and one Asian). All 24 have college degrees (nine of them have graduate degrees). The degrees of 16 are in journalism or mass communication. Fifteen exemplars said they took a course focused on media ethics as part of their college education.

The journalism exemplars represent a broad range of experiences, specialties and accomplishments. They share five Pulitzer Prizes among them; one journalist received multiple Pulitzers. Three of them work as editors or managers of online news organizations; two others are consultants for digital news operations. The group also includes a newspaper editor, a managing editor for a capitol bureau, a foreign-policy editor, a computer-assisted reporting editor, a syndicated columnist, a feature writer and one freelance journalist. The group of selected public relations

Table 3.1   Demographic comparison between journalistic and public relations exemplars.

	JOURNALISM EXEMPLARS	PR EXEMPLARS
Average age	45.6	53.4
Years in profession	22.4	29.3
Number of organizations employed	5	3.9
Years with present organization	6.6	10
Years in present job	5.1	6.3
Years in present community	12.1	14.5
Stance on social issues*	6.75	5.67
Stance on fiscal issues*	5.17	2.75
Stance on foreign policy*	5.08	4.25
Political orientation*	5.92	4.5

* Average based on responses using 9-point scale, with 1 = "Conservative" and 9 = "Liberal."

exemplars includes the president and CEO of a prominent international PR firm, three managing partners from different leading agencies, five current or retired corporate PR directors, an agency executive vice president, a senior consultant for an international firm and a solo practitioner. Several are managers or architects of informational and media campaigns that received the Gold Pick and Silver Anvil awards from the Public Relations Society of America (PRSA).

Some notable distinctions emerge between the journalists and public relations practitioners. The journalists on average are younger and consistently more liberal on all four political orientation-related measures. The PR exemplars have on average about seven more years of professional experience than do the journalists, have stayed with their organizations longer and made fewer job moves than their journalistic counterparts. Fully half of the PR exemplars have between 30 and 35 years of professional experience. More than half of the journalists have 20 years or more of professional experience. Half of the PR exemplars hold executive-level positions—managing partner, CEO, executive vice-president. The journalists represent a more diverse range of ranks.

These groups of public relations and journalism exemplars differ from their peers as well in some ways. There are slightly more women than men among the public relations group, reflecting the gender ratios found in the most recent study based on a random sample of members of the Public Relations Society of America (Sallot, Cameron & Weaver Lariscy, 1998). But whereas that representative sample found nearly 95 percent of the respondents were white, the group of exemplars here is slightly more diverse, with nine of the 12 (75 percent) being white. The group of journalism exemplars features more men than women (seven and five, respectively), which reflects the larger proportion of men in the profession as a whole—67 percent men and 33 percent women— as tracked by the representative sample of journalists used in the study of American journalism by David Weaver and colleagues (2007). The median age of the national sample population for that study was 39.1, compared with the 52.5 median age of this study's exemplars. As with other differences, this likely is a result of the selection process, dependent as it was on nominations by peer-group representatives; older, more established professionals are more likely to be widely known. Weaver and colleagues found that minorities continue to be underrepresented in journalism, with 85 percent being Caucasian (2007, p. 12). Among the journalism exemplars, 75 percent are white.

This chapter details the descriptive data that will provide the foundation of a profile of media exemplars. Looking at how the 24 exemplars responded to all the sections of the extensive survey they were given— their personality traits, ethical ideologies, moral reasoning skills and perceived workplace culture, all taken together with a range of demographic data—helps us to draw a basic outline of a type of media professional committed to quality performance. As such, this chapter provides an initial, basic step toward constructing a multidimensional picture of media exemplars. Subsequent chapters will fill in this picture, using inferential statistical procedures to explore relationships among the data as well as identifying and discussing central themes of the qualitative component of this study—the extensive "life story" interviews conducted with all the exemplars.

PERSONALITY TRAITS

How might you describe your personality in a few brief phrases? How might those descriptions hint at your outlook on the world, explain your relationships, suggest the values you hold or indicate your methods—and degrees of success—in tackling problems and challenges? Over the last several decades, empirical work examining peoples' descriptions of themselves and others, as well as testing of various personality questionnaires, has yielded five robust factors that psychologists say largely capture key features of everyone's personality. Several theorists have recently argued that the five factors—Agreeableness (vs. Hostility), Conscientiousness (vs. Heedlessness), Neuroticism (vs. Emotional Stability), Extraversion and Openness—are traits that we all exhibit to varying degrees. The Five Factor Model is not without controversy; there is continuing debate over whether the factors are actually independent of each other, whether the relationships among the factors are more important than the factors themselves and whether we all have more basic human features that underlie these five factors. Nonetheless, a general scientific consensus has emerged in support of the Five Factor Model over the last two decades. Sonia Roccas and colleagues (2002, pp. 792–793) offered a concise interpretation of each factor:

- *Extraversion.* People who score high tend to be sociable, talkative, assertive and active; those who score low tend to be retiring, reserved and cautious. Extraversion is compatible with pursuing excitement, novelty and challenge.
- *Agreeableness.* People who score high tend to be good-natured, compliant, modest, gentle and cooperative. Those who score low tend to be irritable, ruthless, suspicious and inflexible. Agreeableness is compatible with benevolence values—concern for the welfare of people with whom one has personal contact—while it conflicts with dominance, control over others and other "power" related values.
- *Openness.* People who score high tend to be intellectual, imaginative, sensitive and open-minded. Those who score low tend to be down-to-earth, insensitive and conventional. Openness has been tied to self-direction and universalism—a tendency of understanding and tolerance for all people.
- *Conscientiousness.* People who score high tend to be careful, thorough, responsible, organized and scrupulous, while low scorers tend to be irresponsible, disorganized and unscrupulous. It is related to both the "will to achieve" and to a tendency to control impulsive behaviors.
- *Neuroticism.* People who score high tend to be anxious, depressed, angry and insecure, while those who score low tend to be calm, poised and emotionally stable.

As a group, the journalism and public relations exemplars exhibited clear clustering in surprisingly definitive trait patterns. The vast majority scored higher in Extraversion, Agreeableness, Conscientiousness and Openness compared with their age cohorts (Srivastava, John, Gosling & Potter, 2003). Statistical tests comparing means of scores show that the degree of difference between the exemplars' averages and those of their age cohorts is significant for all five traits (Table 3.2).

Table 3.2   Paired samples t-tests for strength-of-difference means on personality traits.*

VARIABLES	MEAN	STD. DEV.	t VALUE	DF	SIGNIFICANCE
Extraversion scores (Exemplar averages)	.09	.94	−12.77	23	p < .000
Extraversion scores (Age cohort averages)	3.20	.08			
Agreeableness scores (Exemplar averages)	.22	.62	−26.81	23	p < .000
Agreeableness scores (Age cohort averages)	3.9	.11			
Conscientiousness scores (Exemplar averages)	.39	.55	−29.18	23	p < .000
Conscientiousness scores (Age cohort averages)	3.79	.09			
Neuroticism scores (Exemplar averages)	−.98	.68	−27.79	23	p < .000
Neuroticism scores (Age cohort averages)	3.04	.11			
Openness scores (Exemplar averages)	.49	.40	−39.63	23	p < .000
Openness scores (Age cohort averages)	3.86	.05			

* Age cohort averages from Srivastava et al., 2003.

In fact, all but three of the exemplars exhibited higher-than-average Extraversion and Openness scores. Conversely, all but four of the exemplars were overwhelmingly *below* average in their Neuroticism scores compared with their age cohort. This is notable because these traits have been shown to relate to different aspects of job performance. Agreeableness and Neuroticism, for example, have predicted performance in jobs where employees work in groups. Conscientiousness has been shown to be a general predictor of job performance across a wide range of jobs; in other words, the higher the Conscientiousness score, the more successful the worker (John, Naumann & Soto, 2008, p. 142). Extraversion has predicted success in sales and management positions, and Openness is a predictor of success in artistic jobs. Exemplars had the highest degree of uniformity in their above-average scores in these two traits, which have clear roles of importance in journalistic, networking and relationship-building duties. Overall, these results appear to reinforce the claim by many moral psychologists that personality traits play a key role in moral functioning; Lawrence Walker and Jeremy Frimer, studying "caring" and "brave" exemplars in Canada, concluded that "several personality variables clearly distinguished moral exemplars from comparison participants and were found to substantially close the explanatory gap between judgment and action" (2009, p. 251).

ETHICAL IDEOLOGIES

If people's responses to ethical dilemmas are influenced by their worldviews, it follows that understanding the basic elements of their outlooks can illuminate the thrust of their ethical judgments. Two such basic elements are key to individuals' "ethical ideologies." One is how *idealistic* they are—that is, to what extent are they optimistic about the actions of others, and to what extent are they concerned about avoiding harm in principle or more accepting of harmful effects if positive consequences are believed to outweigh them. Another basic element is how *relativistic* they are—whether they tend to make judgments based primarily on their own interests and perceptions of "rightness" that are relative to their own standing or views, or they tend to draw on broader, universal principles to decide what's ethically justifiable. Similar to their "clustering" on personality traits, media exemplars in this study share the same ethical ideology to a striking degree. Their responses to the Forsyth Ethics Position Questionnaire (EPQ) revealed their uniform rejection of relativistic thinking.

Table 3.3   Forsyth taxonomy of ethical ideologies.

Idealism	RELATIVISM	
	High	Low
High	**Situationists** Reject moral rules; ask if the action yielded the best possible outcome in the given situation. *Exemplars: (J) = 0; (PR) = 0*	**Absolutists** Assume that the best possible outcome can always be achieved by following universal moral rules. *Exemplars: (J) = 10; (PR) = 9*
Low	**Subjectivists** Reject moral rules; base moral judgments on personal feelings and interests about the action and setting. *Exemplars: (J) = 0; (PR) = 0*	**Exceptionists** Moral absolutes guide judgments but pragmatically open to exceptions to these standards; utilitarian. *Exemplars: (J) = 2; (PR) = 3*

And more than three-quarters of the exemplars can be described as strong idealists. As Table 3.3 shows, a strong majority of exemplars fall into the "absolutist" quadrant of the Forsyth Ethical Ideology Taxonomy. Scoring highly on idealism-related items but low on items measuring relativistic thinking, absolutists tend to draw on universal principles when making decisions and believe that the best, most ethically justifiable outcome is achieved by doing so. The remaining exemplars, two journalists and three PR executives, fell into the "exceptionist" category, meaning that since they rated both relativism and idealism low, they tended to be more utilitarian in their approach, taking principles into account but being more pragmatic—and thus more willing to tolerate degrees of harm if they were perceived to be outweighed by broader benefits—in their applications of them.

While Donelson Forsyth (1980) emphasized there was no "right" ethical ideology to aspire to, the exemplars' uniform rejection of relativistic thinking does reflect higher stages of moral development. As we grow morally, we do tend to rely less on self-interest and views of what's right that are *relative* to our own sensibilities and move toward a recognition that, as moral agents in the world, we are called upon to act out of a broader concern for others based on principles that are universal in nature, not relative to our personal definitions of goodness. Indeed, the architect of one of the more enduring moral-development theories, Lawrence Kohlberg, had as a central aim of his work to defeat ethical relativism on psychological grounds (Kohlberg, 1971; Lapsley & Narvaez, 2004, p. 190). And recent research has concluded that individuals who were less relativistic in their thinking and who had internalized beliefs prohibiting harming others were less likely to make ethically questionable decisions (Kish-Gephart, Harrison & Treviño, 2010). Examining consumers' attitudes toward advertising, Debbie Treise and colleagues (1994) found that people's degrees of both relativism and idealism were related to their judgments of different types of advertising as ethical or not. "Low relativists," they concluded, were more likely to condemn children's tie-in programs, candy and gum ads and ads targeting minorities for products such as alcohol, cigarettes and the lottery. "High idealists" also took greater offense at ads portraying women as contented homemakers (Treise, Weigold, Conna & Garrison, 1994, p. 67). Elderly consumers also were found to be more Machiavellian (low idealism, low relativism) than the general population (Vitell, Lumpkin & Rawwas, 1991). Jeffrey Maciejewski (2004) found that young women, regardless of their ethical ideology, were opposed to marketers' use of sexual appeals. Until recently, the EPQ has not been widely used in media ethics research. This author applied the EPQ to media ethics students to explore the effect of course content on their degrees of reported idealism and relativism. Using key items of the EPQ in a survey of nearly 2,000 journalists in 18 countries, Patrick Plaisance, Thomas Hanitzsch and Elizabeth Skewes (2012) found that country-level, or ideological, factors rather than individual-level variables appeared to have the greatest impact on journalists' degrees of idealism and relativistic thinking. The results here suggest that these media exemplars have developed, at the very least, a heightened sensitivity to ethical principles, as is underscored by their comparatively high levels of moral reasoning, which will be discussed in the following section.

MORAL REASONING

Both the journalism and public relations exemplars demonstrated a consistent ability to draw on higher-order reasoning when confronted with moral dilemmas. As described in the previous chapter, the Defining Issues Test (DIT) presents six scenarios and assesses individual responses to a series of action-justifying claims for each. The DIT has been shown to be highly reliable over the course of decades and has been used with tens of thousands of research subjects in a wide range of professional and cultural settings. Media researchers also have established baseline data on the moral reasoning levels of hundreds of journalists (Wilkins & Coleman, 2005) and PR practitioners (Coleman & Wilkins, 2009). The valuable body of work by Renita Coleman (2003, 2011) as well as her collaborations with Lee Wilkins (2005, 2009) constitutes peerless research that reveals the theoretical links between the moral-reasoning skills of media professionals and their approaches to various ethical dilemmas. They found journalists ranked relatively high in moral reasoning scores among professional groups (Wilkins & Coleman, 2005), just under seminarians, philosophers, medical students and practicing physicians, with a P score of 48.68 (the average P score for adults in general is 40, which indicates higher stages of reasoning are used about 40 percent of the time, while reasoning representing lower stages is being used 60 percent). Public relations practitioners ranked just a few notches lower, with an average P score of 46.2 (Coleman & Wilkins, 2009) (Table 3.4). They also incorporated journalism- and PR-specific scenarios, as the DIT allows, which suggested both groups have significant "local" expertise in questions of harm, public service and respect for audiences or stakeholders.

Table 3.4 Mean *P* scores of various subject groups.

Seminarians/philosophers	65.1	Veterinary students	42.2
Medical students	50.2	Navy enlisted personnel	41.6
Practicing physicians	49.2	Orthopedic surgeons	41
Journalists	**48.68**	US adults in general	40
Dental students	47.6	Business professionals	38.12
Nurses	46.3	Accounting undergraduates	34.8
Public relations practitioners	**46.2**	Accounting auditors	32.5
Lawyers	46	Advertising managers	31.6
Graduate students	44.9	Business undergraduates	31.35
Undergraduates students	43.2	High school students	31
Pharmacy students	42.8	Prison inmates	23.7

* From Wilkins & Coleman (2005), p. 39; Coleman & Wilkins (2009), p. 333.

Table 3.5 Mean *P* scores of exemplar and professional media groups.

Journalism exemplars	**51.62**	**Public relations exemplars**	**50.38**
Journalists in general	48.68	PR practitioners in general	46.2

This study relied on the profession-specific scenarios developed by Wilkins and Coleman (2005).

Overall, moral reasoning averages among both the journalism and public relations exemplars were higher than those reported by Wilkins and Coleman (2005) (Table 3.5), suggesting a consistent ability to draw on what Lawrence Kohlberg, Charles Levine and Alexandra Hewer (1983) called "postconventional" rationales that emphasize the value of broad moral principles over more legalistic claims that the "right" course of action is that which reflects existing laws and social norms. People who draw on postconventional reasoning appear to have internalized universal principles, such as justice and avoidance of harm to others, and are less likely to be driven by relativistic ideas about what is right or by a utilitarian ethic that more readily accepts harm or compromises when majority interests are served. Fully half of the 24 journalism and public relations exemplars had *P* scores above the averages of the Wilkins and Coleman studies. *P* scores ranged from 41.6 (a journalism exemplar) to 70 (a public relations exemplar). Consistent with the history of research using the DIT, there were no significant differences in the scores between men and women. Two of the 12 PR exemplars did not produce usable scores. One of the effective reliability controls of the DIT is that, for each of the six scenarios, subjects must not only *rate* their agreement of 12 claim statements arguing what's important in deciding the case (some of which are also nonsensical, such as, "Whether the essence of living is more encompassing than the termination of dying"), but they must *rank* which of the 12 statements are most important to them in justifying the course of action they believe is right. If respondents include too many low-rated claims among their highly ranked claims, their scores are thrown out. Scores also are disqualified if respondents highly rank too many nonsense items. Three exemplars (one PR, two journalists) had excessive rating-ranking inconsistencies, which required their scores to be thrown out. This error margin is consistent with the error rate of DIT studies over the last three decades (Davison & Robbins, 1978; Rest, 1979).

WORKPLACE CLIMATE

The exemplars' responses to the 36 items that constitute an assessment of the perceived ethical nature of their organizations show some clear patterns. On the one hand, a solid group of exemplars emphasizes a strong belief that their workplaces embody an ethic of caring for all stakeholders. Yet, another group is of the belief that relativistic thinking dominates their organizational cultures. The former may well be an expression of affirmation in which workplace cultures are perceived as being in line with exemplars' broader concerns of justice and societal welfare. The latter could reflect a concern rather than approval; as we have seen with the ethical ideology profile of exemplars in the previous section, they all are driven by a conviction that they are duty-bound to uphold some principles that transcend their own personal points of view and reject the notion that everyone individually must decide what constitutes the "right" action in a given situation. But clearly, a group of exemplars finds that their workplace culture does not reflect this approach.

As described in the previous chapter, the Ethical Climate Questionnaire developed by Bart Victor and John Cullen (1988) uses a matrix to map out an organization's work climate with items that probe perceptions of employee autonomy and a company's perceived emphasis on rules, social responsibility and accountability. While the responses of the exemplars in this study generally affirmed the validity of Victor and Cullen's categories, an exploratory factor analysis found that their items loaded clearly on five factors that strongly suggested a scale of perceived "organizational" moral development (Table 3.6). While these factors did not clearly reflect Victor and Cullen's levels of referents (e.g., whether respondents identified the workplace ethical culture was rooted in individual-level beliefs, the organization's standards and policies or in a broader, external set of professional norms), they did track the researchers' descriptions of a culture's

Table 3.6 Factor loadings of items assessing workplace ethical climate.

	FACTOR 1: WELFARE & BENEVOLENCE (α = .85)	FACTOR 2: INSTRUMENTAL EGOISM (α = .84)	FACTOR 3: CORPORATE LIBERTARIANISM (α = .77)	FACTOR 4: PROCEDURAL LEGALISM (α = .82)	FACTOR 5: RELATIVISTIC MORALITY (α = .85)
Primary factor is each person's sense of right and wrong.	.568				
Primary concern is the good of all the people in the organization.	.820				
Our major concern is always what is best for the other person.	.352				
Major factor is what is best for everyone in the organization.	.862				
Main concern is what is best for employees in the organization.	.710				
What is best for each individual is the organization's first concern.	.587				
Primary concern is our effects on the customer and the public.	.533				
Each individual is cared for when making decisions here.	.496				

(Continued)

Table 3.6 (Continued)

	FACTOR 1: WELFARE & BENEVOLENCE ($\alpha = .85$)	FACTOR 2: INSTRUMENTAL EGOISM ($\alpha = .84$)	FACTOR 3: CORPORATE LIBERTARIANISM ($\alpha = .77$)	FACTOR 4: PROCEDURAL LEGALISM ($\alpha = .82$)	FACTOR 5: RELATIVISTIC MORALITY ($\alpha = .85$)
In this organization, people are mostly out for themselves.		.617			
Work seen as substandard only when it hurts the organization.		.560			
People here protect their interests above other considerations.		.729			
People here are after what is best for themselves.		.819			
The major responsibility here is to consider efficiency first.			.340		
The most efficient way is always the right way here.			.501		
Each person here is expected, above all, to work efficiently.			.700		
Decisions here are viewed in terms of contribution to profit.			.748		
Efficient solutions to problems are always sought here.			.516		

All are expected to do anything to further organization interests.	.502	
There is no room here for one's own personal morals or ethics.	.344	
All must strictly follow organization procedures.	.625	
Each person here decides for himself what is right and wrong.	.575	
All are solely concerned with the organization's interests.	.584	
Successful people in this organization go by the book.	.707	
The first concern is whether a decision violates any law.	.472	
All must comply with law and professional standards above all.	.180	
Everyone is expected to stick by company rules and procedures.	.387	
People here must strictly follow legal or professional standards.	.474	
Successful people here strictly obey company policies.	.523	
All here are expected to follow their personal and moral beliefs.		.765
People here are guided by their own personal ethics.		.765

Principal axis factoring with Varimax rotation.

ethical orientation as ranging among egoism, a concern for welfare and through to a principle-driven ethos:

- Factor One could be described as "welfare and benevolence." This cluster of items emphasizes that the organization regularly takes everyone's interests into account in making decisions;
- Factor Two could be described as "instrumental egoism," with items that emphasize employees are mostly driven by their own interests;
- Factor Three could be described as "corporate libertarianism," with items that emphasize the primacy of efficiency and bottom-line contributions;
- Factor Four could be described as "procedural legalism," with items that emphasize the organization's regulations and requirements for order;
- And Factor Five could be described as "relativistic morality," with items that emphasize the belief that employees are expected to make decisions based on their personal ethics.

Statistically, these factors were at least as robust as the categories in Victor and Cullen's matrix, and in several cases stronger (with alphas ranging from .77 to .85). All but five of the exemplars had their highest average responses for the items in the "welfare and benevolence" and "relativistic morality" factors, with groups evenly split between the two. Nearly all of the journalism exemplars in the advanced stages of their careers and who were employees of multi-outlet chains or national-level organizations appeared to view their company to have a "welfare and benevolence" culture. Among the group of public relations exemplars, the most senior-level executives decidedly perceived their firms as having a "welfare and benevolence" culture as well, while PR exemplars at other career stages and positions were much more varied in their assessments of workplace ethics.

AN EMERGING PROFILE

The introductory chapter cautioned against using the term moral exemplar loosely, since it implies a set of rigid, definitive criteria and seems to preclude human imperfection. Instead, we are on surer footing when we focus on the presence of discernible virtues, a sense of a commitment to quality and a conscientious harnessing of skills and talents in the service of something bigger than any single person. Abraham Maslow said such a focus described what he called "self-actualizing people": "They are devoted, working at something, something which is very precious to them—some calling or vocation in the old sense, the priestly sense" (1971, p. 43). The agenda of this study is not to assert categorical claims about what constitutes the highest "good" in those who work in journalism and public relations. Such claims easily lead to what moral philosophers have criticized as the naturalistic fallacy—that is, asserting what *ought* to be based on describing what *is*. The normative does not necessarily follow from the descriptive. Merely describing the arguably admirable qualities and traits that these exemplars appear to have does not necessarily lend compelling force to any claim that, ergo, these qualities are those that all upstanding media professionals ought to have or strive to develop. Rather, this study suggests that we can simultaneously set the threat of this fallacy aside and uncover the nature of professional virtue in media by drawing on the virtue theory of Philippa Foot. Instead of getting hung up on the nature of goodness, her framework enables us to focus instead on the everyday-life connections between human activity and "objective" reasons for acting morally:

> In spite of the diversity of human goods—the elements that can make up human lives—it is . . . possible that the concept of a good human life plays the same part in determining goodness of human characteristics and operations that the concept of flourishing plays in the determination of goodness in plants and animals.
>
> (2001, p. 44)

In other words, rather than enter the age-old debate over what constitutes goodness, Foot argued that people are hard-wired to seek the good in their lives—a type of "flourishing"—so the things that people do to ensure or promote such qualities are, by definition, virtuous. "Virtues play a necessary part in the life of human beings as do stings in the life of the bee," she said (2001, p. 35). Her deft reframing of the virtues in longstanding philosophical debates serves as a way to link ethics theory with the kind of empirical findings presented here. The tentative outline of a profile of exemplary journalists and public relations practitioners suggested by this data indeed indicates a perception of their work as some sort of "calling," a professional stance driven by a broader sense of public service and a concern that their work contributes to a notion of "flourishing," on the personal, the interpersonal and the public levels.

The journalism and PR exemplars clearly demonstrate a well-developed appreciation for the value of striving to apply key moral principles to all, as evidenced by their relatively high moral-reasoning scores as well as their uniform rejection of relativistic thinking. The importance of justice could be said to be a key thread that summarizes their profile: a fine-tuned awareness of their impacts on others, a conscientiousness of the welfare and interests of others, an agenda driven largely by values of equal treatment and respect. Their high scores on Agreeableness as a personality trait meshes well with these so-called "benevolence" values. So, too, do their high scores on Conscientiousness and Openness as personality traits, reflecting their motivation to apply universal principles to everyone and to cultivate tolerance for others who might be different. These traits are what psychologists have called enduring dispositions: "Traits describe 'what people are like' rather than the intentions behind their behavior" (Roccas, Sagiv, Schwartz & Knafo, 2002, p. 790). And their role in moral action is increasingly clear. As Robert McCrae and Oliver John (1992) noted, Agreeableness and Conscientiousness seem to be "classic dimensions of character, describing 'good' versus 'evil' and 'strong-willed' versus 'weak-willed' individuals" (p. 197). Summarizing decades of research into personality traits and moral functioning, Dan McAdams wrote: "Certain dispositional profiles—high conscientiousness and agreeableness, and at least moderately high openness to experience—tend to be associated with patterns of behavior and thought indicative of high moral functioning. Most generally, conscientiousness and agreeableness tend to predict prosocial behavior whereas openness to experience tend to predict principled moral reasoning" (2009, pp. 15–16). Indeed, while low Conscientiousness scores have predicted a wide range of outcomes that carry negative moral meaning (Bogg & Roberts, 2004; Roberts & Hogan, 2001), the personality trait that may be most closely associated with moral reasoning is Openness to experience. High Openness scores tend to predict higher-stage, or postconventional moral reasoning in adults:

> People who are dispositionally high on openness tend to be
> highly imaginative, reflective, intellectual, and broadminded.
> They welcome change and complexity in life, and they show high
> levels of tolerance for ambiguity. By contrast, individuals lower
> in openness tend to be more concrete, dogmatic and traditional.
> Openness tends to be positively associated with both educational
> level and intelligence. (McAdams, 2009, p. 15)

Emphases on these traits also comport with most of the exemplars' high levels of idealism; the exemplars appear to reject, as a group, any Machiavellian tendencies or a motivation to succeed at the expense of the welfare of others. As shown, many of the exemplars expressed appreciation that such values were reflected in a "welfare and benevolence" culture they found in their organizations, while at the same time other exemplars indicated concern when their workplace culture appeared to conflict with these values and instead exhibited more of a culture that encouraged relativistic thinking. Chuck Huff and colleagues (2008) termed this organizational dimension one's "moral ecology," which cultivates "a profoundly social vision of the good life with members both cooperating and competing but sharing at least overlapping visions of the good" (p. 286). The term also nicely comports with Foot's vision of virtue as that which allows individuals and groups to "flourish." Alasdair MacIntyre (2007) argued that people's social surroundings provide a range of goods and values from which members select to fit into their own personal narratives. Thus, exemplars' perceptions and worries about their moral ecologies are important, as we will see later when we examine their narratives describing their professional lives. The exemplars' perceptions of their workplace culture, or moral ecology, also probably has something to do with the fact that most of the exemplars have solid roots in their community and have invested much of their careers in the organizations for which they work.

Of course, such data provide the basis for nearly endless speculation about the motivations and values of media exemplars. These data, it must be emphasized, provide only the most general, though suggestive, outline of a profile of virtue. The following chapter will use inferential statistical tests to explore the relationships among all these factors in more detail and suggest how those statistical relationships underscore some central themes of courage, justice and internalization of morality into self-identity that emerged in the extensive "life story" interviews with all the exemplars. One thing that does emerge clearly from this tentative profile of excellence is a commitment to quality and to the welfare of others. The profile does suggest the outline of a "self-actualizing" media professional who embraces the professional ethos of public service. The exemplars indeed emphasize a sense of flourishing—of their craft, of the values that ensure their work is respected and of the public they are called to serve.

REFERENCES

Bogg, T., & Roberts, B.W. (2004). Conscientiousness and health-related behavior: A meta-analysis of the leading behavioral contributions to mortality. *Psychological Bulletin 130*, 887–919.

Coleman, R. (2003). Race and ethical reasoning: The importance of race to journalistic decision making. *Journalism & Mass Communication Quarterly 80* (2), 295–310.

Coleman, R. (2011). Color blind: Race and the ethical reasoning of blacks on journalism dilemmas. *Journalism & Mass Communication Quarterly 88* (2), 337–351.

Coleman, R., & Wilkins, L. (2009). The moral development of public relations practitioners: A comparison with other professions and influences on higher quality ethical reasoning. *Journal of Public Relations Research 21* (3), 318–340.

Davison, M.L., & Robbins, S. (1978). The reliability and validity of objective indices of moral development. *Applied Psychological Measurement 2* (3), 391–403.

Foot, P. (2001). *Natural goodness.* Oxford: Oxford University Press.

Forsyth, R.D. (1980). A taxonomy of ethical ideologies. *Journal of Personality and Social Psychology 39* (1), 175–184.

Huff, C.W., Barnard, L., & Frey, W. (2008). Good computing: A pedagogically focused model of virtue in the practice of computing (part 2). *Journal of Information, Communication and Ethics in Society 6* (4), 284–316.

John, O.P., Naumann, L.P., & Soto, C.J. (2008). Paradigm shift to the integrative Big Five trait taxonomy: History, measurement, and conceptual issues. In *Handbook of personality: Theory and research* (O.P. John, R.W. Robins & L.A. Pervin, Eds.), 114–158. New York: Guilford Press.

Kish-Gephart, J.J., Harrison, D.A., & Treviño, L.K. (2010). Bad apples, bad cases and bad barrels: Meta-analytic evidence about sources of unethical decisions at work. *Journal of Applied Psychology 95* (1), 1–31.

Kohlberg, L. (1971). From is to ought: How to commit the naturalistic fallacy and get away with it in the study of moral development. In *Cognitive development and epistemology* (T. Mischel, Ed.), 151–235. New York: Academic Press.

Kohlberg, L., Levine, C., & Hewer, A. (1983). *Moral stages: A current formulation and a response to critics.* Basel, Switzerland: Karger.

Lapsley, D.K., & Narvaez, D. (2004). A social-cognitive approach to the moral personality. In *Moral development, self and identity* (D.K. Lapsley & D. Narvaez, Eds.), 189–212. Mahwah, NJ: Lawrence Erlbaum Associates.

Maciejewski, J. J. (2004). Is the use of sexual and fear appeals ethical? A moral evaluation by Generation Y college students. *Journal of Current Issues and Research in Advertising,* 26(2), 97–105.

MacIntyre, A. (2007). *After virtue: A study in moral theory* (3rd ed.). Notre Dame, IN: University of Notre Dame Press.

Maslow, A. (1971). *The farther reaches of human nature.* New York: Viking Press.

McAdams, D.P. (2009). The moral personality. In *Personality, identity, and character: Explorations in moral psychology* (D. Narvaez & D.K. Lapsley, Eds.), 11–29. New York: Cambridge University Press.

McCrae, R.R., & John, O.P. (1992). An introduction to the five-factor model and its applications. *Journal of Personality 60,* 175–215.

Plaisance, P.L., Hanitzsch, T., & Skewes, E.A. (2012). Ethical orientations of journalists around the globe: Implications from a cross-national survey. *Communication Research 39,* 641–661.

Rest, J.R. (1979). *Development in judging moral issues.* Minneapolis: University of Minnesota Press.

Roberts, B.W., & Hogan, R. (Eds.). (2001). *Personality psychology in the workplace.* Washington, D.C.: American Psychological Association.

Roccas, S., Sagiv, L., Schwartz, S.H., & Knafo, A. (2002). The big five personality factors and personal values. *Personality and Social Psychology Bulletin 28* (6), 789–801.

Sallot, L.M., Cameron, G.T., & Weaver Lariscy, R.A. (1998). Pluralistic ignorance and professional standards: Underestimating professionalism of our peers in public relations. *Public Relations Review 24* (1), 1–19.

Srivastava, S., John, O.P., Gosling, S.D., & Potter, J. (2003). Development of personality in early and middle adulthood: Set like plaster or persistent change? *Journal of Personality and Social Psychology 84,* 1041–1053.

Treise, D., Weigold, M.F., Conna, J., & Garrison, H. (1994). Ethics in advertising: Ideological correlates of consumer perceptions. *Journal of Advertising 23* (3), 59–69.

Victor, B., & Cullen, J.B. (1988). The organizational bases of ethical work climates. *Administrative Science Quarterly 33,* 101–125.

Vitell, S.J., Lumpkin, J.R., & Rawwas, M.Y.A. (1991). Consumer ethics: An investigation of the ethical beliefs of elderly consumers. *Journal of Business Ethics* (May), 365–375.

Walker, L.J., & Frimer, J.A. (2009). Moral personality exemplified. In *Personality, identity and character: Explorations in moral psychology* (D. Narvaez & D.K. Lapsley, Eds.), 232–255. New York: Cambridge University Press.

Weaver, D.H., Beam, R.A., Brownlee, B.J., Voakes, P.S., & Wilhoit, G.C. (2007). *The American journalist in the 21st century: U.S. news people at the down of a new millennium.* Mahwah, NJ: Lawrence Erlbaum Associates.

Wilkins, L., & Coleman, R. (2005). *The moral media: How journalists reason about ethics.* Mahwah, NJ: Lawrence Erlbaum Associates.

CHAPTER 4

Patterns That Point to Virtue

In his 2002 book, *Truth and Truthfulness,* philosopher Bernard Williams set forth a complex argument for understanding the idea of truth as resting on two basic virtues: accuracy and sincerity. These, he argued, are nonnegotiable for all successful human social life, even though they take different forms through history and across cultures. It has never been enough for people to simply *pretend* to care about telling the truth; if that were the case, most all reasons for trusting others fall away. Williams argued that it is only by enshrining truth-telling as a virtue—a stance that other people can regularly rely upon because it becomes regarded as a characteristic of anyone who is known to be or who claims to be virtuous—that truth-telling can contribute to human flourishing. Williams's argument can be extended to virtue in media. Public service as a "calling," their worldview framed by a belief in universally applied ideas of justice and concern for the welfare of others, their self-identity emphasizing character traits of conscientiousness, a knack for working well with others and openness to different experiences—all appear as key characteristics in the profile of media exemplars that emerges from descriptive data explored in the previous chapter. The exemplars in this study clearly "cluster" in ways that tell us some important things about their ability to achieve the level of sustained quality they have reached. They also point to key enduring virtues that appear to be inextricably linked to their professional statures—not only virtues of habit, in the Aristotelian sense of the term, but also that some important personal and professional motivations and dispositions—what drives them, what makes them tick—are closely bound up with a notion of professional "flourishing," as Philippa Foot (2001) described virtue in human life.

Defining features of quality, care and commitment to public service clearly emerge from the descriptive statistical data detailed in the previous chapter. But that does not provide a full account of the profile stemming from the information provided by the exemplars in the survey. We can also perform some inferential statistical analyses to further flesh out the profile of exemplar motivations and dispositions. While descriptive statistics give us a basic idea of where exemplars *on average* fall amid a range of scales and measurements, inferential statistical tests allow us to explore potentially valuable relationships among the various factors in the data. This chapter does just that, extending the quantitative analysis of the exemplars' survey data and thus more precisely identifying patterns among exemplars' responses that point to and underscore notions of virtue, which seem to be central to their sense of self. Here we'll also begin to discern connections between the resulting quantitative profile and important themes that recur in the second component of this study: the exemplars' qualitative "life story" interviews. These links set the stage for us to explore, in the subsequent chapters, the key themes that dominate the exemplars' self-narratives. Taken together, the statistical analyses and the close reading of their life story narratives result in a compelling "moral psychology of excellence" that can inspire and instruct anyone interested in making virtuous behavior among media professionals more pervasive and routine.

KEY LINKS IN THE DATA

Both groups of exemplars, the journalists and the public relations practitioners, have comparatively higher moral reasoning scores than groups of their cohorts tested in other research. They draw on higher-order reasoning, emphasizing concerns of universal application of moral standards and concern for welfare of others. As the previous chapter described, people who do so, drawing on so-called "postconventional" reasoning, appear to have internalized universal principles such as justice and avoidance of harm to others and are less likely to be driven by relativistic ideas about what is right or by a utilitarian ethic that more readily accepts harm or compromises even as majority interests might be served. Also, when their "ethical ideologies" are assessed, the exemplars as a group "cluster" strongly in the "absolutist" camp, where they are characterized as rejecting any tendencies to base judgments on primarily their own personal viewpoints (low relativistic thinking) while also expressing strong concern about the harmful impacts that any decisions might have on other stakeholders (high idealistic thinking). But how exactly might these factors—moral reasoning, relativistic thinking and idealism—be related to each other? A statistical analysis shows a correlation does

Table 4.1 Pearson correlation coefficients for moral reasoning (DIT) *P* score and ethical ideology.

		DIT *P* SCORE	IDEALISM SCORE	RELATIVISM SCORE
DIT *P* score	Pearson Correlation	1	−.508*	.004
	Sig. (2-tailed)		.032	.986
	N	19	18	19
Idealism score	Pearson Correlation			.157
	Sig. (2-tailed)			.473
	N			23

* Correlation is significant at the 0.05 level (2-tailed).

exist (adjusting for the differing numbers of items that constitute valid measures for the relativism and idealism scores). While levels of moral reasoning do not appear related to exemplars' relativism scores, they are negatively correlated with their levels of idealism. That is, the higher the exemplars score on the Defining Issues Test, the less they appear to embrace idealistic thinking (Table 4.1). This may first appear counterintuitive; wouldn't it stand to reason that people with higher DIT scores, associated as they are with greater application of universal principles in moral judgments, also would be rather idealistic in their outlooks? However, it is important to remember that *all* of the exemplars scored low in relativistic thinking (which also explains the lack of correlation between this factor and DIT scores); so the issue is not that the exemplars would be more or less Machiavellian depending on their DIT scores but to what degree their belief in universal moral standards, and perhaps primarily their concern for harming others, could be applied rigidly or not. Those who score low in their relativistic thinking yet also low in their idealism fall into the "exceptionist" category, so what we are seeing is a relationship with exemplars' DIT scores as they are spread along the "absolutist" and "exceptionist" continuum, where the exceptionalists tend to be more pragmatic in their application of moral absolutes depending on what specific situations allow. The negative correlation with moral-reasoning scores, then, arguably reinforces the suggestion of comparatively greater moral development in that exemplars with the higher DIT scores exhibit a greater ability to adapt their principles to best fit the often complex range of contingencies in which they find themselves having to work. Too wise to believe they can insist on a rigid application of moral rules that can fit all circumstances, the exemplars' correlations here appear to represent the American pragmatist strain of philosophy that strives to balance a principled life with a sense of accountability regarding necessary outcomes. A critical distinction between the strength of one's moral beliefs and how successful one is at manifesting those beliefs in daily life is useful here. In their landmark study of moral exemplars of various walks of life, Anne Colby and William Damon concluded that their exemplars did not stand out because their moral beliefs were stronger than those of average people or that they were more morally resolute:

> [E]xemplars' moral commitments are extensions in scope but not in kind from most people's typical moral engagements. Such extensions are made possible by a progressive uniting of self and moral goals during the course of development. This progressive uniting does not rest upon greater capacities for moral reflection, . . . [but] reflects an increasingly functional integration between one's sense of self, one's moral beliefs, and one's habits of social conduct.
>
> (Colby & Damon, 1992 , pp. 307–308)

This point also can be tied to another important aspect of moral development theory: that the DIT isn't intended to categorize people into neat boxes of moral reasoning. Rather, it rests on the notion of "schemas," taken from cognitive psychology. Schemas are the mental links we form about concepts, allowing us to access general impressions and judgments without having to retrieve vast amounts of detail or analysis. Such mental "shortcuts" allows us to synthesize things and apply ideas to new situations quickly. James Rest and other researchers (Rest, Narvaez, Bebeau & Thoma, 1999) who worked on the DIT argued that people have schemas for ethical issues, which they draw upon to help them work through dilemmas. The DIT, then, assesses what kinds of ethical schemas people draw on, based on the premise that if a person has developed a schema representing the highest stage of ethical reasoning, statements at that stage on the DIT will activate them. Otherwise, lower-stage schemas are used. Thus, rather than understanding moral development as a rigid set of steps, it should be seen as the ability to activate schemas that represent higher-order ethical thinking. Not only is that ability influenced by life experiences and personal principles but also by a variety of factors that define specific situations. Regardless of how secure or resolute media exemplars may be in their beliefs in the primacy of concerns such as avoiding harm to others, they are intimately familiar with the endless clashes of competing stakeholders and interests—and the often inevitable harm that occurs in most any decisions about reporting controversial stories or choosing one's battles in the corporate PR boardroom.

Some notable correlations also emerge among exemplars' personality traits and demographic data, particularly when it comes to details of their education and career training. Recall that, as discussed in the previous chapter, both the journalism and public relations exemplars "clustered" strongly in their high degrees of four traits: Extraversion, Agreeableness, Openness and Conscientiousness. All of them also had uniformly low scores on the fifth trait, Neuroticism. When analyzing these scores in the context of their demographic data, some compelling correlations emerge. For one, Neuroticism scores appear related to exemplars' educational backgrounds: Exemplars with lower Neuroticism scores (e.g., described as being calm, poised and emotionally stable) are more likely to have majored in journalism or communication in college (Table 4.2). As with all fields and professions, journalism and media work often draw certain "types" of people; granted, there are no doubt plenty of highly strung, anxious and insecure people in journalism and PR, but the professional success of exemplars here may have something to do with their ability to work gracefully under pressure. Their emotional stability appears to be a definite factor in what they have accomplished. Also, their Agreeableness scores (e.g., described as being good-natured, compliant and modest) show a relationship to the exemplars' stated political orientation (Table 4.3). In other words, the higher their Agreeableness score, the more they are likely to describe themselves as politically liberal. Other significant correlations emerge when considering journalists and PR exemplars separately. Journalists with higher Openness scores (e.g., described as being intellectual, imaginative and sensitive) also tended to have had further professional training and workshops (Table 4.4). Journalists with higher Conscientiousness scores (e.g., described as being organized, thorough

Table 4.2   Independent samples t-tests for Neuroticism scores by college degree.

VARIABLES	JOURNALISM/ COMMUNICATION MEANS (& SD) (N = 16)	OTHER MAJOR MEANS (& SD) (N = 8)	t VALUE	DF	SIGNIFICANCE
Neuroticism scores*	−.79 (.687)	−1.36 (.543)	2.03	22	p < .055

* Recoded variable to reflect degree of difference among exemplars' scores and those of age cohorts.

Table 4.3 Pearson correlation coefficients for Agreeableness scores and exemplars' political orientation.

		POLITICAL ORIENTATION
Agreeableness$^\lozenge$	Pearson Correlation	.480*
	Sig. (2-tailed)	.018
	N	24

* Correlation is significant at the 0.05 level (2-tailed).
$\lozenge$ Recoded variable to reflect degree of difference among exemplars' scores and those of age cohorts.

Table 4.4 Independent samples t-tests for journalists' Openness scores by postcollege training or workshops.

VARIABLES	WITH TRAINING MEANS (& SD) (N = 11)	WITHOUT TRAINING MEANS (& SD) (N = 1)	t VALUE	DF	SIGNIFICANCE
Neuroticism scores*	.62 (.255)	–.48 (. . .)	4.13	10	p < .05

* Recoded variable to reflect degree of difference among exemplars' scores and those of age cohorts.

and responsible) also tended to say they took a media ethics course as part of their college education (Table 4.5). Public relations exemplars with lower Neuroticism scores tended to have majored in journalism or communications, whereas those with higher scores majored in other subjects in college (Table 4.6). The only significant gender-based difference among the exemplars' personality traits emerged with their Extraversion scores, where the women tended to score higher than the men (Table 4.7).

A final portion of the survey asked exemplars to indicate how much they agreed with a host of statements intended to measure the ethical "climate" of their workplace. As discussed in the previous chapter, the resulting data suggested five distinct factors, or organizational climates, that emphasized different approaches: efficiency and bottom-line contributions, reliance on employees to use their own sense of right and wrong, stability and regulatory order, employees' pursuit of their own interests and an ability to take everyone's interest into account when making a decision. Analyzing patterns among these perceived workplace climates and other exemplar data yielded two noteworthy relationships.

Table 4.5 Independent samples t-tests for journalists' Conscientiousness scores by media ethics college course.

VARIABLES	WITH ETHICS COURSE MEANS (& SD) (N = 10)	WITHOUT ETHICS COURSE MEANS (& SD) (N = 2)	t VALUE	DF	SIGNIFICANCE
Conscientiousness scores*	.47 (.624)	−.002 (.101)	2.26	10	$p < .05$

* Recoded variable to reflect degree of difference among exemplars' scores and those of age cohorts.

Table 4.6 Independent samples t-tests for PR exemplars' Neuroticism scores by college degree.

VARIABLES	JOURNALISM/ COMMUNICATION MEANS (& SD) (N = 8)	OTHER MAJOR MEANS (& SD) (N = 4)	t VALUE	DF	SIGNIFICANCE
Neuroticism scores*	−.54 (.67)	−1.42 (.405)	2.38	10	$p < .05$

* Recoded variable to reflect degree of difference among exemplars' scores and those of age cohorts.

Table 4.7 Independent samples t-tests for Extraversion scores by gender.

VARIABLES	MALE MEANS (& SD) (N = 12)	FEMALE MEANS (& SD) (N = 12)	t VALUE	DF	SIGNIFICANCE
Extraversion scores*	.41 (1.11)	1.2 (.503)	2.27	22	$p < .05$

* Recoded variable to reflect degree of difference among exemplars' scores and those of age cohorts.

The first involved exemplars who characterized their workplaces (for better or worse) as having a culture of "corporate libertarianism"—that is, they indicated their organization seemed to place a premium on efficiency and bottom-line contributions (Table 4.8). Exemplars who indicated this climate agreed strongly with statements such as "Each

Table 4.8 Pearson correlation coefficients for perceived workplace climates, idealism and Neuroticism scores.

		"CORPORATE LIBERTARIAN" WORKPLACE	"PROCEDURAL LEGALISM" WORKPLACE
Idealism	Pearson Correlation	.553**	
	Sig. (2-tailed)	.008	
	N	22	
Neuroticism	Pearson Correlation		.418*
	Sig. (2-tailed)		.047
	N		23

* Correlation is significant at the 0.05 level (2-tailed).
** Correlation is significant at the 0.01 level (2-tailed).

person here is expected, above all, to work efficiently" and "Decisions are viewed in terms of contribution to profit." Exemplars who indicated this culture as descriptive of their workplace also were likely to have shown a high degree of idealistic thinking as part of their own ethical ideology—they tended to be highly mindful of issues involving the welfare of others and expressed heightened concern for the potential of causing them harm when grappling with a problem or decision. While seemingly counterintuitive and contradictory, this disparate pattern in the data could indicate that the perceptions of the former serve to underscore the value of the latter. In other words, the correlation could be indicative of exemplars' concerns about their organizations; these exemplars may well have a keen sense that the comparatively self-interested goals of their organizations fall far short of their own concerns and expectations. The second noteworthy relationship involved exemplars who characterized their organization's workplace as placing a premium on the company's regulations and requirements for order—a culture of "procedural legalism," in other words. Exemplars who indicated this culture tended to identify with statements such as "All are solely concerned with the organization's interest" and "All must strictly follow organization procedures." Exemplars who indicated this culture as descriptive of their workplace also tended to have higher Neuroticism scores on their personality traits assessment. This relationship, in contrast, may well be an affirmative indication; people with high Neuroticism scores tend to emphasize short-term decision making and be anxious, insecure and highly strung. Such individuals may value more hierarchical and rule-bound workplaces.

From these statistical analyses of the survey data, a definite profile emerges. Chosen for their sustained commitment to quality and their reputations as outstanding professionals defined by integrity and effectiveness, these journalists and PR practitioners appear to manifest the notions of care and respect for others, duty, concern for harm and proactive social engagement that characterize the higher stages of moral development. In his 1991 book, *Varieties of Moral Personality,* psychologist Owen Flanagan challenged researchers to work toward a more holistic conception of moral functioning rather than remaining wedded to a strictly rationalist, Kantian understanding of the moral life. "Every moral conception," he wrote, "owes us at least a partial specification of the personality and motivational structure it expects of morally mature individuals, and that conception will need to be constrained by considerations of realism" (1991, p. 35). The quantitative results of this study move some distance toward a contribution of such a conception, taking into account as they do moral reasoning, personality traits, ethical ideologies and perceived workplace climates. But as a moral psychology of media excellence, it is far from complete. The black-and-white quantitative outline of exemplary journalists and PR practitioners needs the color, texture and comprehensive shading that only an exploration of their personal and professional narratives can provide.

KEY LINKS IN NARRATIVE THEMES

"In order to explore the depths of moral commitment—its origins in a person's life, its meaning to that person's life, its development and sustenance throughout the person's life—we need to go beyond laboratory experiments, personality assessments, or discrete bits of family background," wrote Anne Colby and William Damon in their landmark 1992 study of 23 selected moral exemplars. "We need to understand the person's life and how the person makes sense of it. The method of investigation must set the moral commitment in the context of a life history. It must establish the person's own perspective on both the commitment and the history" (1992, p. 8). The five pervasive themes that Colby and Damon found were defining characteristics of moral exemplars provide a good place to start. Their selected exemplars exhibited a distinct evolution in their moral life and goals; they seldom saw themselves as moral paragons working in isolation but rather as part of an enabling community; they possessed remarkable degrees of moral courage and a clarity about their purpose; their sense of optimism and confidence in their mission remained intact despite setbacks and obstacles; and they all had incorporated their moral principles so that these principles became part of the fabric of who they were. These themes largely mirror the central themes of the media exemplars' life stories, which will be explored in subsequent chapters. Some of these themes also became the focus of a study of exemplars in computer science by Chuck Huff and colleagues (2008a, 2008b).

The development transformation of moral goals

"Moral commitment," wrote Colby and Damon, "is a continually evolving process that implicates every part of one's personal and social world" (1992, p. 14). The researchers were struck by the fact that, while their exemplars might have been affected by significant events early in their lives that may have helped set them on their paths, a "pattern" of increasingly greater awareness of moral concerns, and a corresponding motivation to act accordingly, defines much of their narratives. This increasing awareness is tied to two things. One is what Colby and Damon called a "reciprocity of influence." Exemplars found and cultivated networks or circles of friends, supporters and acquaintances who served to reinforce and enable exemplars' focus on moral concerns. The other was an "active receptiveness" to new experiences, claims of injustice and calls for change—even when exemplars might not have the ability to articulate why such things would resonate with them. These patterns, the researchers said, suggest "a propensity toward ethical growth even late in life" (p. 13). In many instances, the journalism and PR exemplars recounted their growing awareness of what they wanted to do with their lives and the evolution of their moral concerns and guiding principles. Jeff, now president of an online news organization and living in Maryland, pointed to a confrontation he had with an editor when, early in his career, he was a brash part-time sportswriter for a major metropolitan daily newspaper:

> I think the personal responsibility [value] changed, only because I really was, all the way up to that argument I had with that editor, one of these people who had a little bit of an entitlement thing. Like, "I should have that job, and it's an outrage that I wasn't interviewed for that job, and it's an outrage that this, and it's an outrage that"—I'm getting screwed. I'm doing great work and they're screwing me. The truth is I wasn't doing great work; I was just too entitled. And so ever since that moment, that's been the big one for me, which is, you know, you'll get passed over for things, but I don't ever want to look back in the rear-view mirror and

say, well of course I didn't get that job, I shouldn't have—I was unqualified for it. So that one—the personal responsibility one has been locked in since then.

Mick, a Chicago resident who retired from a career in corporate communications for an international food conglomerate, talked about how his ability to work with and appreciate others evolved since his gung-ho experiences as a special forces soldier in Vietnam:

I think that 40 years ago, that young lieutenant that went to Vietnam was very narrow-minded, very homophobic. . . . I was very, very conservative as a young person, and by being homophobic, I mean, I would make fun of gays, and I would tell jokes that would be hurtful, and things like that. And I think politically, I was very conservative. You know? And didn't look—and didn't have the tolerance to look at the other side. I think over the years I've become more tolerant and moderated, and—you know, like when I was in Vietnam, I thought that was so the right thing, and that was—you know, I wanted to go. I couldn't wait to go. I went. When I got home, I remember I came home, I wrote Nixon a letter. And I believed in it so strongly. Today, I have a different view of it. Now, by the way, I still—the experience was still worth—incalculable to me. The experience—and I don't think it was all wrong, but I don't think it was all as one-sided as I thought it was then. Because I think I was pretty narrow in my—and I think that over the last 30 or 40 years, because of a lot of people and a lot of experiences, and a lot of people that I've been influenced by that I see that, you know, what—there's another perspective. There's always another side to this. Very rarely are things as black and white as sometimes people perceive them, and, of course, I have a lot more tolerance.

Don, a computer-assisted reporting specialist and editor in Washington, D.C., arrived at his "calling" of journalism relatively late in life as he struggled through a period of aimlessness, yet he was all the while motivated by a sense of obligation to put his talent to use in a line of work that had public service at its core:

I was right around, you know, 29 or whatever, at the time. I was kind of the small biz dropout, OK? I kind of dropped out of society and started working and eventually managing a small, you might call it an outdoors shop or whatever, that sells tents and backpacks and canoes and skis. . . . I was missing some kind of personal satisfaction from all those years studying literature. And, I missed some of the kind of—I'm going to call it, civic engagement. I wouldn't have called it probably that back then, however. Because, I had an interest in politics growing up and a minor in history, but then continually I read history all the time—still. So then, I was missing kind of that, and I thought, "Well, what am I going to do?" And I came to kind of a crossroads, deciding in the late '80s, should I do journalism or should I go to law school? And it's obvious which one I chose.

As these examples suggest, most of the media exemplars took years to see their professional goals and moral concerns coalesce into something they could identify as a sort of purpose or mission. Any sort of moral clarity often was long and slow in coming.

The reciprocal nature of social influence

The term "exemplar" can be misleading, as historical and social narratives tend to focus on the drama of individual stories while minimizing the coterie of supporters and colleagues that enabled an exemplary figure to achieve accomplishments and who often walked along the same paths of hardship, perseverance and courage. We see this dramatization of the individual clearly in the accounts of famous moral leaders such as the exiled Soviet scientist Andrei Sakharov (1990; Damon & Colby, 1987) and Mahatma Gandhi (Gardner, 2011). The relationships among exemplars and their support networks, Colby and Damon found, were consistently "reciprocal in their influence" and "mutually transformative": "Initially, there is a partial match of goals between the two. Then there is a communication of new information and concerns, followed by an engagement in new activities, followed finally by the adoption of broader moral goals. In this manner, transformative social influence continues through one's life span" (1987, pp. 14–15). While the media exemplars of this study would never presume to occupy any sort of moral stature like those of Sakharov or Gandhi, their stories do tell similar tales of being surrounded by important supporters whose influence is reciprocal and mutually transformative on some level. "Each step, almost, in my life, I felt very fortunate to be where I was, and under the circumstances that I was—under and who I worked with, or who I was influenced by both personally and professionally," said Mick, the retired corporate communications executive. "[The company], because of the leadership, was tremendously ethical. And the people I worked with, the people who I worked with there and worked for, believed in that as strongly as I did. And you know, I remember when I took that job in 1981, the job that I didn't want, I told [the supervising executive], I said, 'I'll take the job but I'll never lie for you. I'll never do anything that is illegal or immoral.' And he said, 'Deal.' And that was the deal, because I never lied, to my knowledge, on behalf of [the company]. Even to protect the business." Mick said he came to rely on the same candor and support as he rose through the ranks to eventually become chief of corporate communications and media relations:

> I want that from my friends. I want that—you know, candor, and that honesty, even if they're telling me that I am full of it. You know? . . . The hardest thing in the world as you grew in the corporate world, was having people be honest with you. They tell you what they thought you wanted to hear rather than what you needed to hear. And when I was running the crisis management task force, I didn't have time for people to give me a bunch of shit and tell me what they thought I wanted to hear. I needed their opinion. . . . And I needed their best shot, and I have a tendency sometimes, just because of the way I am, to overwhelm a little bit. OK? And, as I said, as I grew, you know—you get a bigger title, it's harder to get people to be honest with you. You know? That's why I think that I brought value to [the company]. Because the chairman—we used to call it sucking around—so many people always sucking around him, you know, and everything. I couldn't stand that. And I never did it. I never played those games. But I was lucky because I had guys who I worked for who let me be honest. They gave me the freedom, and that's what they wanted from me.

Certainty and moral courage

Colby and Damon said they were struck by how their exemplars demonstrated "a combination of great certainty about moral principles . . . with an open-mindedness about new facts and their implications. Seldom did they ever discuss or even acknowledge the notion of moral courage; more often, they talked as if, when faced with hardship or challenges while standing upon principle, they had no choice." This combination often proved to be a powerful one and often explained the exemplars' perception by others as "leaders." "Perhaps this seems a curious combination on its surface," Colby and Damon wrote, "but it is a highly effective one for moral leadership, for it enables one to be both steadfast and adaptive"

(1987, p. 16). The journalism exemplars repeatedly referred to their journalistic "mission" using this framework. The words of Keith, a foreign affairs editor in Washington, D.C., are typical:

> I guess I don't spend a lot of time trying to fit into some larger—to fit a philosophy and try to figure out how to live by it. It's more instinctive than that, but when it comes to doing my job, for me, it comes down to not about personal glory or ambition, it comes down to trying to get good stories, get them right, and get them early. So you try to call bullshit when you see bullshit, try to hold people to what they say, you try to call them out when they screw up. And so that's what I've tried to do all along. I don't know quite how to articulate that as a coherent philosophy.

Ava, a corporate communication chief in Long Island, New York, recalled spending afternoons as a child in the office of her father, an advertising executive, and later finding herself building a similar career. Even while in college, she said she never questioned her sense of certainty about doing what was needed to ensure future opportunities:

> [W]hen I came in freshman year, [my future husband] was going into his junior year, and his program was five years, so he was there an extra year at Hofstra, so he was playing on the football team, enjoying the college life, going to parties, and I was working full-time so I could pay my tuition. So we completely had two different types of experiences. But the reason why I say that growing up the way that I did through my college years—it was difficult, it was very, very difficult at times, so I wonder if the way that I was brought up with just, you know, "Keep going, don't give up, there's light at the end of the tunnel, hopefully it's not train headlights! You'll make it through"—probably did prepare me for that, so that's why I could still term that as "survival of the fittest": Just keep trying and you'll make it through. And then always finding a creative way in how you can get things done.

Positivity and faith

A capacity for finding hope and joy even while frankly facing the often dreary truth was a striking characteristic that Colby and Damon saw in most all their exemplars. Sometimes this manifested itself as an unshakable religious faith; in others it was rooted in a more humanistic belief in the intrinsic goodness that dwells within all people. "It is a capacity that enables them to endure circumstances that would be dispiriting for others," they wrote (1987, p. 16). Faith, a corporate PR director in Virginia Beach, Virginia, referred to her Christian roots as a source of strength and guidance, both personally and professionally:

> It is not about [the company] and it's not about my job, it is about me being the best Christian that I can be and be a representative of Christ in my work and in my dealings and in my communications, in my daily walk, in the excellence of my work, meaning he does not want us to put forth sloppy reports in my judgment. You know, God is everywhere. He doesn't stop at church. Even when I do a press release, it should be done with excellence because that is how God operates.

Yet, this sense of positivity also was sometimes counterbalanced by a tone that was often angry, defiant and bitter—responses stemming from having to endure perceived injustice or hardship because of their principled stands or from a perceived sense of ineffectiveness despite best efforts. Keith, the foreign affairs editor who wrote stories raising questions about the intelligence that provided the basis for the military invasion of Iraq, expressed frustration about the limits of his work's effects:

> To the degree that you look back and there are things that you wished you could have done more, or better or whatever, it's the run-up to the Iraq War—I'm still proud of what I did, but to me it still wasn't enough because it still didn't make a lick of difference, right? So, is that a failure? Is that a regret? Not exactly, but I can't help but wonder what else I could have done, what else—did I need to write more stories, did I need to write them better, did I need to—you know—was there some other piece of information that I could have gotten that would have changed something? I don't know the answer to that. The answer is probably no, but that's not satisfactory.

Uniting self and morality

This pattern is a bit different than the others in that Colby and Damon saw it both as the cumulative result of the other patterns and as a valuable way to explain their exemplars' moral, cognitive and social *development* into who they ultimately become. As they develop in each of these areas, their moral concerns become an increasingly intrinsic aspect of how exemplars see themselves; their moral concerns increasingly shape who they are. Since Colby and Damon's 1992 study, researchers and theorists have extensively examined the relationship between one's identity and one's moral sense. And the debate over the precise nature of that relationship continues. Most agree, however, that "when morality is important and central to one's sense of self and identity, it heightens one's sense of obligation and responsibility to live consistent with one's moral concerns" (Hardy & Carlo, 2005, p. 234). Most also either rely or elaborate upon Augusto Blasi's "model of moral identity" (1983, 1995, 2004). His model suggests our motivation to act on moral principles and concerns is influenced by the degree of people's self-awareness, their desire for self-consistency (e.g., making sure their daily lives reflect the values they believe are important) and how they see themselves as obligated, or responsible, for enacting moral values. "In the end, moral behavior depends on something beyond the moral beliefs in and of themselves," Colby and Damon wrote. "It depends on how and to what extent the moral concerns of individuals are important to their sense of themselves as people. For some strongly committed people, these concerns are of absolute and undeniable importance to their sense of who they are. But the reason for this lies less in the nature of their moral concerns than in the way they integrate these concerns with their sense of self" (1992, p. 307). This integration of moral concerns into their self-identities recurred often as a key part of the media exemplars' narratives. Edward, a veteran PR executive who served as a Chicago-based managing partner for an international PR firm, said his drive to be well-liked and to empower those around him also defined his talent in the PR shop:

> Well, I just see both sides. . . . I think more people ought to be
> in charge that, you know, will listen. I think the ability to listen
> to both sides is the key, and probably what's made me successful
> in PR for the most part, is just an ability—I, my logo for my
> business was two rabbit ears because I just listen. A lot of people
> don't listen. They just start pontificating. And I'd rather listen,
> and you're going to tell me what probably is the right course
> of action if I ask the right questions, and I listen, and I kind of,
> "What do you mean by this?" "Or what do you mean by that?"
> And you're going to get to the right—and you're going to come to
> the conclusion, which means you are going to implement it better
> than if I tell you to do it.

Mitchell, a Pulitzer Prize-winning editor in Washington, D.C., said his ingrained concern about issues of justice permeated his outlook as a journalist:

> I'm an A.J. Liebling follower—"Afflict the comfortable, comfort the afflicted." [laugh] If I have to figure out how I live my life, that's it. If you're rich and powerful, I gotta figure out somehow if you're doing something illegal, or something—. . . I feel very strongly about our court system. Because the administration of justice is important. Because it is so easy for elite groups to do unjust things, and not even know they're doing them. So I think if you don't have a good court system that understands the issue, that you're in trouble. I wrote down, "We *are* our brother's keeper." And I really think that's true. We should be looking out for those people who can't look out for themselves. You should ask yourself whether you've engaged in an injustice, and you should try to rectify those injustices that you see. And you should ask of yourself all the time, which I always try to do; did I do—what I should have done?

A clear and noteworthy evolution of moral concerns; an ability to cultivate a supportive network of colleagues that clarify those concerns and augment their ability to act on them; an unwavering confidence in their perspective and a willingness to bear negative consequences stemming from standing on principle; an enduring optimism and sense of faith; a merging of moral concerns and who they are. The key patterns discerned by researchers in important studies of exemplars in the past also emerge clearly in the narratives of these media exemplars. Clearly, they are not saints, and nearly all of the exemplars talk as much or more about their failures and mistakes as they do about their triumphs. But as we will see, their narratives add a profound richness to the profile outlined by the psychological and demographic data. The next several chapters attempt to do justice to that richness, exploring the central themes that characterize exemplars' moral concerns, that trace the evolution of their sustained commitment to quality and that show how, through personal and professional stories, these exemplars point to what virtuous action in media can look like.

REFERENCES

Blasi, A. (1983). Moral cognition and more action: A theoretical perspective. *Developmental Review 3*, 178–210.

Blasi, A. (1995). Moral understanding and moral personality: The process of moral integration. In *Moral development: An introduction* (W.M. Kurtines & J.L. Gewirtz, Eds.), 229–253. Needham Heights, MA: Allyn & Bacon.

Blasi, A. (2004). Moral functioning: Moral understanding and personality. In *Moral development, self and identity* (D.K. Lapsley & D. Narvaez, Eds.), 189–212. Mahwah, NJ: Lawrence Erlbaum Associates.

Colby, A., & Damon, W. (1992). *Some do care: Contemporary lives of moral commitment*. New York: Free Press.

Damon, W., & Colby, A. (1987). Social influence and moral change. In *Moral development through social interaction* (W. Kurtines & J. Gewirtz, Eds.), 3–19. New York: Wiley.

Flanagan, O. (1991). *Varieties of moral personality: Ethics and psychological realism*. Cambridge, MA: Harvard University Press.

Foot, P. (2001). Natural goodness. Oxford: Oxford University Press.

Gardner, H. (2011). *Creating minds: An anatomy of creativity seen through the lives of Freud, Einstein, Picasso, Stravinsky, Eliot, Graham and Gandhi*. New York: Basic Books.

Hardy, S.A., & Carlo, G. (2005). Identity as a source of moral motivation. *Human Development* 48, 232–256.

Huff, C.W., Barnard, L., & Frey, W. (2008a). Good computing: A pedagogically focused model of virtue in the practice of computing (part 1). *Journal of Information, Communication and Ethics in Society* 6 (3), 246–278.

Huff, C.W., Barnard, L., & Frey, W. (2008b). Good computing: A pedagogically focused model of virtue in the practice of computing (part 2). *Journal of Information, Communication and Ethics in Society* 6 (4), 284–316.

Rest, J.R., Narvaez, D., Bebeau, M.J., & Thoma, S.J. (1999). *Postconventional moral thinking: A neo-Kohlbergian approach*. Mahwah, NJ: Lawrence Erlbaum Associates.

Sakharov, A. (1990). *Memiors*. (Trans. R. Lourie) New York: Knopf.

Williams, B. (2002). Truth and truthfulness: An essay in genealogy. Princeton, NJ: Princeton University Press.

CHAPTER 5

Professionalism and Public Service

The connection between the moral functioning of individual media exemplars and the notion of public service as a crucial virtue may not be immediately apparent. What does it mean for media exemplars to "serve" the "public"? Why should public service be considered a normative term? Does it have to be present for moral excellence in journalism and public relations to exist? What exactly do we mean by the public "good"? To these questions, some compelling answers emerged from the exemplars in this study. This chapter is the first of four that focus exclusively on predominant themes found in the extensive, face-to-face "life story" interviews conducted with the two dozen selected exemplars and that synthesize their narratives with related theories and philosophical claims. In many ways discussed later, the anecdotes and the phenomenological analysis presented in these chapters illustrate the values and dimensions of these themes, and they also reinforce some of the patterns in the exemplars' statistical data discussed in Chapters 3 and 4. Regarding the concept of public service, the exemplars embraced it almost unanimously as a critical, if often implicit, part of their professional and moral identities. Most important was the moral link between how the journalism and public relations exemplars saw themselves in their roles and how theorists have articulated a devotion to the "common good" as an essential feature of what it means to be "professional."

Before getting to the media exemplars' own claims, it is worthwhile to consider what the authors of a landmark study of moral exemplars found on the same theme of public service as a virtue. Anne Colby and William Damon (1992) were struck by the deep connection between the moral self and focus on the common good among the 24 exemplars they worked with:

> Often in public discourse we confuse altruism with self-denial. We take personal suffering as the truest sign of moral commitment. We expect our heroes to figuratively (or even literally) punish the flesh, lead woeful lives, go about their grim business grimly. Perhaps we acquired such notions by observing the decidedly woeful consequences that have befallen the many moral leaders who have been crucified, shot, imprisoned, or consigned to lives of poverty and deprivation. But these are merely the external misfortunes that too many people with enduring moral commitments have had to endure. Unhappy as these misfortunes are, they are still no more than external consequences. They do not speak to the inner experience that determines the true quality of life for such highly committed persons. The exemplars expressed to us the kind of inner harmony characteristic of those who dedicate themselves to purposes beyond themselves. As [psychologist Martin] Seligman has pointed out, the persons at greatest risk for depression and other psychological disharmonies are those who do not have "lives of meaning"—often manifested, Seligman writes, in an overcommitment to self and an undercommitment to the common good.
>
> (p. 300)

The common good—that vague, definitely moral-sounding term was not often explicitly mentioned by the media exemplars in their stories about themselves. And yet their narratives repeatedly came back to the notion in one way or another, circling it and hovering over it while they focused on more concrete examples of their personal and professional experiences. This chapter will tease out the various ways exemplars touched on this notion of the common good and the role public service plays in their perceptions of their professional selves. In doing so, it will provide brief explorations into the theories of public service and its two critical components: the idea of common good, or public good, and the notion of professionalism. It also will explore the different applications of each to the fields of journalism and public relations. As it surveys the relevant stories and anecdotes from the media exemplars in this study, the chapter then will articulate how public service, as a motivating force behind excellent work in media, should be considered a virtue, drawing from Alasdair MacIntyre's notion of "practice."

A DAY JOB WITH "MORAL IMPLICATIONS"

We assign value to many different kinds of work in many different ways. Landscaping laborers, Taco Bell employees, medical-office receptionists—performance in the vast majority of existing jobs is assessed through the delivery of services or products to specific customers. These kinds of workers deliver what Alasdair MacIntyre (2007) refers to as "external" goods—things that are concrete in nature and are deliberately limited in their benefit to only single individuals. They involve the application of a relatively limited set of skills, and their legitimacy is not dependent upon anything more than the successful completion of discrete transactions (e.g., the planting of a healthy tree, the delivery of a reasonably tasty burrito, the courteous handling of appointment requests and paperwork). But the category of work we refer to as "professional," or *professionalized*, is different. The legitimacy of physicians, lawyers, engineers, ministers and others with specialized expertise—and the enjoyment of the public authority that expertise confers—is quite dependent upon something more than how well they might deliver goods or services. These and other professions are held to a constellation of standards and expectations, not least of which is that they are expected to work in service to a broader notion of the "public" and not just to individual clients or customers. In other words, they are *trusted* to serve some sort of public function. It is this sense of public trust so deeply embedded in the notion of professionalism that explains why we are so disturbed by stories of corrupt attorneys, predatory ministers and corner-cutting doctors—such stories represent violations of the trust attached to their positions of authority. It is this distinction that Dennis, editor of a metropolitan newspaper in the southeast United States, referred to when comparing his accomplishments as a pastry chef in his 20s with later winning a national photojournalism award:

> [I]t was kind of a culmination of this 35-year journey I was on. I finally had figured something out. I didn't figure "it" out, but I figured something out, and I had excelled at something that I wanted to do that I felt was a noble cause and a noble profession. I didn't consider being a pastry chef particularly noble. There's nothing wrong with it. It's a good profession, and I got good write-ups and reviews by food writers, and I was really good. But I never considered it noble. I consider the profession of journalism to be a noble profession.

A similar point was made by one of this study's PR exemplars, Ava, a corporate communications specialist on Long Island, when she discussed how she arranged to have her CEO invited to participate in a segment on online commerce on CNN's "The Situation Room":

> [T]he difference between PR people—like, who is a publicity placer and who is just making a lot of noise with no substance, and a person who is a strategic communications professional, there's a clear difference. Their whole thought process is very different. . . . And so I said, "You know, part of my job as a communications person is to think proactively and how to get you in those unique positions where you can be part of a hot topic that is still going to position you in a good light and gets you to a relevant audience. A lot of people [are] watching 'Situation Room.' Hey, you're never going to be in the 'Situation Room' because of how great you are. It just doesn't happen. It's the 'Situation Room.' They pull the news that's about controversial topics." I said, "But as long as we're positioned in a good light and it helps us with whoever our partner is, then I consider that a home run."

Theorists have long debated what exactly constitutes the requirements for a type of work to qualify as a profession (Appelbaum & Lawton, 1990; Koehn, 1994; Kultgen, 1988). Law and medicine, the classic professions, have rigorous training and licensing requirements as well as regulatory bodies that police members. But many other professionalized lines of work may not have all these and yet still are considered alongside them. Regardless, fundamental to the definition of professionalism is that its legitimacy involves some expectation that the work's benefits extend beyond an immediate customer or client—that by definition it is serving a broader conception of the "public." A profession, according to two theorists, "consists of a group of people organized to serve a body of specialized knowledge *in the interests of society*" [emphasis added] (Appelbaum & Lawton, 1990, p. 4). It should be clear here that any work that claims the mantle of professional, or that describes itself as professionalized, embraces an explicitly *moral* dimension in its relation to the public. Daryl Koehn argued that this moral dimension is rooted not in training requirements or licensing boards but in the work's claim to be a form of "public trust":

> A professional is an agent who freely makes a public promise to serve persons (e.g., the sick) who are distinguished by a specific desire for a particular good (e.g., health) and who have come

into the presence of the professional with or on the expectation that the professional will promote that particular good. . . . The Greek *prophiano* became the Latin *professio,* a term applied to the public statement made by persons who sought to occupy a position of public trust.

(1994, p. 59)

Such professionals have developed a "highly internalized sense of responsibility" (pp. 55–56), which is the basis of trustworthiness. This trustworthiness, in turn, is the key trait of any professional's moral legitimacy. "The trustor's expectations that the trustee will exhibit good will toward him constitutes trust," Koehn explained. "And it is trust, not the perceived power of the professional to manipulate things or people, that bestows moral legitimacy" (1994, p. 58).

Public trust and the media

The media have long been considered as being more than just a business or commercial enterprise: a sector of the economy that also carries a moral responsibility to serve the broader public. Government agencies, Hollywood film studios, newspapers, Google and other media-based groups with keen interests in how the Web can be profitable continue to debate the need for regulation to preserve and promote this public-service mission. But the ongoing argument over the Web's public responsibilities is actually a recycled one. In the debate over the exciting new technology of radio in the early 1920s, President Herbert Hoover was among the first to articulate a standard of public interest to be applied to media, which became law in the Radio Act of 1927. Years earlier, Hoover gave a speech on the issue:

Radio has passed from the field of an adventure to that of a public utility. . . . It must now be considered as a great agency of public service. . . . It is our duty as public officials, it is our duty as men engaged in the industry, and it is our duty as a great listening public to assure the future conduct of this industry with the single view to the public interest.

(Dempsey & Gruver, 2012, p. 97)

Since then, theorists have regularly insisted that media enjoy a special place in society because of this moral dimension of the business and that, in treating media simply as a commercial venture, society ignores media's public-service duties at our peril:

> [T]here has been a recognition that the media are not like other commercial services such as banking. They play a major part in creating shared frameworks of information and entertainment, and thus in the formation of national and regional cultures. They are perceived as having moral implications, are associated with concepts of public service and are the object of important rights set out in national and international instruments.
>
> (Born & Prosser, 2001, p. 659)

The claim, then, that public service constitutes a critical part of our definition of media and that it represents an important virtue of media practice is rooted in two more fundamental concepts: the idea that certain kinds of media work, such as journalism and public relations, are professionalized, and that such work must be informed by a solid appreciation of the notion of the public or common "good." All three components of this equation, professionalism, the public good and public service, have been internalized to a remarkable degree by the journalism and public relations exemplars in this study.

MEDIA AS PROFESSIONALIZED PRACTICE

In 1933, Supreme Court Justice Louis Brandeis famously described a profession as "an occupation for which the necessary preliminary training is intellectual in character, involving knowledge and to some extent learning, as distinguished from mere skill; which is pursued largely for others, and not merely for one's own self; and in which the financial return is not the accepted measure of success" (1933, p. 2). For the public relations exemplars in this study, professionalism meant going beyond merely polished communication skills to a commitment to deep public engagement and strategic thinking about relationships—with clients, with government, with public audiences. "I'd like the PR business to be recognized as more than either spin or hype," said Rich, the Manhattan-based CEO of a prominent international PR firm. "I'd like it to be seen as a serious management tool." Emily, a veteran corporate communications chief living in Colorado, said she felt her value as a professional lay not in crafting specific messages but in helping organizations maintain important perspective on their relationships to other stakeholders:

> My role was to bring some of an agency's outside perspective to the teams. Because what happens, in my observation, too often, to corporate teams—and it's not a criticism, it's a reality—is you just get caught up in all of the stuff around the corporation—the internal politics. You start navel gazing and you start looking inside out, rather than outside in. And that was probably one of my biggest struggles, was trying to get people to shift [outside the bubble].

Bill, a San Francisco-based senior corporate communications consultant, agreed:

> The top corporate communications jobs in major corporations are essentially political jobs—political and administrative. You're not writing press releases, you're trying to weigh in and stop people from doing stupid things or saying stupid things. You know, fighting against the chief legal counsel and the chief financial officer and taking flak from all quarters.

One of the secrets to professionalism in PR, according to Edward, a veteran corporate communications chief in Chicago, is good listening skills—quite different from message control:

> I think more people ought to be, you know, in charge that, you know, will listen. I think the ability to listen to both sides is the key, and probably what's made me successful in PR for the most part, is just an ability—I, my logo for my business was two rabbit ears because I just listen. A lot of people don't listen. They just start pontificating. And I'd rather listen, and you're going to tell me what probably is the right course of action if I ask the right questions, and I listen, and I kind of, "What do you mean by this?" "Or what do you mean by that?" And you're going to get to the right—and you're going to come to the conclusion, which means you are going to implement it better than if I tell you how to do it.

Several PR exemplars likened this aspect of their work to law. "Law and PR are very similar in that you are manipulating people with the spoken or the written word," said Karen, a new-products specialist in

Boston. "And, you know, it's pleading your case. Writing all your counterpoints to be able to defend whatever side you are on. I think that there a lot of synergies there." Ava, a corporate communications chief for an online retail company on Long Island, agreed:

> As a PR person you have a working knowledge to every single function. You don't master in it. But I can speak to what we do. So I typically know, and I like to also sit in meetings so that I can learn more, because the idea is I want to understand everything that we do. This is when I feel like a PR person turns lawyer. So you're sitting in a room. It's so funny when everyone is together. So you have your colleagues who are the day-to-day people, and then you have your executive management team. And sometimes you feel, because you're the person who is the liaison with the outside person, they don't realize that you're actually on their team. So we're talking about our practices, going back and forth, and I started to feel like they were building a story for me, and I'm actually the insider. So at one point I said, "Guys, this is when a PR person turns lawyer. I need to know everything. Pay me a dollar—retain me, if that makes you feel better and you want to look at me as a lawyer. I'm trying to help you."

Mick, a retired corporate communication chief in Chicago, recalled organizing his global company's communications department when the corporate world first began realizing such a thing was needed:

> But we were also starting to have things happen in the company that I'll call a crisis, where something bad would happen and there really wasn't anybody that had the responsibility of dealing with it except for, well, if it happened here, the regional vice president in that area or someone in operations or the legal department or whatever so, we started something called a crisis management task force, and I ran it, and it involved people from all major departments in the company, and representatives from legal and operations and human resources, or what they called personnel then, and different functions, and marketing, and generally when something bad happened, we were the ones that jumped in and took the management control of it, and I got to be the Vice President of Bad News.

Many of the PR exemplars' favorite stories involved working with the public in some way, either to avert a problem or to effectively explain a mishap on behalf of a client. Rich, the Manhattan-based CEO, described an episode involving a client whose work inadvertently triggered flooding in downtown Chicago:

> Like in the Chicago River. So, they were doing a job in the Chicago River, and putting a piling in, and all of a sudden, "Oh my God, the water is getting sucked down." It turns out there was a tunnel under the Chicago River, and it took water from the river and put it into the middle of downtown and created a flood, and they had to close all of the stores and the office buildings because there was a flood. So, we were going through the crisis preparation for these guys, because we got hired. I was home in Chicago [at the time], and this guy called me up from [the company]—"Can you help us?" So, we came up with this idea. Show us the map. Show us the map that they gave you. Map: No tunnel. Then we found out that the cable TV guys had been using the tunnel for wires. What kind of a map did they give the cable guys? Cable: Our map. And we did a press conference on a Saturday morning. The CEO said, "Look, I feel horrible because I'm a Chicagoan and I don't want downtown to be flooded, but let me just show you what we had." Because the mayor was saying we're suing [our client] for billions of dollars. And the story just turned like that. . . . That was fun.

Ava, the Long Island communications executive, said the challenges of corporate PR were vastly different than agency work—challenges that put added demands on professional conduct:

> And to be honest with you, half of the time I think for PR people, and I wonder, when you're in-house, in an agency or such, depending on who your in-house contact is, a lot of the stress comes from the education part, internally. That's really what it comes from. And that's why a lot of people sometimes like to work on the agency side, because you look to your left, you look to your right, everyone understands PR, and they know what you do, they understand what you need to do to be able to go in and achieve what you have to get. In house, it's an [education job]—the great part is, you can really integrate yourself into the marketing plan, become 360 [degrees] and really see this consistent message on so many different levels, and the impact it can have to the brand. The flip side is you have to explain your [role] . . . and this is what I try to help my team with. You're not limiting your conversation, but you have to understand when there's too much conversation, when

there's too much information that you're giving them that becomes confusing. And it is a fine line. Because it's like, "I need to educate you, but I'm not going to take you through the process of what we need to do as PR people, because it's going to sound like I'm speaking a different language to you. And it's also not fair to you. Your job is not to understand exactly what I do; my job is to tell you what you need to do to get the impact in my world."

Other PR exemplars spoke more broadly of being attracted to the idea of public service rather than putting out fires. J.P., a Manhattan-based former managing partner of an international PR firm, spoke fondly of his opportunity to take his interest in public-health issues and put it to work for the Food and Drug Administration earlier in his career:

And another one is getting the job with the FDA, which really took me out of the kind of the consulting business, where you can make money, and kind of continuing doing it, or—and then this whole public concept, of the whole FDA stuff, but I think more importantly, the whole concept of public service—policymaking is part of the FDA, but the whole concept of not doing it for the money. I mean, when you are a consultant, you're, "Why am I doing it? I'm doing it for the money. I'd rather play tennis." You know, on a nice day, but I'm working and want to make money. At the FDA, it was, "I'm doing the public good. I'm actually giving back. And getting a lot of it as well." And then having an actual impact on national policy—wow, really heavy stuff.

The notion of public service was often made more explicit by the journalism exemplars, who more readily drew on journalism's deep, traditional roots that involve respecting the ideal of impartiality, scrutinizing society's centers of power and interpreting events to help audiences make sense of the world. Historians have shown clearly how the notion of public service is woven into the culture of American journalism and is intimately tied to journalists' conception of themselves (Hallin, 2000; Harris, 2007; Schudson, 1978). "I think being able to help people understand the policies, the world around them, how it affects them, is incredibly important and very hard to do," said Keith, a foreign-affairs editor in Washington, D.C. He continued:

So to the degree that I have a cause, it is to try to call bullshit when I can call bullshit, and ferret out what people need to know

and aren't being told—I mean, that's the cause. That's enough.
And on a more basic level, just explain what's going on. I think
explanatory journalism is, if anything, just as important and maybe
more important than investigative journalism. . . . And maybe it's
also just become more important amid the noise and speed and
overload of today's media. I just feel that there's so much—there's
so many headlines floating around, that people are losing track
of what's actually behind all this stuff—what's actually going on.
What worries me, much more deeply, is that there is enough biased
media sources that have emerged, that people are just going to
what's going to tell them something that just reinforces something
that they already believe. And we're sort of losing the idea of an
agreed-upon set of facts.

Martha, a veteran newspaper journalist who now leads a local online
news site in Missouri, also emphasized her role as "an honest broker of
the discussion" for her audience:

So, there is a lot of discussion in journalistic circles about
objectivity, and so on and so forth, and I believe that any human
being has limitations on how "objective" you can be, but I think
it's really important for journalists to try. . . . To try to understand
that your responsibility is to go out and talk to people with lots
of different points of view, and try to represent those views fairly,
and try to tease out what the crucial questions—what are the most
relevant and interesting points of view on those? That's how we
can help our communities move forward and understand what's
happening. [The news site's] slogan is "News that matters," so that
kind of a slogan, there's a lot of judgment woven into that. And
of course, your judgment about what's important is formed by, I
guess, your political philosophy and so on, but I hope that what
we're getting across to people is that we're kind of an honest broker
of the discussion, and it means that they [do not have to] waste a
lot of time with, sort of, superficial balance, but can kind of cut
through to some really interesting things that are not limited by
one ideology or another. So that's my social mission, and that's my
political philosophy, really.

The journalism exemplars had no shortage of what they perceived
were examples of work that was successful in serving a vital function for
the public. Jeff, manager of an online news company in Washington, D.C.,

recounted his experience helping to coordinate the coverage of the September 11, 2001, attacks for his employer at the time, America Online:

> [A]nd we did, I thought, considering the limitations AOL has as a journalistic entity—not a whole lot of our own resources—like how we did a really good job on that story, of doing some things that a lot of other news organizations didn't do, because we decided that 9–11 coverage had to permeate every single one of the 18 channels that AOL had on its service. So Kids was a channel, and we decided how to talk to kids about 9–11, and got experts saying something there, and the Travel channel—obviously there wasn't much travel going on for a couple of days, but it was staying on top of when the FAA was going to reopen airspace. And so we used every single property on AOL to tell the 9–11 story, because there were no other stories then—there was no point in talking about anything else for five days. So basically the entire service was repurposed as a, basically, "how to handle 9–11" thing. And I think that was what we did better than others; the *Post* and the *Times* did phenomenal jobs covering the news on the ground and what was the military response, and who's responsible. We did some of that—what we did for the most part is partnered with some really good news organizations that did that. But what we did better, was getting right into how to talk to your kids about it, and what's the effect on the markets. So I was really proud of that coverage.

EMBRACING THE COMMON GOOD

Business ethicist Daryl Koehn usefully synthesized the theories explaining work that implies a devotion to a larger public service into four key components of "the public good":

- It is the sum of the good of individuals who are members of the public in question;
- It needs to be understood as that system of checks designed to curtail attempts by the powerful to inappropriately and arbitrarily control the lives of individual citizens;
- It includes a structure for effective citizen action;
- It includes mechanisms to balance individuals' competing goods (1994, pp. 155–164).

The relevance of the last component may not be readily apparent, but for Koehn it is critical, and it is particularly resonant for public relations practitioners. "The professions will lose their moral authority if they permit or require the individual professional to sacrifice another's well-being as part of promoting another's good. . . . For insofar as the pledge is professed before the entire public, potential and actual clients are equally recipients of the professional's attention" (1994, p. 162). She continues: "While professionals are under no obligation to serve some vague, amorphous good such as 'public welfare' or 'societal happiness,' they do concern themselves with the well-being of other members of the community when promoting the good of an actual client" (p. 174).

As a professionalized practice that is still maturing, public relations' embrace of this concept remains uneven, as a steady stream of scandals can attest. The tension between the aspiration of being recognized as a practice with public service at its core and the centrality of client loyalty enshrined in the public relations code of ethics (Public Relations Society of America, 2012) continues to pose difficult dilemmas for corporate and agency practitioners alike. But when PR practitioners, or any other professionals, fully understand and embrace this notion of the public good, Koehn argues such conflicts should be reduced:

> The pledge-based professional ethic . . . is consistent with and promotes the public good in all four senses of the term. When the public good is interpreted as an arrangement for weighing competing claims, the power of the pledge-based ethic becomes especially apparent. Since the pledger commits to aid any and all members of the audience who hear the pledge and need the good which is being promoted, the pledger must attend to the claims of all members of that audience. . . . Rigorous application of this principle enables the professional to avoid many problems which necessarily arise if and when professionals falsely assume that they must act as the unconditionally loyal servant of the individual client at hand.
>
> (1994, pp. 172–173)

Echoing this, several of the PR exemplars articulated clear distinctions between their work and the business of "spin or hype" on behalf of a specific client. The career of Bill, the San Francisco-based senior communication consultant to multiple international companies, has been defined by his commitment to promoting a culture of corporate social responsibility—even when his efforts fell on deaf ears:

> [A] good chunk of my career is on corporate social responsibility, and I think what I like about—one of the things I'm satisfied about

my career is that people think all these heartless corporations—they never think about the moral issues. What I know is, I raise those issues. Sometimes I won, and sometimes I lost. I never got, "How dare you say that to me?" I never got that. . . . So to the extent that I've been able to influence—I pretty much introduced corporate social responsibility at [a nationwide car-rental company], which is the largest fleet in the world. Now they have the largest non-gas fleet, and if you look, they've really done an impressive amount. . . . But when I went in there, it was, "What the hell is he talking about?" So I've gone in, and I'm doing it with [a national retail chain] now, and I'm doing it with [an international petroleum company], and whatever. And have exerted influence on major corporations, which is really—in a lot of ways, they have more resources than anyone else. And by their leadership behaviors, they pull others, even within their industry, in a certain direction—and it's almost always behind the scenes, but I'm very satisfied by the sort of cumulative amount of good I've done, particularly for the environment in my various corporate incarnations.

J. P., the Manhattan-based former managing partner who specializes in health-care communications, said his involvement in critical issues of public policy was the most gratifying part of his career:

Yeah. I tell people here in the health-care practice, I think the health-care public relations is more important than anything else, because when you succeed, you actually help people's lives. I mean, we sell razors. Gillette is one of our biggest clients. That's great. I'm all for selling razors. You know, some razors are better than others. But when you help somebody with their health, that's a higher calling.

For the journalism exemplars, this notion of the common good appeared to be more seamlessly aligned with their daily work. Indeed, many talked as though it were their reason for being. Linda, an investigative journalist in Denver, said she remembers being concerned about questions of social justice as a little girl:

I think I can trace this to an afternoon spent with my grandparents in St. Charles [Missouri], where we were down by the river and we saw this guy breaking into a parking meter and stealing the change. And my sister and I and my cousin and, I believe, his little brother was there too. He was a little bit younger than the three of us, but I know the three of us were there and um, my grandmother—so we stopped a police officer and said we had seen this crime, this terrible crime occur, and we felt very good about what we had done, and my grandmother, who was a first-grade teacher, then took us home to her house and made us write a little story about it. So, I wrote my story, which I can't remember any of, but I remember my cousin's story very clearly, because he ended it with a picture of the American flag and the word "Justice." [laugh] So, actually, I'm in this business because I have been trying to, you know, outdo my cousin's story.

Elaine, a Pulitzer Prize-winning feature writer in Florida, described her outlook with a similar kind of missionary zeal:

I mean, I don't want to say I think of my job as like a ministry, but I think a part of the challenge and the honor and the purpose of being a journalist is to show the humanity in everybody and to help people, Jesus-like, not judge. You know? And to witness, to find that there is this commonality, that even the sex offenders living under the bridge miss their kids. You know, even the guy who killed his mother and buried her under a sand dune wants his old guitar so he can sing a song to his dad. You know? . . . There's people inside all of these statistics and these news stories that so many times don't—you don't get to the heart of that or the core of that. I like to say I like to write about people in the shadows. . . . I think that's my ideology, and in a very roundabout way of saying, it is like, expose the humanity in people and believe that everybody not only has a story but has something in them that is good and human and worth sharing. That you just shouldn't judge. You know you need to walk around in someone's moccasins.

Mitchell, another Pulitzer-winning journalist who is now a managing editor for a large Washington, D.C. bureau, shared Elaine's ideology but worried it was eroding:

I think we're very guilty of being very conventional, and one of the problems that I think newspapers have is that they're very boring. In the post-Watergate years and—if you go back to, say, the run-up to the Iraq war, newspapers weren't courageous, they didn't ask questions. . . . And I often wonder, how is it that so many media competitors got it so wrong? And people who were so easily intimidated by their own readers. You know, it's an interesting question, because I do think the values that we admired as we became journalists, some of them slipped away, in some news organizations. And I know I encounter editors all the time who I wonder how did you become so conservative—I don't mean that politically, I don't mean in your personal life, but what you're willing to talk to your readers about.

Martha, editor of an online news site in Missouri, said her organization has learned how to use technology to serve its audience in a different way, to cultivate public engagement:

[W]e were just talking about this yesterday, because we're going to relaunch the [news site] with some new technology that's going to enable us to do some things a lot better than we're doing them now. [S]o we're thinking about, "What is it that we are really doing, and how are we going to talk to people about this?" And we realized that the heart of the [news site] is really two things: It's the in-depth journalism, but it's also community engagement. . . . It wasn't that we were indifferent to—you know, "Is anybody going to pay attention to this?" We were interested in that, but now we really see that our job isn't just to sort of take the thing and throw it out the door and throw it onto somebody's lawn; our job is to think about, "How does this get into somebody's head in a useful way? What can we do?" And then also, "How can we tap the knowledge and experience that others have in a way that makes it accessible and useful to people?" In a way, it's a subtle shift, but it's also a very fundamental change in how we think about our world.

James, manager of online content for a national broadcasting organization based in Washington, D.C., said he is inspired by the possibilities that technology poses to give journalism, community dialogue and storytelling, new power:

We've just never had a document like Wikipedia. Something that— they have this saying that's stuck with me for a long time: truth is an asymptote. If you can always say something true, then you can always say something truer. And that—I think journalism at its most powerful, would be about a constant quest to describe the world, ever more truly, and that process doesn't exactly have an end, but the better we can understand ourselves—I think it means we'll start asking ourselves questions, not just like what's the most important thing happening today, or this week. . . . That we're constantly trying to find the best contrary truth for the information we present. I love that idea, we're constantly—the truth that life is a wrestling match, to constantly find the best contrary truth, to really explore it. I think that—that the asymptote, approaching ever closer, I think, is a powerful idea.

But neither new digital opportunities nor the implosion of journalism as a business changes the core public-service function of the work, all the exemplars emphasized. Here is Mitchell:

> I wrote down, We *are* our brother's keeper. And I really think that's true. We should be looking out for those people who can't look out for themselves. You should ask yourself whether you've engaged in an injustice, and you should try to rectify those injustices that you see. And you should ask of yourself all the time, which I always try to do—did I do what I should have done? . . . My life's theme is to challenge authority, to be always testing. And, nothing is as it seems. Anyone in authority who's telling you something, you have to examine the argument, ask what are they getting out of it. And so I would say that's my life theme. [laugh]

DRIVEN BY A SENSE OF "THE PUBLIC"

Appreciation for what it means to act as a "professional," added to a deep understanding of and concern for the "common good," equals work defined by its commitment to public service. The media exemplars in this study repeatedly acknowledged this equation in their personal and professional stories about themselves. While many spoke in generalities, as in the examples above, they also could be quite concrete about what public relations work and journalism driven by public-service concerns actually looks like. The manifestations of their ideas of public service were wide-ranging. Mitchell, the Washington bureau editor, recalled flying over the destruction of Hurricane Andrew in 1992 after it roared across Florida:

> We embarked on an investigation of housing codes in south Florida, basically because I asked a question, after an over-flight of the area a couple of days after it got hit by the hurricane—we had all these aerial photos out there, and a lot of them were just rows and rows

of roofless houses, and I said, "Here's what I want to know: Was this a huge hurricane, or is this a lot of crappy houses?" Turned out they were a lot of crappy houses. And we went out and got an engineer who went out and examined the houses, and in four or five days, we basically had a story that said these houses weren't built to code, we dug down into the building code itself, and it really had a long-term impact on south Florida, and getting people to think about things like how long their roofing nails ought to be. It turns out, that's an important calculation. How thick should your felt be, on your roof? That turns out to be important. Is it plywood, or something else? Is it quarter-inch plywood, or three-quarter-inch plywood? And those are things that people didn't think about that turned out to be critical in how destructive that particular storm was going to be.

Linda, the Denver-based investigative journalist, recalled work she did that uncovered systematic corruption in an eastern U.S. state police crime lab:

So, two women had been abducted and raped from the [local mall] right around Christmas time, and that sort of thing just didn't happen, right? So, it was big. They found this guy and they—you know, prosecuted him, and they put him in prison. And all the while, of course, he's saying, "You've got the wrong guy." He finally got a lawyer to persuade a judge to give him a DNA test, and it was one of the first DNA tests in the country, in a courtroom. Sure enough, they had the wrong guy. And when I got there, I had found out that, well, the state paid this man . . . $1 million. Which doesn't seem so unusual now, but then, it was—you know, all my red flags went off. This is more than just, "Oops, we screwed up. Here you go. Sorry for taking seven years of your life." [But the state] didn't have a million dollars lying around to give away as an apology. And I found out that the head of the State Police crime lab had faked evidence to convict him. And the end of the story is the State Supreme Court actually wound up reopening 134 rape and murder cases after we reported. I know for sure, six people have been released from prison because of that. So, having had some role in seeing innocent people released from prison—I was hooked. I would never do any other kind of reporting.

That same embrace of the public-service imperative also made many exemplars keenly aware of examples when they felt the media failed to embody it. James, the online content manager, said he remembered being embarrassed by local television news as an intern at a Florida affiliate:

> [S]ummer after sophomore year, I ended up doing a broadcast internship—in Orlando, actually, at WESH. And, it was a production assistant internship, because I said, newspapers are wonderful, but seems a bit too rigidly tracked, maybe the broadcast world would be a little bit more my speed. So, I tried an internship at WESH, had great fun, really liked the editors, loved running the Teleprompter, getting to see the crazy weather guy, but, the journalism—I remember specifically, one night, being in the newsroom, when a man had—the details are fuzzy to me, but a man had walked into a house, and taken a family hostage. I remember there was some detail, indication, that it couldn't end well, that someone would end up being shot. And it felt like the type of story you saw on the evening news all the time, but being in the newsroom made it just incredibly powerful, very vivid, of this family being in this house, fearing for their lives. . . . And the realness of it, was palpable. And I just remember being horrified by this family, and then went home, watched the broadcast that evening. And it was such a sort of oddly disconnected or dry presentation of what I'd felt. It somehow reduced this element, this story, to 90 seconds of abstract shots of police caution tape, a shot of the mailbox, police officers milling around, sort of out-of-focus shots of the house—it was—the language of broadcast journalism had become so stultified that you couldn't actually tell that story.

Several exemplars recounted experiences where they felt they might have failed to fulfill their own public-service ideals. Keith, the foreign-affairs editor in Washington who made several reporting trips to Iraq soon after the American invasion, has mixed feelings about his coverage:

> To the degree that you look back and there's things that you wished you could have done more, or better, or whatever it's the run-up to the Iraq War, or whatever—I'm still proud of what I did, but to me it still wasn't enough because it still didn't make a lick of different, right? So, is that a failure? Is that a regret? Not exactly, but can't help but wonder what else I could have done, what else—did I need to write more stories, did I need to write them better, did I need to—you know—was there some other piece of information that

I could have gotten that would have changed something? I don't
know the answer to that. The answer is probably no, but that's not
satisfactory.

Emily, the veteran corporate communications specialist living in
Denver, talked about her frustration as PR director for a global food
chain's European operations when so-called "mad cow" disease caused
hysteria across the continent in the 1990s:

> I was still living and working in London, I was working with a
> British company to help manage the impact on the business. It was
> hitting all over Europe. Even though it was in the UK, everything
> was going—think about it today—it was "viral." It was bad enough
> the story being picked up on SKY TV and so on. The global
> communications head said: "We're not going to do anything." My
> counsel was that: "You can't *not* do anything! You know, people
> listen with half an ear—consumers are not going to differentiate."
> And it was really difficult, because he's sitting in [the United
> States], and the story is not even on the radar screen [there]. Yet
> sales are off 50% to 75% in the UK, and the managing director of
> France is calling, the managing director of Belgium is calling—of
> Holland—and they're beside themselves, because customers are
> asking questions and their sales are dropping as well. And they're
> saying, "Our customers need to know." I am counseling my client
> that "We've got to put something in the restaurants," and [the
> global communications head said] "No, no, no, it'll just fan the fire!
> It'll just fan the fire!" Well, and the Europeans just said, "Screw
> 'em, we'll do it our own way." And instead of having a cohesive
> approach, people were going rogue because they had to reassure
> their customers. You know, in France, it's French beef, so "screw the
> bulldogs." It's French beef. Don't worry about it.

In some cases, the media exemplars admitted they were unsure how
exactly to fulfill a public-service function. Ava, the corporate communications director for an online retail conglomerate on Long Island, said
she struggled over how, or whether, her company should respond when
Osama bin Laden's killing by U.S. forces in May 2011 triggered a surge
of patriotic fervor:

> [F]or instance, like the passing of Osama bin Laden. A lot of
> retailers jumped at the opportunity to have materials out there that

celebrated that, and you have to ask yourself as a person, is it OK to do that? Now, how do you have that conversation at work? Do you condone it? It was funny, because my boss and I happened to be on the same page with that, which I was completely shocked by. Not shocked at him, and nothing against him whatsoever but, he came into my office and he said, "You know, it was a thing that needed to be done, but as a corporation you can't celebrate this." And I'm sitting here, like, "Thank God! I feel the same way." But I was never going to get into that battle with him, because I didn't even know if we were going to have to talk about that. But the question is as a PR person, when you see all these retailers, you think to yourself as a corporation, "Are they going to come to us and ask us how we feel about the fact of throwing red, white and blue things up on the site now all of a sudden because people are feeling so patriotic?" How do you handle that? And how do you handle that in a most subtle way that you don't come across like [you're celebrating death?] I said to him, "We need to be very, very careful. It is a thin line to walk. I don't want us to celebrate it, and I don't want us to be read as an organization that's doing that."

PUBLIC SERVICE AS A VIRTUE IN MEDIA

These accounts by media exemplars suggest how valuable the concept of public service is to excellence in media work. But we can be much more precise in situating the concept's philosophical value within virtue theory. In his landmark work *After Virtue,* philosopher MacIntyre made the important observation that Homeric and Aristotelian accounts of virtue always assume the fact that features of our social and moral lives are widely accepted as important and as necessary conditions for the enactment of virtuous behavior. In the Homeric tradition, virtues are presented as qualities crucial for effectively performing certain *social roles.* Similarly, for Aristotle, the virtues as he often described them are not ends in themselves but are instrumental in the broader aim of achieving "the good life," or *eudaimonia* (MacIntyre, 2007, p. 148; Prior, 2001). "[T]his notion of a particular type of practice as providing the arena in which the virtues are exhibited . . . is crucial to the whole enterprise of identifying a core concept of virtues," MacIntyre argued (2007, p. 187). Earlier, this chapter referred to MacIntyre's idea of "external" goods—things or acts that benefit single individuals. In contrast, he referred to the social benefits resulting in some work as "internal" goods. The medical profession's importance to general public health, as opposed to single patients, is an example of an internal good. The kinds of (often specialized) work that we value primarily for the internal goods they provide, MacIntyre argued, constitute the basis for virtue in professional behavior. We must understand this work as a "practice" that is distinct from other work focused on delivering strictly external goods (e.g., factory work, retail transactions, etc.):

> By "practice" I . . . mean any coherent and complex form of socially established cooperative human activity through which goods internal to that form of activity are realized in the course of trying to achieve those standards of excellence which are appropriate to, and partially definitive of, that form of activity, with the result that human powers to achieve excellence, and human conceptions of the end and good involved, are systematically extended.
>
> (2007, p. 187)

Practices involve "standards of excellence and obedience to rules" and are aimed at attaining internal goods, or things that contribute to the common good regardless of who actually receives them. Media professionals, when deliberately informing their work with the "standards of excellence" that are attached to their "practices," are able to deliver internal goods such as providing information and analysis that enables the public to participate in a vigorous democratic life (journalism) or providing messages and advocacy of perspectives that contribute to a vibrant marketplace of ideas (public relations). As Sandra Borden summarized, "an occupation's purpose provides it with moral justification, from a virtue perspective, if it can be integrated into a broader conception of what is good for humans" (2007, p. 16). In her book *Journalism as Practice*, she made the compelling case that journalism should indeed be treated as a MacIntyrean *practice*. Victor Pickard, too, eloquently described the "practice" of journalism having internal goods as its aim:

> [Journalism] is an essential public service with social benefits that transcend its revenue stream. In its ideal form, journalism creates tremendous positive externalities. It serves as a watchdog over the powerful, covers crucial social issues, and provides a forum for diverse voices and viewpoints. As such, journalism functions as democracy's critical infrastructure.
>
> (2011, p. 76)

While there is as yet no counterpart who has made a similarly explicit case for public relations, many PR practitioners and theorists have suggested such. "The fundamental marketplace principles of access, process, truth and disclosure provide an ethical floor on which public relations practice standards can be built," wrote Kathy Fitzpatrick (2006, p. 17). Here are just a couple of the many similar claims that imply PR is a MacIntyrean practice:

> The social justification for public relations in a free society is to
> ethically and effectively plead the cause of a client or organization
> in the freewheeling forum of public debate. It is a basic democratic
> right that every idea, individual, and institution shall have a
> full and fair hearing in the public forum—and that their merit
> ultimately must be determined by their ability to be accepted in
> the marketplace.
>
> (Cutlip, 1994, p. xii)

> Through rhetoric, individuals and organizations negotiate their
> relationships. To do so, they form opinions of one another, decide
> on actions, set limits, and express obligations that influence how
> each is to act toward the other. . . . Opinions that are formed
> set standards of ethical performance to which organizations are
> expected to adhere, and they foster understanding of public policy
> issues, such as the impact manufacturing processes have on the
> environment.
>
> (Heath, 1992, pp. 18–19)

The question of loyalty in public relations

"We have to accept as necessary components of any practice with internal goods and standards of excellence the virtues of justice, courage and honesty," MacIntyre argued. "For not to accept these . . . so far bars us from achieving standards of excellence or the goods internal to the practice that it renders the practice pointless except as a device for achieving external goods" (2007, p. 191). For all the aspirational theorizing about public relations as a maturing *profession*, the tension between internal goods obviously supported by PR and the premium practitioners place on client "loyalty" continues to result in stark ethical lapses. "Loyalty" and "advocacy" are institutionalized as "key professional values" in the Member Code of Ethics promoted by the Public Relations Society of America, yet these values can be described as merely "external" goods in a MacIntyrean sense. It is useful to recall the definition of professionalism by business ethicist Koehn in which the practitioner pledges service to all actual and potential "clients"—that is, to the broader public, primarily. Koehn argued that a professional who is exclusively focused on serving the interests of individual clients "ignores the professions' own understanding of themselves as having responsibilities to persons other than their current client base." To argue otherwise, she said, is "naïve." "Lawyers," she argued, "historically have seen themselves as 'officers of the court,' ministers as 'servants of the church.' These roles are the professionals' way of talking about responsibilities they have to members of the public who are not actual clients but who certainly qualify as potential clients" (1994, p. 145). She could have been speaking directly to public relations practitioners when she continued: "[I]f the professional is indeed bound to do whatever the client wants as long as the client's desires do not interfere with others' desire satisfaction, then the professional is little more than a hired hand" (1994, p. 38). So might another business ethicist, John Kultgen, when he wrote: "Professionals serve clients and employers and, ostensibly, society as a whole through this service. Sometimes service to patrons does indeed redound to the public good and is justified by the principle of special responsibilities. But sometimes it does not. Patron loyalty takes priority over public interest. This pollutes the stream of professional practice at its spring" (1988, p. 4). If PR practitioners continue to insist that their craft be considered professionalized work, the field will need to mature in its understanding that its moral authority lies not with the narrow value of client loyalty but in its dedication to the broader internal goods of dialogue and democratic exchange—as illustrated by the PR exemplars in this study.

In contrast to the failures resulting from the implosion of journalism's commercial business model, and despite the ethically questionable cases in which PR client interests are placed above the common good, the narratives of the media exemplars in this study illustrate what can happen when media "professionals" understand the concept of public service and its deep normative connection to their work. Not only do their examples ringingly affirm the definition of a "practice" as work supporting the common good through virtuous behavior, they also underscore another philosopher's call for media to promote the moral imperative of pluralism. "An adequate view [of media's obligations] would have to identify practices of toleration that sustain the presuppositions of public communication, in forms from which nobody is excluded," wrote Onora O'Neill (1990, p. 167). When practiced with a deep appreciation of their work as a public service, as these media exemplars demonstrate, journalists and PR practitioners truly do contribute to human "flourishing" in Aristotle's sense of the word.

REFERENCES

Appelbaum, D., & Lawton, S.V. (Eds.) (1990). *Ethics and the professions.* Englewood Cliffs, NJ: Prentice-Hall.

Borden, S.L. (2007). *Journalism as practice: MacIntyre, virtue ethics and the press.* Burlington, VT: Ashgate.

Born, G., & Prosser, T. (2001). Culture and consumerism: Citizenship, public service broadcasting and the BBC's fair trading obligations. *Modern Law Review 64* (5), 657–687.

Brandeis, L. (1933). *Business – A profession.* Boston: Hale, Cushman and Flint.

Colby, A., & Damon, W. (1992). *Some do care: Contemporary lives of moral commitment.* New York: Free Press.

Cutlip, S. (1994). *The unseen power: Public relations; a history.* Hillsdale, NJ: Lawrence Erlbaum Associates.

Dempsey, J.M., & Gruver, E. (2012). "The public interest must dominate": Herbert Hoover and the public interest, convenience and necessity. *Journal of Radio & Audio Media 19* (1), 96–109.

Fitzpatrick, K. (2006). Baselines for ethical advocacy in the "marketplace of ideas." In *Ethics in public relations: Responsible advocacy* (K. Fitzpatrick & C. Bronstein, Eds.), 1–17. Thousand Oaks, CA: SAGE.

Hallin, D.C. (2000). Commercialism and professionalism in the American news media. In *Mass media and Society* (3rd ed.) (J. Curran & M. Gurevitch, Eds.), 218–237. London: Edward Arnold.

Harris, R.J. (2007). *Pulitzer's gold: Behind the prize for public service journalism.* Columbia: University of Missouri Press.

Heath, R.L. (1992). The wrangle in the marketplace: A rhetorical perspective on public relations. In *Rhetorical and critical approaches to public relations* (E.L. Toth & R.L. Heath, Eds.), 17–36. Hillsdale, NJ: Lawrence Erlbaum Associates.

Koehn, D. (1994). *The ground of professional ethics.* New York: Routledge.

Kultgen, J. (1988). *Ethics and professionalism.* Philadelphia: University of Pennsylvania Press.

MacIntyre, A. (2007). *After virtue: A study in moral theory* (3rd ed.). Notre Dame, IN: University of Notre Dame Press.

O'Neill, O. (1990). Practices of toleration. In *Democracy and the mass media* (J. Lichtenberg, Ed.), 167. Cambridge: Cambridge University Press.

Pickard, V. (2011). Can government support the press? Historicizing and internationalizing a policy approach to the journalism crisis. *Communication Review 14,* 73–95.

Prior, W.J. (2001). *Eudaimonism* and virtue. *Journal of Value Inquiry 35,* 325–342.

Public Relations Society of America. (2012). PRSA Member Code of Ethics. Available: www.prsa.org/AboutPRSA/Ethics/CodeEnglish/index.html Retrieved 19 July 2012.

Schudson, M. (1978). *Discovering the news: A social history of American newspapers.* New York: Basic Books.

CHAPTER 6

Moral Courage

Richard G. Starmann had taken his wife out for a birthday dinner in downtown Chicago in July 1984 when the calls started coming. A Vietnam veteran walked into a McDonald's restaurant in southern California and opened fire with his M-16 rifle. He shot 40 people, including children, killing 21 and wounding 19 before he was killed by a police officer. Starmann, chief of McDonald's worldwide communications efforts, was quickly forced into crisis-communication mode by what became one of the deadliest massacres in U.S. history. Over the next few frantic days, he was the center of the company's public responses, from managing the flood of media calls, cancelling TV ads and arranging support for funerals and victims' hospital bills. But two moments in particular stood out for Starmann. One was the formation of what later became known as the "Horwitz Rule":

> It was expressed by Don Horwitz, then executive vice president and general counsel of the company, who the day after the incident told a few of us who were responding to more than 1,000 media calls, "I don't want you people to worry or care about the legal implications of what you might say. We are going to do what's right for the survivors and families of the victims, and we'll worry about lawsuits later." "We're going to do what's right" became the "Horwitz Rule."
>
> (Starmann, 1993, p. 309)

The second moment occurred several days later, when Starmann and other McDonald's executives were on a corporate plane flying to San Ysidro, without any public announcements, to attend funeral services of the victims. A pressing question emerged: what to do with the restaurant, where a makeshift shrine of candles, photos and notes for victims had sprung up. "[W]hen we flew out to San Diego, there had been a heated discussion about whether or not to reopen the restaurant," Starmann wrote. "While I truly could see both sides of the argument, I had strongly urged that we close the site—forever" (1993, p. 315). Other executives felt just as strongly that doing so would be to capitulate to the violence, instead arguing that the store should be reopened as soon as possible, to send a message of the company's resilience and resolve:

> Within six hours after the shooting, the president of McDonald's USA, with all good faith and intention, had concluded in his mind that the best thing for us to do after this was all over was to rebuild and reopen that restaurant. I was diametrically opposed to that. On the way out there, [the executive] and I went toe to toe, and I thought . . . he was going to throw me out of the plane. And we went toe to toe for three and a half hours, screaming and yelling at each other. I wanted it torn down, and he wanted to rebuild it, and he had people coming from different states—new seating, new equipment, new packages—and he was all set, and [the police] hadn't even turned the store back over to us. . . . The end of the funeral service, we were getting ready to get in the cars to go back to the airport, and I said to one of the SWAT team guys—I said, "Is it possible for us to go by the store on our way back to the airport?" The guy says, "No problem." Anyway, pretty rough in there. Worst that I've seen since Vietnam. Blood all over everything. We get in the cars and get to the airport and get out of the car at the airport, nobody says a word. [The executive], who had beaten the shit out of me on the plane the night before—the day before for three hours—he turns to me as we were getting on the plane, and he turns to me and says, "I want that goddamn store torn down immediately. And you're responsible for doing it. Do you understand?" I looked at him and I said, "Good decision." I believe that was the right decision. Now, I didn't know for sure. I almost lost my job over it. So, it was instinctively—I think I did the right thing. I think, in retrospect, I did the right thing.

Richard's story is a particularly public example of taking a stand on a controversy that could well undermine one's own interests. It is a powerful illustration of what is known as moral courage. The personal and professional stories of the media exemplars in this study are studded with examples of variations on the theme of moral courage, of controversial stands taken on principle, of well-being risked and hardship endured to act on what the journalists and PR practitioners believed was right, despite the potential or actual costs. Some are "trial by fire" experiences that helped shape the exemplars' careers and priorities. Some involved pivotal moments; others were struggles that spanned years. Many were much less "public" than Richard's story yet no less momentous. Danielle, a PR agency specialist in Colorado, recounted her handling of what could have sprouted into a full-blown crisis for a prominent ski resort:

> When we were dealing with the *Today* show episode that I mentioned. One death and having one person in jail. And having literally about a half an hour to figure out, "How do we make this work?" Because this is not a crisis for [the ski resort]; this happens all the time—people die on ski resort hills, it's what happens. But I could hear this producer's tone. It was going to be a slam, right? So we said, "OK, call the boss, the CEO of the resort." I said, "[Rob], legal is saying I can't take these people up to see the scene. The scene is wide open, there are barely any trees. If we show them this, we can prove this is just one those weird accidents." So, he fought legal and said, "[Danielle] knows—I trust what she's doing, let her do this." So, we managed it properly. I sat with the producer. And I said, "Take your camera guy up—ski patrol will take you up and show you where it was." I counseled ski patrol, and I said, "Just don't say—don't chatter with these guys, 'cause that's not going to help our situation. Just take them and show them." They come back down, they interview my boss, it was all fine. And the next day on the *Today* show, Matt Lauer said, "You know, it sounds like just one of those unfortunate incidents that happens sometimes when people ski." And I was like, "Oh, thank God. Thank God I fought legal on this. What are you thinking, people?"

Repeatedly, the media exemplars described these decisions to do what they felt was "the right thing" in terms of duty rather than choice. Psychologists call this the successful integration of morality into the self: Once individuals embrace or internalize a moral principle, they not only feel obligated to live their lives accordingly, but the moral principle can actually become intertwined with how they see themselves. In a sense, what looks like courage actually becomes just examples of duty. This is a recurring theme among the exemplars. Here is Mitchell, a veteran editor working in Washington, D.C.:

> And then, in the professional life, the struggle there was always to get people to do the right thing. I'm a firm believer in the idea that if you're reporting the conventional wisdom, you're wasting

your time. Everybody already knows the conventional wisdom and understands that's how the world is. And I think our job as journalists is to show you that that's not how the world is, or at least there are some alternatives you ought to be thinking about. I've never understood journalists who don't want to do something controversial, who object to being deluged with hate mail. What'd you get into the business for? I mean, that's the goal. The more people hate you, the better job you're probably doing. [laugh]

UNDERSTANDING THE CONCEPT OF COURAGE

In one of his *Dialogues,* Plato recounted how Socrates interrogated two prominent Athenian military generals to teach them about the nature of courage. "Then, Laches, suppose that we first set about determining the nature of courage, and in the second place proceed to inquire how the young men may attain this quality by the help of studies and pursuits. Tell me, if you can, what is courage" (Plato, 1996, p. 134). After beguiling and exasperating them with a very Socratic cross-examination of their reasonable-sounding claims, the humbled generals finally agree with Socrates that "we have not discovered what courage is" (p. 143). Despite changes in the types of actions praised for courage over the millennia, courage itself is valued universally across cultures. Shane Lopez and colleagues (e.g., Lopez et al., 2010; Pury & Lopez, 2009; Snyder & Lopez, 2007) proposed that most types of courage share three common features: the presence of personal risk, the development of courage as an asset over time and the influence of a socio-environmental context that both reinforces the value of courageous behavior and allows for its incorporation into everyday life. Winston Churchill, often referred to as a paragon of both physical and moral courage, said courage was the "first" human quality, because it guaranteed the possibility of all others.

Moral courage has been defined in several ways:

- Being courageous involves being fully aware of and accepting the threat of a long-term health concern, solving problems using discernment and developing enhanced sensitivities to personal needs and the world in general. Courageous behavior consists of taking responsibility and being productive (Finfgeld, 1998).
- "Men whose abiding loyalty to their nation triumphed over all personal and political considerations" (Kennedy, 1961, p. 20) (in describing U.S. senators with political courage).

- "Dispositional psychological courage is the cognitive process of defining risk, identifying and considering alternative actions, and choosing to act in spite of potential negative consequences in an effort to obtain 'good' for self or others, recognizing that this perceived good may not be realized" (O'Byrne, Lopez & Petersen, 2000, p. 6).
- Critical components of courage are freedom of choice, fear of a situation and the willingness to take risks in a situation with an uncertain but morally worthy end (Shelp, 1984).

In much of the moral psychology research over the last several decades (e.g., Blasi, 1985; Blasi & Milton, 1991; Colby & Damon, 1992; Huff, Barnard & Frey, 2008a, 2008b), one of the most urgent questions has been how individuals manage to blend the abstract claims of morality with the stuff of daily living. That is, what exactly is the process by which we incorporate the moral into the self? Those who are most successful at integrating morality with their self-identity arguably respond to ethical challenges in ways that are different than others. To be motivated by principle in the face of daunting adversity, to persevere in a course of action despite great personal risk or hardship, to eschew expedience in the service of what is perceived to be a "right" or just cause—such behavior can be considered examples of a high degree of integration of morality into the self. We often call examples of this behavior moral courage. "The self is progressively moralized when the objective values that one apprehends become integrated within the motivational and affective systems of personality and when these moral values guide the construction of the self-concept and one's identity as a person," explained Daniel Lapsley, a prominent moral psychology theorist (1996, p. 231). In other words, we successfully blend the moral with the mundane when we fully understand the compelling nature of the universal concerns of dignity, respect and justice and when we feel "the weight of obligation" to promote these claims *independent* of our own personal desires, goals and preferences. Developmentally speaking, this is miles beyond the whatever-it-takes-to-get-ahead mentality that so often characterizes Western culture. Lapsley continued:

> The integration (or integrity) of the moral personality is revealed, first, by our felt sense of accountability, or by the "ownership" we assert over our actions. Many of us have been in situations when we just could not muster the agency, or the strong will, to put into effect what our good will demanded of us. We desired to do the

right thing but were let down by our "agentic system." But when our rational understanding of morality is integrated with our character (strong will, or agentic system), we should feel a sense of ownership over our actions, a sense of mastery over the moral demands that we place upon ourselves, and consequently, a sense of moral accountability toward ourselves and others. . . . If we then feel guilt, shame, regret, hypocrisy, and allied emotions, we can be sure that our moral understanding is well integrated within our personality. If we don't feel these moral emotions, our moral sensibilities are split off from the rest of our personality.

(1996, pp. 232–233)

The ancient Greeks referred to *andreia*, best translated as "manliness" and understood primarily as among the traditionally masculine aspects of virtue concerned first and foremost with the behavior of soldiers on the battlefield. Later, Thomas Aquinas used the Latin *fortitudo* to describe the "endurance" of a martyr as representing the purest form of courage. The fourth century Confucian Mencius wrote of *da yong*, or "great courage," referring to what we understand as moral courage through personal acceptance of moral claims. With long practice of self-cultivation, virtuous people are able to choose moral action undeterred by any difficulty or danger (Ivanhoe, 2002). Christopher Rate and colleagues (2007, 2010) established the presence of several major features that constituted the concept of courage, including external circumstances that influence one's actions, volition or exercise of free will, and, notably, "motivation toward excellence": "One's actions are directed toward, for example, the good of others, a noble purpose, or worthy aim" (2010, p. 56).

More specifically, moral courage is defined as "a prosocial behavior with high social costs and no (or rare) direct rewards for the actor" (Osswald, Greitemeyer, Fischer & Frey, 2010, p. 150). It is important to distinguish moral courage from other "helping behaviors," such as lending aid to victims of a natural disaster, that are not characterized by the threat of social costs to the actor. It also has been characterized through such famous acts as the decision by Rosa Parks in December 1955 to refuse to give up her seat on a Montgomery, Alabama, bus to a white man. Daniel Putman (1997) defined this moral courage as the absence of fear while defending deeply rooted moral claims despite the risk of hardship or social disapproval. Shane Lopez and colleagues similarly explained the power of moral courage by saying that "authenticity and integrity may be the fulfillments most closely associated with the expression of personal views in the face of dissension and rejection" (2003, p. 187).

Yet, theorists are still debating what exactly constitutes the "elements or components of courage" (Lopez, O'Byrne & Petersen, 2003, p. 189). Debate continues among those who say we should understand courage as a manifestation of subjective experiences, positive individual traits and institutions that enable them (Petersen & Seligman, 2004; Seligman & Csikszentmihalyi, 2000) and those who argue that courage is better understood as an attribute of an act rather than as an attribute of the person (Rachman, 1990; Rate, Clark, Lindsay & Sternberg, 2007). Indeed, Rate itemized 20 distinct ways researchers have conceptualized courage (pp. 52–53). All of them, however, "seem to acknowledge the multidimensional nature of courage, identifying dimensions such as intentionality, fear, risk, and noble purpose" (Rate, 2010, p. 51):

> In many ways, the field has ended up where Socrates began; following several attempts to define courage and describe its nature, Socrates and his two interlocutors failed, regrettably, to reach a consensus definition. . . . One may wonder whether Socrates and Plato would be surprised—despite their unsuccessful attempts to understand courage—that similar discussions persist over 2,000 years later.
>
> (2010, p. 51)

MEDIA EXEMPLARS: STANDING ON PRINCIPLE

Yet, the continuing debate over the concept does not preclude an exploration of its many manifestations and expressions. Indeed, it quickly became clear in this study that moral courage was among the handful of unifying features of the media exemplars. Moral courage, Sandra Borden (2007) argued, is among the central virtues necessary to ensure journalism's ability to deliver "goods" available only through its "practice," in Alasdair MacIntyre's sense of the term. The presence of moral courage as a theme running through the exemplars' narratives is striking because the life story interview format used in this study (Foley Center, 2008) is not explicitly designed to solicit accounts of moral courage. Rather, the exemplars repeatedly volunteered examples of difficult choices and challenges in their lives—moments of fear and risk that they drew upon to illustrate events that shaped their behaviors and outlooks and that simultaneously suggested the presence of moral courage. So closely did they seem to identify with notions of perseverance amid adversity and a motivation to translate the ideas of virtue into their daily lives with good work, that the idea of moral courage became an intrinsic, if often implicit, part of their personal and professional narratives. "I have a very, maybe overly strong sense of right and wrong," said Linda, an editor of an online news organization. "I think people should do what's right, and I'm really bothered when they do what is wrong. I'm sure that drives in part what I do with my life." Ann, a journalist who worked in Maryland and now in Mexico, agreed:

> I think to stand, to fight for what you believe. And of course not doing any harm to others. I believe that having an ethical life is more difficult; it gives you more challenges because you have to respect everyone, and you have to find a way to do less harm to reach your goals. So I believe in considering all human needs and animals.

Mitchell, the Washington, D.C. editor and Pulitzer Prize recipient, said he quickly learned that the idea of courage was a paradox that challenged any decent manager:

> And the other thing is, am I behaving, actually, courageously enough? Am I avoiding a confrontation because I just prefer not to have it? Am I taking the right stance or doing the right thing here? And I'm always asking myself that—have I defended my position here, have I let somebody down, because they needed my ability to defend them, and I didn't step up? And that's always an ongoing conversation. . . . I talked about that before—did I behave courageously in these situations, et cetera et cetera, and I always think back, "Well, should I have defended this person early on, or was I allowing this person to be picked on, or singled out, and I could have stepped in and maybe have stopped it, or made their supervisor do a better job?" I mean, I tend to be very critical of how people deal with—I don't want to say less talented, but people who it can be problematic to help them achieve, whether it's writing a great story, or a series of stories, or organizing their thoughts, or whatever it is. I believe an editor's worth is shown not by whether he was able to take the most talented person and direct them, but whether he was able to take the least talented person and direct them. And I always look back and say, did I do the right thing by that person?

J. P., a PR veteran in New York and former managing partner of one of the country's largest firms, talked of the demand for courage in a business that often appears to place the relatively narrow value of client loyalty above all values:

> Twenty percent of the time, I was impressed with kind of the cogitation process of the client. Fifty percent of the time, I was not impressed, and 30 percent of the time, I was nauseous. . . . And I just couldn't believe—and again, this is just my naiveté. Going back to my upbringing. I grew up in a very innocent time. You know, I was brought up in a time where, you know, I was patriotic, and I followed the rules, and you didn't do bad things. You got rewarded if you behaved like that. And so, when I discovered that people actually weren't always honest, and were often devious— and oftentimes did things that were for their own benefit to the distress of others. To this day, I can't—I find I am a very naive person when it comes to that. I can't ascribe bad behavior in people. I have a hard time doing it. I want to give people the benefit of the doubt. . . . But people tell you these things—it's like, I can't believe—oftentimes, [clients viewed my work] as, "I said that to you in confidence." I'm not a lawyer. I'm not. There is no client-attorney privilege between us. If you are doing something immoral or illegal, and I don't bring it up to you, then I'm complicit in that. I'm not going to do that. And that is a big issue in any business, but especially in the business where you are a party to somebody else's messaging. You know, if that messaging is illegal or immoral or wrong, and you know it, and you facilitate communicating it, you know, are you any better than that? Not making any moral judgments, but I wouldn't do it.

General indications of courage as a value

While the journalism and PR exemplars often spoke a different language in terms of the aims and challenges of their work, the ways in which they sought to describe their values as media professionals, referring repeatedly to the need for bravery or fortitude, were remarkably similar. Several exemplars fell back on broad, abstract appeals in a defensive way, as if having to justify what others might view as quixotic behavior or self-righteousness. "I guess I don't spend a lot of time trying to fit into some larger—to fit a philosophy and try to figure out how to live by it," said Keith, a foreign-affairs journalist. "It's more instinctive than that, but when it comes to doing my job, for me, it comes down to not about personal glory or ambition, it comes down to trying to get good stories, get them right, and get them early. So you try to call bullshit when you see bullshit, try to hold people to what they say, you try to call them out when they screw up. And so that's what I've tried to do all along. I don't know quite how to articulate that as a coherent philosophy." Others were more explicit about their driving philosophies that enabled them to weather ethical challenges. Faith, a corporate communications veteran in Virginia, referred to her Christian beliefs: "[Christ] wants the best in me. He wants me to get the best out of others and he wants a presentation to him that is great. So, that's my motivation to do what is best, to be a representative of Christ," she said. "I've made mistakes, but the one thing, I just don't do, I just will not out-and-out tell you a bald-faced lie right to your face. And I've had people do that. And it's very hard for me to go back because . . . you cannot learn character, you cannot grow character; you have it or you don't. So I do think I sometimes can be a little rigid in that regard but your character is your integrity, and if that is flawed, then everything is." Unprompted, Dennis, editor of a metropolitan newspaper in the southeast United States, drew on Immanuel Kant:

Live your life as if your every action will become a universal law. Do I always do it? No. Hell no. But that's kind of my philosophical direction in life. I'm not religious. I grew up and went to Catholic school for 12 years. That will always be with me—the Catholicism is inbred in me. It taught me a lot. It helped formed who I am. But, you know, I think that Kant put it best: "Live as if every action will become a universal law." And if you think about that, you tend to do the right thing.

Similarly, Emily, a veteran corporate PR specialist, said fairness was a concern underlying her career:

That probably comes from being a Libra; I'm always seeking balance and fairness. But I tend to be a champion of the underdog and tend to stand up for people who don't have a voice. . . . I'm a believer in "do unto others," and also to give people their space as long as it doesn't impinge or impose and harm someone else. I don't believe in strict dogma . . . because it's all based on intolerance, and it's all based on "I'm right and you're wrong," and it's all based on "my way or the highway," and I don't believe in that.

While Don, a computer-assisted reporting editor in Washington, D.C., is white, heterosexual and never reported on national politics, the debate over gay rights animated his sense of fairness as justice:

I still believe passionately about civil rights, and it was interesting because, growing up in the '60s, and the experience of African Americans and their fight and determination and everything through civil rights, certainly affected me. No question about it— and the whole '60s. And I didn't approach it initially, but looking at gay rights initially, you know, looking at it pragmatically, or whatever, and trying to listen to both sides, but then, you know, in the end it got down to, it's like, you know, a lot of that could have been said during the push for African American civil rights. This is a civil rights issue, and you give people their rights, and you know what? Show me an instance, just one instance, where marriage has been damaged. . . . Like, where has it been damaged by gay people? So I still think of civil rights as a fundamental cause that sits fine with my view of myself as a journalist.

Others expressed more direct struggles that challenged their ability to put their values into practice. Martha, an accomplished national-affairs journalist who now leads a fledgling online news organization, recounted her years-long struggle with entrenched gender discrimination in the business:

I'm 62, so when I was a kid, the expectations for women were so different than they are now, and that really shifted about the time that I was in high school and college—like, a lot of opportunities opened up, or at least if not in actuality, the aspiration for those opportunities—so I guess the challenge, earlier on especially, would be dealing with the kind of barriers that were still in place, that in some ways I was oblivious to. When I was in college and planning to have a career in journalism, [my hometown metropolitan newspaper] still had not hired a single woman directly onto the city desk. . . . There were a couple that had been hired and eventually made their way over there, but just a couple. And so, those kinds of limitations were still very much in play when I started my career, and the expectations that people had of what a woman would do were very different, and so I guess sort of sorting out my own aspirations and trying to not overreact or under-react to the situation, and then to create the kind of life that I wanted to live—I think that's probably been the biggest challenge.

Other exemplars credited what researchers (Huff et al., 2008b) have called the "moral ecology" of their work environments as being an important influence that cultivated their abilities to imbed key values into their careers. Bill, the veteran PR executive, recounted the culture shock he experienced when he became chief of communications for an international manufacturing company:

> I came in at a director level, and I was promoted to VP, but I'm not talking about title, I'm talking about a culture of leadership. So I mean, for example, I'd been working at [another company], and especially in media relations, you're working, like, 80-hour weeks. I mean, just hard-ass, hardcore, full-tilt. So, I come to [the new, California-based employer], and I'm used to everyone just, like, slamming! Well, we're all called downstairs to this meeting. We have two OD facilitators assigned to our staff, there's about a 30 people, and they stand us in a circle. I had never heard of organizational development, let alone have permanent, full-time OD specialists assigned to your department, which I inherited. What do you do? So, we did this exercise where we passed balls around in circles and tried to get some learning around it. And I called back my people in the Midwest and said, "You cannot believe what I just did. I mean, this is shit." Now, I fully embrace it, I understand what they were getting at. In fact there were valuable lessons that I learned from that experience that I still repeat today. So the one corporate environment I've seen people change their behavior to be more ethical and more mindful of what they're doing is [that company], because it was tied to compensation. I was judged on my values, and it was always 360 degrees. And the way we were doing it at [the company] at the time was, the values came first. How did you perform against the set of values? . . . It's tougher than it sounds, because, for example, ethical behavior is one of those things. So you don't break a law, you don't steal from the company, whatever—that's a C. That's what's expected. How do you get on the 'up' end of the curve on ethical behavior? That's really tough. How do you do it on respect for diversity, especially if you're not hiring? You can't change the mix of your people. You know, you can do it when you're hiring, you can gradually change that so there are sort of optics around it. But what about that? Then what do you do to show respect for diversity?

MOMENTS OF COURAGE IN MEDIA:
SOME PIVOTAL STORIES

Despite the different types of courage identified over the decades by psychologists—physical, moral, psychological—and despite the wide array of definitions, any worthwhile definition needs to include actual instances of courageous behavior, regardless of the kind. "[T]heories of the courage phenomenon should account for how courageous behavior is manifested in the lives of all people, in public and behind closed doors," Lopez and colleagues wrote (2010, p. 42). Some theorists have even worked on a "predictive model" that sets out the key factors necessary for anyone to exhibit moral courage:

> Before a person can act with moral courage, he or she has to perceive an incident as a situation of moral courage, and he or she has to take responsibility and has to feel competent to act. Furthermore, the person should possess a variety of reaction options that he or she can promptly realize. Moral courage situations mostly happen fast and are often dangerous and quite unsettling. Therefore, fast reactions are necessary. In the model, the availability of reaction options besides self-efficacy and high self-esteem as well as salience of prosocial norms, empathy, and moral outrage act as promoting factors of moral courage. As inhibiting factors, anticipated social costs, fear of being evaluated and judged, and the (mis)perception of having not enough intervention skills are proposed. Indeed, in moral courage situations people feel less competent to intervene than in other prosocial incidents.
>
> (Osswald et al., 2010, p. 159)

Few exemplars ever actually used the word courage to describe any of their experiences that clearly fall under the concept. Yet, the narratives of hardship endured, of actions taken at great professional or social cost and of triumphs achieved over adversity are among the most compelling, inspiring and instructive ones collected in this study. They include stories of key points in exemplars' professional careers as well as formative challenges in their personal lives.

Courage in a professional media context

For the media exemplars in this study, their successful integration of moral concerns into the self has proven to be a critical element of their professional lives and has resulted in recurring examples of decision making and perseverance despite adversity and hardship. Some of these examples have already been mentioned. Others are just as compelling. For journalists, this sense of professional moral courage often takes the form of crusading journalism that is met with hostility and derision. Ann, a journalist who worked in Maryland with extensive experience with the Mexican press, recounted the challenge posed when her newspaper's publisher became publicly implicated in a political corruption scandal:

> He was sponsoring illegal things, like—politicians, careers, in order to obtain contracts, because he has a construction business—he gave—someone put cameras in his office, so everyone in Mexico saw on TV, how people from the left-wing party, went to his office, and he put a suitcase filled with dollars, and politicians putting it in their pockets, and everywhere, like people starving for food, they were taking the money and putting them in their pockets, everywhere. So it was disgusting. And everyone saw that in national TV, and that was the owner of the paper. So we were really—we knew it was the end of the newspaper. What credibility were we going to have there? Who was going to read that? And the general editor of the newspaper said, we have to continue. We had a meeting that day . . . and said, What are we going to do? Do we have to excuse ourselves in the front page, or what do we say, or do? And I said, we haven't done anything. Why do we have to excuse it? We didn't know about this. It's like, I have seen him twice in my life. In which way am I related to him? And so we had very tough discussions, and we decided we had to—we published something about it. We decided to cover the story, as if the owner wasn't the owner. [laugh] So we did it. And he was really mad. He was really mad.

Linda, the veteran investigative journalist now running an online news site, talked about how she was long haunted by, and ultimately vindicated for, her work probing chronic health problems apparently linked to the nation's nuclear weapons facilities:

> [T]he other big story that changed—really changed the course of my career, was about Oak Ridge. [P]eople had sent us a message— sent us a letter saying, "We're sick and we think it is because of our jobs and nobody is taking us seriously." Which launched what is now going on a 12- or 15-year story. We were the first to report about people's health concerns around nuclear weapons

reservations. . . . I [wrote] about Rocky Flats. The same kind of
thing around every major nuclear weapons facility, and it was really
interesting in that—we as a newspaper, were vilified for even raising
these questions. So, what we did was go to every major site and see,
OK, are there people complaining about the same kinds of things.
It was not a scientific survey, and we clearly said that it wasn't, but
we got vilified by, "Oh, this is not a scientific survey." It was merely
a story saying, "Look, there are people who have been sounding
an alarm. They are clearly sick. Their doctors say they can't figure
out why but that weird things are happening to their bodies. Their
immune systems are attacking their own bodies. Their neurological
systems are breaking down." . . . [It] got the attention of the federal
government, and they created the Energy Employees Occupational
Illness and Compensation program, and they've now handed
out almost $5 billion to people who they say, "Yes, indeed. Your
illnesses are related."

Such stories are also common among the PR exemplars, though
often not as public in nature. Deb, now working in higher-education in
Nebraska, recounted how, as communications chief for a national nonprofit agency, she challenged the veracity of a "60 Minutes" segment on
a program run by her organization:

I looked to the lawyers and said, "I'm going to write a letter to '60
Minutes' because," I said, "number one, we've got enough data to
challenge the story, and number two, we've got to take a stand."
I'm sitting there going, there's this girl from Council Bluffs, Iowa,
who is going to write to "60 Minutes" and tell them, "You've got to
retract something." [It was] another life-altering moment, because
I knew in my gut it was the right thing to do. . . . The head of
CBS called me, and said they would be more diligent about their
reporting efforts. And I think that served me well.

Mick, the retired Chicago-based corporate communications executive, said behind-the-scenes showdowns, often with one's job hanging on
the line, were common:

I never lied to them. I never sugar-coated anything. They used to
beat the shit out of me. Pardon me. OK? I got scars all over my
back from [the executives]. And—but, you know, [the president], he
fired me twice. Whenever they'd beat me up they'd always, within

24 hours in some way, shape or form, let me know everything was fine. [He] would put his arm around me and tell you that you were still one of his boys. . . . And you know, I got to be honest with them. They gave me permission to be honest with them. And that is the only way I could work. And I always told them the truth. No bullshit. Right down the middle. No nonsense.

Many episodes with the PR exemplars are focused on challenges that never reached publicity levels but were rather more internal struggles. Karen, a new-products specialist in Boston, discussed a dilemma involving her financial relationship with a former agency client:

I have a client whom I adore and who adores me, that fired us when I got back from being sick last year because he was very angry that the agency continued to bill him, and no one cared about his business, and he has been—he wanted to fund me. . . . Anytime he has an issue, he calls me and he needs my advice. One of his products just got pulled from shelves because of an FDA issue, and he wanted to know, "What should I do? How do I communicate to my customers?" This has been going on for three or four months now, and I've just been doing it. It's, like, my time. . . . I haven't been billing him, and I'm fine with that. But he just came to me with a more sizeable project that, he's made it clear, "I don't want to work with your agency. I only want to work with you." So, I said to my husband, and I'm dying to go to Nantucket for the Fourth of July, and of course, a giant tuition payment [for children's private school] is due, and I said, "You know, I could do this for him and just send him an invoice, and he'll pay it." And I could say, "I'm going to send you a bill for $2,000 but if I run it through my agency, it's going to be $10,000." And he doesn't care. He's going to say, "I'll pay you whatever. You know, I want to give you money. I don't want to give it to [the agency]." 'Cause he doesn't like [the agency president]. . . . And I said, "I don't feel like it's the right thing to do." And it's because, you know why? It's not honest. It's not honest. . . . I'll have to figure out another way to get to Nantucket. I will. I'll figure it out.

Some exemplars also recounted struggles that, in their eyes, ended unsatisfactorily, yet remained important experiences that informed their professional lives. Deb, the PR veteran in Nebraska, described how she clashed with her president over the cover of the organization's national magazine after the September 11 attacks:

> We had a tabletop magazine, 60,000 copies, and we had just done 9/11. Huge. I worked for six months straight without a day off. . . . I had a beautiful picture of a worker helping someone, basically, who was covered in ash. It was just the most poignant depiction of a volunteer. . . . And we were meeting with the president and the building surrounding her. The magazine's been done, and I have the layout. Anyway, so we're going through it, and she says, "Deb, tell me about this picture on the front cover." And I said, "It basically says what the [organization] is all about—it's those volunteers helping others, and I just think it's a poignant—" And she said, "I want my picture on the front cover." And I looked at my boss, and he didn't say a word. This was a defining moment for me. And I said, "In all due respect, this is a volunteer organization—you're a paid professional. I believe what conveys to the country what we did in 9/11 is how all of our volunteers helped those in need." She said to me, "In all due respect, Deb, my picture will be on the cover." I thought I was fired on the spot. And we walked out, and . . . I thought I was gone. I think she respected me for standing up to her because nothing happened.

Bill, the California-based corporate communications consultant, talked about an episode that raised the question of corporate social responsibility—a theme that came to dominate his communications career with an array of Fortune 500 companies:

> So, [my corporation] was building a plant [in Asia], and I went to look at the plant. And it's tropical conditions and the humidity is unbelievable—I can barely stand the heat. Up on these steel girders, I see hundreds of workers covered head to toe with hard hats, steel toes and whatever, hitting rivets in the plant, and I asked how much they were paid, and it was like a dollar an hour or something like that. And I thought, "If I were asked to dress like that and go up and work like that, I would collapse. I would just physically collapse in minutes." Now, the hard hats and steel toes were for their safety. It took a lot to get them to do that, because they were used to going barefoot, but it's a heavy construction site. So I went back to the vice chairman, and I said, "[Frank], I understand they're not even our workers, they're a contracting construction company,

but it's unconscionable that we're paying the wages that these people are getting for the work they do." So [Frank] did the worst possible thing he could do to me, and he said, "OK, so what do you want to do about it?" And I had no answer. So . . . I commissioned a white-paper study . . . and they came back and said, "We don't have an answer for you." So I never solved it, but I know I raised it.

Others were more light-hearted in nature—at least in hindsight. Nonetheless, their stories echoed the same broad themes of perseverance amid adversity. Elaine, a Pulitzer Prize-winning journalist, recalled when she was told to cover the Outer Banks fishing industry early in her news-writing career:

We covered 120 miles of coastline, had eleven hurricanes in seven years, you know? My beat became commercial fishing, which is kind of ironic, because I really hate fish. [laugh] They freak me out. Ever since I was a little kid, I can't go to an aquarium. You know, I have a fish—I have some kind of "ick" phobia, and the guy that was covering commercial fishing left, and they were like, "[Elaine], we want you to cover this." [laugh] Is God testing me? [laugh] The thing you fear the most. So, I did that for about six years.

Courage in exemplars' personal lives

Elaine's anecdote hints at a broad truth about the challenges that are not easily compartmentalized into "professional" and "personal." An overlap of the two realms is often the norm. As anyone might, the media exemplars in this study often reached back into their childhood and early adult years for stories that mattered to them, that they felt were important for understanding who they were. They talked about rising proudly to some challenges and regretting their responses to others. They talked of some as having helped forge meaning in their lives, of some as having cast values or concerns permanently onto their characters. Dennis, the editor of a southeast U.S. metropolitan paper, said he could identify a series of moments in his life where he was challenged to do something he felt unprepared to do. He looked back at the times when he turned away, when his courage failed him, as moments of regret. But the times in which he was able to overcome fear and self-doubts seem, in hindsight, to magically open doors of opportunity and success. One of those moments occurred as he struggled over whether to pursue his interest in photojournalism, when little of his background had prepared him to do so. In a moment, a cliché seemed to have decided his fate:

I've always said I have a guardian angel. I've had stuff happen to me my whole life that you wonder, "How did that happen?" There's something, combined with my intuition, there's something that pushes me in certain directions, and I always end up better for it. So, I've always felt like somebody is watching out for me. And I had a really vivid experience, a very weird experience when I was trying to decide what to do when I had applied to Syracuse and Missouri. I was really petrified about going to grad school. I didn't want to ever go to grad, back to school. When I got out of college and I graduated from Temple, I was like, "I'm never going back to school." But, it was the best way for me to get into the field. If I wanted to do it. I had learned over about a year and talking to a lot of people, the best way to do is go to grad school, get some experience, get some internships. But, I was really petrified. And then I hadn't been accepted by Syracuse. I had been accepted by Missouri, but I had not decided yet that I was going to go. I remember thinking either I go to Missouri or I go get a job as a bartender. And, but it was like, you know—"Well, bartending is not so bad." And I was driving down the road. I don't know where I was going. I don't remember. And came to a stoplight, and next to me was this beat up junker car. I think it was a Datsun 1200. This crusty old guy driving it, smoking a cigarette, ashtray open, filled with butts, and there was a piece of paper ripped up, not neat—a ripped-up piece of paper that had been ripped out of a notebook. And it said on it, "Do the thing you fear to do." And I could read it, 'cause I was in the driver's seat, and he was right next to me, and I swear that was a sign. That was a sign. It was a message. It didn't immediately make me flip, but I—that made me think. And it gave me direction and helped me make that decision. And I—you know, call it what you want. A coincidence. But that to me was a spiritual experience. Because that just doesn't happen. It doesn't happen. I was at the point where I had to decide within days and here's this message. "Do the thing . . ." And I still live by that. And that was the first time I'd seen it. That was the weirdest—I remember sitting there. I could still—holding on to the wheel, and I look over and there's this guy, and it's taped, hanging crooked . . .

Mitchell, the Washington, D.C. editor, talked of a more light-hearted moment in high school that, in hindsight, illustrated a willingness to confront the status quo that has defined his prize-winning journalism career:

> And this is kind of an odd thing. But we had a rebellion about wearing ties in high school. This was the late '60s, and we said, "What were we doing wearing ties?" [laugh] So that was our cause. And I was actually invited to speak to the parents association on why we should be wearing ties or not. And my parents recall it as being their most horrifying night [laugh], but I recall it as, one, I was able to make an argument, I was able to be fairly positive in my approach, and several parents actually stood up and said, "Well, I don't know where I come down on the ties, but you know, you've got a good place in public relations." [laugh]

While many such stories were suggestive of the notion of moral courage, other narratives of personal challenges were of a different, and darker, type. Several talked of times that involved feats of physical courage. Mick, the retired corporate communications chief from Chicago, looks back with pride on his service in the Army's special forces during the Vietnam War:

> An intelligence wing, and it's small teams in the early '60s. . . . That's where the whole concept of the Green Berets came from. And it was fascinating to work, and what we did in Vietnam was—Delta Project was classified reconnaissance. Where we went was pretty highly classified. What we did, it was everything from long-range reconnaissance: six-man teams, two Americans, two South Vietnamese Special Forces and two of what they called Hmongs—Chinese, Hmongs who were on our teams with us. And we did everything from interdiction on the Ho Chi Minh Trail of North Vietnamese coming down with arms and ammunitions— we'd interdict them, we'd ambush them. It was small teams. Real quick, lightening—stuff to get in and out, and then a lot of reconnaissance. It's our job, our primary job over there—this isn't anything classified today; God, it's been 40 years ago—but our job was usually . . . go into an area and find out what was there, and on the basis of what we found out, we'd put teams in. We'd go out for, normally—if you didn't have a problem, you'd go out somewhere between three and five days and you'd come back for a few days

and then go back out. These small six-man teams. Depending upon what we found, then we'd be everything from B-52 airstrikes to Marine forces, or whatever, going in and our job was done. We were—needless to say, we got into some pretty interesting stuff. . . . Again, as I said, it's like, you've never lived until you've almost died. And there have been times in my—there have been times in Vietnam, when I got through something that I didn't think I was going to make it.

Allen, a Pulitzer Prize-winning syndicated columnist, talked about dealing with his often violent alcoholic father:

. . . [P]robably any given moment, when he came in and, you know—spoiling for a fight. I don't know if there is any one [moment] that [was] worse than the others, but just any given moment when he came in spoiling for a fight. . . . That whole thing of lying in bed and, you know, waiting to see if, you know, you'd hear him hit the door, you know, at 11 or 12 or whatever it was, and you're lying in bed, couldn't go to sleep. Me and my sister, we would be lying in bed, and you'd sort of wait to see what kind of mood he is going to be in. If he comes in and he's in a quiet mood. then you can go to sleep. If he comes in and he's spoiling for a fight, then you got tense and be ready to run out there and jump between them and keep him from hitting her. You know, that was probably, you know, the worst thing about my childhood.

Larissa, a solo PR practitioner in California, talked about her unusual, and unexpected, coping strategy after a painful divorce:

It was very hard. My parents had gone through a divorce; I swore it would never happen to me, but I didn't have any choice in the matter. So my kids would go spend time with their dad every other weekend, and I felt bereft. . . . So I was at loose ends, and a friend said, "Why don't you go up and go skiing?" And I hadn't skied since I was 14 years old. So, it turns out that you have something called muscle memory. I went up to Tahoe, and what I found was that it was the only place where the noise in my head just went silent. And what I found was I could stand at the top of a hill that scared me shitless, and there were no other noises, there was nothing but the hill. I loved it—oh God, I loved it. And there were these black-diamond slopes, and I was pretty fair intermediate skier, but I couldn't do these hills, and I wanted to do those hills. I wanted to go straight down as fast as I could go and not be afraid, and so I rented an instructor for a day—I found a really good one, and so she said, "What do you really want to do?" And I said, "I want to do that hill before the end of the day." And so—this is a great life lesson. She said, "You don't have to ski the whole hill; you only have to ski to the next turn." I had never thought of it that way. She said, "You just have to get there, and then you turn, and you ski to the next turn." And I went down the hill, and when I got to the bottom and she said, "Turn around and look at what you just did." It was a great analogy for life. And you don't have to ski the whole hill, just the next turn. Life lesson. And after that, I could conquer pretty much any hill. And I forced myself to. If it scared me, I had to do it. And I did.

Larissa's story straddles what psychologists have identified as distinct types of courage: the physical kind and the psychological, or "vital" type, denoting the willpower and endurance exhibited by those dealing with trauma, addiction or other illness (Synder & Lopez, 2007, p. 225). Karen, the Boston-based new-products specialist, discussed her lifelong struggle with eating disorders—a clearer case of psychological courage:

When I was younger, I had an eating disorder. So that was, I think— and that has stayed with me. That's like—I think having an eating disorder is like being an alcoholic. It's—you're never not. And I struggled with that when I was—I think I was 18. And it wasn't like—I didn't throw up or anything. I wish I did. But I just ceased eating. And I have an ability, and always have been very focused and determined. I stopped eating. I will not eat, and I lived on nothing but diet pills and Diet Coke and pretzels for a couple of years. And I whittled myself down from 130 pounds down to, like, 90. And I stayed like that for a while. I was very unhealthy. I mean, just as a young woman to do that to myself. But it was a control issue, and I realize that now, and I got better, and had a boyfriend that liked to go out and eat submarine sandwiches every night. You know, so I started to. And I still feel a twinge of it when I get out of control, and I don't feel like I'm centered, and I have my outlets, I revert back to it. I know myself well enough that—not so much soda, because I try not to drink Diet Coke, because I think it is poison now—but the pretzels. Go back to the pretzels, and I'll go back to the not eating. And I won't eat until dinner time. I just did it recently. You know, and I ended up dropping five or six pounds just because I stopped having lunch. Would work through, and for me it has always been a control thing, so that is something I need to really watch.

MORAL COURAGE AS A VIRTUE IN MEDIA

These narratives of perseverance amid adversity show that the media exemplars in this study would not be who they are without the deep integration of moral concerns that they so often exhibit. They serve as compelling examples of people whose sense of self has become "progressively moralized," as Bebeau and Monson (2008, p. 558) said, to the point where their embraced virtues come to drive behavior and identity to a remarkable degree. Since claims of what it means to be a "good" person and a "virtuous" professional have become so intimately connected with exemplars' self-identities, taking controversial stands or risking their own interests feel less like choices and more like unavoidable duties. Not only have they acknowledged the importance of key virtues such as honesty, transparency and justice, their embrace of these has actually reinforced their notion of autonomous agency, enabling them to directly feel a sense of accountability for their conduct. Embrace of these virtues has cultivated an expectation of themselves, a standard of conduct, that paradoxically has enabled them to "claim ownership" of their actions in ways not possible if their self-identities were less integrated with their moral concerns. One result, as these narratives show, is the recurring demonstration of moral courage.

At least three important connections emerge between the likelihood of morally courageous behavior and other dimensions of the exemplars' moral psychology. For one, the high degree of integration of moral concerns suggests cultivation by the exemplars of "schemas," or cognitive shortcuts, they can use to envision how their concerns can actually be manifested in their behavior. This is analogous to the schema theory behind stages of moral development, where, as discussed in Chapter 4, some people have developed, and are able to activate, mental links representing higher-order moral thinking—nearly automatic responses rooted in firmly embraced universal values that explain scorers in the higher moral-development stages on the Defining Issues Test (Rest, Narvaez, Bebeau & Thoma, 1999). The tighter their embrace of moral concerns, the better able the exemplars appear to be at seeing the link between virtues and their behavioral manifestation, and thus the more likely they are to exhibit moral courage. Another link suggested here involves the exemplars' "moral ecology" (Huff et al., 2008b). In ways direct and indirect, exemplars repeatedly indicated the importance of organizational culture as a factor that either encouraged or hindered behavior driven by moral concerns. Cultures that prioritized ethical concerns and that systematized expectations of value-driven behavior clearly were effective, at least with these exemplars, in reinforcing their links between their own values and their self-identities. And third, the pervasiveness of morally courageous behavior among these exemplars also suggests the presence of some kind of connection with their personality traits of Openness and Agreeableness in which their personality assessment scores show they "clustered" to a remarkable degree (see Chapter 3). While many theorists caution against seeing moral courage as an attribute of an individual or a result of an array of social, environmental and personal factors, researchers have recently uncovered some apparent links between personality traits and inclination to exhibit moral courage. (Morally courageous behavior may be inversely related to high Agreeableness scorers, however.) After they assessed subjects' personality traits, researchers ran an experiment in which the subjects witnessed how an experimenter insulted and discriminated against a foreign student (actually a confederate researcher). They then assessed whether the subjects intervened and defended the foreign student:

> Results revealed that the higher participants scored on the Openness dimensions of the Big Five, the more likely they showed moral courage. This is an interesting result because in most studies of the relationship between personality variables and prosocial behavior the Agreeableness dimension of the Big Five was found to be related to prosocial behavior. . . . Nevertheless, it makes sense that only a very slight relationship exists between Agreeableness and moral courage: Being agreeable and friendly does not foster answering back a rude experimenter. On the other hand, openness to new experiences and a broad mind promote acceptance of different ways of life and of persons from other countries and cultures. It therefore seems plausible that open-minded persons are more likely to intervene against discrimination and to show moral courage.
> (Osswald et al., 2010, pp. 157–158)

As these exemplar narratives arguably show, an institutionalized tendency toward morally courageous behavior is essential for the health of professionalism in journalism and public relations. Its cultivation cannot be limited to a few select "elites" of industry but rather must be a pedagological, educational, organizational and ideological priority. Moral courage should be considered an essential element that constitutes excellence in media work, despite the economic organizational and structural forces that may discourage it, and not an ethical "luxury" to be honored only when it serves an interest to do so.

REFERENCES

Bebeau, M. J., & Monson, V. E. (2008). Guided by theory, grounded in evidence: A way forward for professional ethics education. *Handbook of moral and character education* (2008): 557–582.

Blasi, A. (1985). The moral personality: Reflections for social science and education. In *Moral education: Theory and application* (M.W. Berkowitz & F. Oser, Eds.), 433–443. Hillsdale, NJ: Lawrence Erlbaum Associates.

Blasi, A., & Milton, K. (1991). The development of the sense of self in adolescence. *Journal of Personality 59*, 217–242.

Borden, S.L. (2007). *Journalism as practice: MacIntyre, virtue ethics and the press.* Burlington, VT: Ashgate.

Colby, A., & Damon, W. (1992). *Some do care: Contemporary lives of moral commitment.* New York: Free Press.

Finfgeld, D.L. (1998). Courage in middle-aged adults with long-term health concerns. *Canadian Journal of Nursing Research 30* (1), 153–169.

Foley Center for the Study of Lives. (2008). The life story interview. Available: http://www.sesp.northwestern.edu/foley/instruments/interview/. Retrieved 2 April 2012.

Huff, C.W., Barnard, L., & Frey, W. (2008a). Good computing: A pedagogically focused model of virtue in the practice of computing (part 1). *Journal of Information, Communication and Ethics in Society 6* (3), 246–278.

Huff, C.W., Barnard, L., & Frey, W. (2008b). Good computing: A pedagogically focused model of virtue in the practice of computing (part 2). *Journal of Information, Communication and Ethics in Society 6* (4), 284–316.

Ivanhoe, P.J. (2002). The virtue of courage in the Mencius. In *Courage* (B. Darling-Smith, Ed.), 65–79. Notre Dame, IN: University of Notre Dame Press.

Kennedy, J.F. (1961). *Profiles in courage.* New York: Harper and Brothers.

Lapsley, D.K. (1996). *Moral psychology.* Boulder, CO: Westview Press.

Lopez, S.J., O'Byrne, K.K., & Petersen, S. (2003). Profiling courage. In *Positive psychological assessment: A handbook of models and measures* (S.J. Lopez & C.R. Snyder, Eds.), 185–197. Washington, D.C.: American Psychological Association.

Lopez, S.J., Rasmussen, H.N., Skorupski, W.P., Koetting, K., Peterson, S.E., & Yang, Y.-T. (2010). Folk conceptualizations of courage. In *The psychology of courage: Modern research on an ancient virtue* (C.L.S. Pury & S.J. Lopez, Eds.), 23–45. Washington, D.C.: American Psychological Association.

O'Byrne, K.K., Lopez, S.J., & Petersen, S. (2000). Building a theory of courage: A precursor to change? Paper presented at annual convention of the American Psychological Association, Washington, D.C.

Osswald, S., Greitemeyer, T., Fischer, P., & Frey, D. (2010). What is moral courage? Definition, explication and classification of a complex construct. In *The psychology of courage: Modern research on an ancient virtue* (C.L.S. Pury & S.J. Lopez, Eds.), 94–120. Washington, D.C.: American Psychological Association.

Petersen, C., & Seligman, M.E.P. (2004). *Character strengths and virtues: A handbook and classification.* New York: Oxford University Press.

Plato. (1996). *The collected* Dialogues *of Plato* (E. Hamilton & H. Cairns, Eds.), Princeton, NJ: Princeton University Press.

Pury, C.L.S., & Lopez, S.J. (2009). Courage. In *Oxford handbook of positive psychology* (C.R. Snyder & S.J. Lopez, Eds.), 375–382. New York: Oxford University Press.

Putman, D. (1997). Psychological courage. *Philosophy, Psychiatry & Psychology 4* (1), 1–11.

Rachman, S.J. (1990). *Fear and courage* (2nd ed.). New York: Freeman.

Rate, C.R. (2010). Defining the features of courage: A search for meaning. In *The psychology of courage: Modern research on an ancient virtue* (C.L.S. Pury & S.J. Lopez, Eds.), 47–66. Washington, D.C.: American Psychological Association.

Rate, C.R., Clark, J.A., Lindsay, D.R., & Sternberg, R.J. (2007). Implicit theories of courage. *Journal of Positive Psychology 2* (2), 80–98.

Rest, J.R., Narvaez, D., Bebeau, M.J., & Thoma, S.J. (1999). *Postconventional moral thinking: A neo-Kohlbergian approach*. Mahwah, NJ: Lawrence Erlbaum Associates.

Seligman, M.E.P., & Csikszentmihalyi, M. (2000). Positive psychology: An introduction. *The American Psychologist 55*, 5–14.

Shelp, E.E. (1984). Courage: A neglected virtue in the patient-physician relationship. *Social Science and Medicine 18* (4), 351–360.

Snyder, C.R., & Lopez, S.J. (2007). *Positive psychology: The scientific and practical explorations of human strengths*. Thousand Oaks, CA: SAGE.

Starmann, R.G. (1993). *Crisis response: Inside stories on managing image under siege* (J.A. Gottschalk, Ed.), 309–321. Detroit: Visible Ink Press.

CHAPTER 7

Humility and Hubris

Be modest! It is the kind of pride least likely to offend.
—Jules Renard, 1964

Let us be a little humble; let us think that the truth may not be entirely with us.
—Jawaharlal Nehru, 1957

"It wasn't me." "I was blessed with a fabulous team." "I didn't see what they saw, but people believed in me." "I was just incredibly lucky." Over and over, the media exemplars in this study demurred from taking credit for accomplishments, often minimizing their hand in their own success. Expressions of humbleness came regularly and repeatedly during the hours of interviews. However, this group of successful professionals also would not be described by many as having small egos. They exude self-confidence. They are masters of self-assertion, many proudly recounting acts of unusual boldness and ambition even in childhood. And while the line between what psychologists call "authentic" or well-earned pride and "hubristic" or presumptuous pride may be a clear one, the exemplars exhibited both in talking about themselves and their work. These expressions of humility and self-assertion—occasionally spilling over into hubris—emerged as one of the most intriguing dichotomies as the media exemplars' "life story" interview transcripts were analyzed. They add complex layers to the moral psychology profile of these exemplary people, often reinforcing other findings related to their personality traits and their ethical ideologies, yet also at times raising questions that illustrated how much more research is needed to fully understand the intricate interplay of environmental, personal and professional factors that shape people's moral agency.

This chapter attempts to do justice to the media exemplars' rich stories by exploring this recurring humility-hubris dichotomy and by integrating it with the latest psychological research on these and related concepts. Both concepts, of course, have deep philosophical roots reaching back to the earliest writings. Humility has long been considered a key virtue among the classical Greek philosophers. It receives less attention than courage, temperance and the other virtues—not because it was perceived as less important but because humility's role in human affairs was so obvious that it was considered to be a starting point for the virtuous life, not an end in itself. This point is emphasized in the Stoics' opening chapter of *The Art of Living:* "Happiness and freedom begin with a clear understanding of one principle: Some things are within our control, and some things are not" (Lebell, 1995, p. 3). More recently, some psychologists have argued that the widely held theory of the "Big Five" personality traits should be amended as the Big Six, since research has suggested the existence of a separate, identifiable "Honesty-Humility" trait that is distinct from Agreeableness, Openness to new experience, Extraversion, Neuroticism and Conscientiousness (Ashton & Lee, 2005; Exline & Hill, 2012). And business researchers are increasingly refuting the relevance of the headstrong, larger-than-life ideal of the corporate executive glamorized in the popular press. Instead, they argue that a close look at the characteristics of nearly all business leaders who have moved their companies from good to great reveals a common, essential yet often-overlooked quality: humility (Collins, 2001; Morris, Brotheridge & Urbanski, 2005; Vera & Rodriguez-Lopez, 2004). This quality is encapsulated perfectly by one unassuming company chief, who over his 20 years as CEO outperformed all others in his industry yet never was the focus of a *Wall Street Journal* profile, said at his retirement, "I never stopped trying to become qualified for the job" (Collins, 2001, p. 138).

Hubris, or "an overweening pride" (Ford, 2006, p. 483), also has deep roots, going back to Greek myth: The goddess Nemesis monitored the mortal world for those who grabbed excessive power or prosperity and who claimed more than their due, swooping down to deliver justice. Psychologists have looked closely at what motivates our need for "self-enhancement" and how that need is linked to other personality traits. In many cases, hubris is as much about how we are perceived by others as it is about the manifestations of our own self-regard, intertwined with notions of security, self-esteem and our ability to relate to others. While it is human nature to believe we are better than average at what we care about (Alicke & Govorun, 2005), such feelings of superiority can easily become the basis of a mode of interaction that suggests bullying and intimidation. What psychologists call excessive self-enhancing behavior, then, or hubristic dealings with others, often backfires, as it evokes hostility and disengagement from others (Hoorens, 2011). Indeed, some argue that since we are predisposed to protect and promote prosocial behaviors, we have built-in sensors to detect hubristic behaviors among others. Such warnings "have been essential for our species, as strivings for power and status endanger pro-social behaviors critical for survival" (Trumbull, 2010, p. 341).

The duality of hubris and humility also speaks to an even more fundamental dimension of the human condition. It is the yin and yang of human assertion upon reality versus a stance of muteness before the universe. As philosopher David Cooper (2002) described, this tension is rooted in questions posed by the earliest religions: Does the world exist apart from human perception and apprehension, or is human articulation of how we see things in the world the only way through which the world *is*? Taoist philosopher Chuang Tzu challenged Confucianism's claim that our conceptions of the world were authentic representations of reality, retorting that our perception no more reflects actual reality of the world than do the "peeps of baby birds." In contrast, Protagoras claimed that "of all things man is the measure, of things that are and of things that are not." Sartre stated that humans are those "by whom it happens that *there is* a world" (as quoted in Cooper, 2002, p. 2, p. 3). This tension certainly can't be understood in strictly absolutist terms; the debate suggests a spectrum on which philosophers have argued that the world, to varying degrees, is dependent on human imposition of structure, or that some realities indeed exist independently of human apprehension. But the argument over the nature of human reality reflects, on a grand scale, the concepts of hubris and humility that have occupied social psychologists, whose observations inform much of this chapter. This tension has animated the work of Kant, Berkeley, Nietzsche, Heidegger, James and a host of other classical and contemporary philosophers. Thomas Nagel, for instance, dismissed the "humanist" idea that the facts of the "real" world are strictly derived from how we humans apprehend them. On the contrary, Nagel argued: "the world is not our world even potentially," and that "to deny [this] shows a lack of humility . . . an attempt to cut the universe down to size" (Nagel, 1986, p. 109). Similarly, Iris Murdoch complained about our Western "egocentric" style of thought in which "our picture of ourselves has become too grand. . . . We have lost the vision of a reality separate from ourselves" (1997, p. 338). Similarly, the dispositions of hubris and humility are also regions on a spectrum: Some people are motivated toward self-assertion, others toward a deferential stance and most of us exhibit both behaviors from time to time.

The point here is not to signal that this chapter will present a grand philosophical treatise in the guise of a psychological study; rather, it is to put the media exemplars' explicit hubristic and humble behaviors in the context of the rich, ongoing metaphysical debate over how we perceive ourselves in the world and how that perception shapes our understanding of virtuous behavior. Cooper discussed hubris and humility in the service of his larger argument that we must embrace the existence of an objective "mystery" or unknowable reality, but his description of hubris-humility tension is useful here: "The vocabulary of humility versus hubris, presumptuousness versus modesty, freedom versus servitude, and even decadence versus responsibility is . . . liberally invoked in discussions of the 'human world' thesis, and by . . . warring parties" (2002, p. 12).

HUMILITY IN MORAL PSYCHOLOGY

Chapter 2 discussed how the selection of media professionals widely respected for their ethical leadership by their peers was based largely on the criteria established by the landmark work of Anne Colby and William Damon (1992). Among the criteria they used to identify individuals whose lives were defined by "moral commitment," Colby and Damon looked for "a sense of realistic humility about one's own importance relative to the world at large, implying a relative lack of concern for one's own ego" (p. 29). While this project has consistently avoided presuming that this group of news and PR professionals are actually *moral* exemplars, analysis of their life story interviews reflects the themes found among Colby and Damon's subjects. Their summary is instructive:

> Moral exemplars have some humility about their own importance in the world. They maintain a sense of perspective about their goals and their ability to accomplish them. Moreover, morally exemplary people are dedicated to missions, values, or persons beyond their own self-aggrandizement. They are not taken, therefore, by the majesty of their own power or the sweep of their own influence. They are oriented to the task at hand and realistic about their expectations for success. [Humility] does not imply that exemplars show a false modesty about their often impressive achievements. But it does rule out these who are egotistically directed, who

glory unduly in their own honors, or who set themselves above 'less worthy' members of society. Moral exemplars may well express pride in their own good deeds, but they do not look down contemptuously at those who have accomplished less.

(pp. 31–32)

One of their exemplars, an antipoverty activist, expressed this sense of humility:

Henry Nouven, in *Calling in Rome*, talks about the acts of history like a circus. And there's the big center stage and there are the side ones. And I had wanted to look at myself as being center stage. And I realized that I was on one of the side ones, one of the clowns that would stumble and fall and get up and start again. But the interesting thing about the clowns was that they were always there. And they would never make the center stage, but they would always be there to remind people of the humanity, to remind you of what a fool you are, to remind you of how ridiculous we human beings are.

(Colby & Damon, 1992, p. 272)

HUMILITY AMONG MEDIA EXEMPLARS

J.P. believed he reached the pinnacle of his career when he was asked to serve as a communications chief for a federal regulatory agency. But then he was thrust into a situation where a national debate—whether or not a group of antidepressant drugs might be linked to suicides among teenagers—became the stage for a humbling, watershed moment for the typically self-confident PR veteran:

And we believed—at the agency, and I believe now that the science is not robust enough to make that claim. There are a lot of things that factor into it. But I had a meeting, because that was part of my job as an outreach person. I met with about a dozen moms whose kids had committed suicide, whose kids had been on anti-depressants and committed suicide. And I walk into the room, and my job was kind of to explain to them why I felt that that was not true, and I walk into the room, and I recognized instantly that was not going to happen at this meeting. I was—this was about my listening to their stories. We went around the table, and they all told these horrible, horrible stories. I can't imagine having a kid commit suicide. It's got to be the worst—it's got to be even worse than having a kid die by natural causes. The guilt that these women had was so profound. I'm thinking about it now—I can't really get my hands around it. And after the meeting, this one woman said to me, "Thank you so much for letting us come in and talk to you." It was just—to this day, it's probably the most intense experience I've ever had. And I realized that they needed to believe it was the drugs. I could have spent an hour explaining why it wasn't, and it would have been cruel. Even if I was right, it would have been cruel. They needed to talk about it.

Keith, a young journalist with a privileged background, said his searing experience trying to work as a magazine correspondent amid the horrors of the genocide in Rwanda in 1997 was a valuable lesson about his own abilities:

So in '97 I went down to Rwanda, flew into Rwanda, stayed there one night, scared out of my mind, because I was getting into a professional experience, in a place—I had no idea what the hell I was doing. I went with—I didn't even have a computer. I didn't have a [satellite] phone, I didn't have anything. I went in with a notebook and a camera. A photographer was going to come in later, so I was going in by myself, arranging it all by myself. Going into what was a war zone—I was going into Zaire, behind rebel lines, going into Kisangani, so I was hopping U.N. aid flights into Kisangani, Zaire. I had no idea where I was going to stay. I had quasi-arranged—I thought I had arranged something with Doctors Without Borders, although it turns out the people on the ground had no idea I was coming, but I thought I had arranged to stay with the Doctors Without Borders people. They're the ones I'd really wanted to feature. Anyway, I walked in—what I didn't know when I planned all this, was that I was walking into a huge news story. Because at that point, there was no massive news coming out of it—there were refugee flows, there were rebel lines that were advancing, but it was sort of a relatively obscure story. But as I was flying in, the rebels shut off access to the camps, and there were massacres in the camps. And these camps were basically Rwandans—they were filled with Rwandans, who had fled. And some of them were the ones who had helped orchestrate the genocide, and a lot of others were people who had been brought along with them, either because they were family or because they were forced to, or because they were in a community and they were scared they were going to get slaughtered in return. So it was a very—the morality of that whole episode—it was one of the more confusing and difficult, and I still—I don't know that I got half of that at the time. I look back on that and I realize that I didn't get the story fully because I walked into something I was not ready for. But, at the same time, I was in the middle of what I thought was an incredibly important story that the world needed to know about, and that was an exciting, thrilling amazing, scary thing.

In her high-stress role as communications chief for an American food company's European operations, Emily felt constantly challenged to literally bridge disparate worlds:

It wasn't necessarily easy, because I had to straddle what the Americans wanted done, and yet understand and support what the Europeans wanted done. I needed to understand what was going on on the ground in Europe, and often help the Americans understand the sentiments and feelings of the Europeans. And this in every different country and how they would view things. What I learned—and this is what, I guess, was one of the high points of my European experience—is I learned to listen more and to not try and impose or mandate my point of view, but to sit back and say, "Well, how can we make what the Americans want to happen, happen, but do it in a way that they, the Europeans, can own it—that the Norwegians can own it? the French can own it?" To remove the barriers and the resistance or opposition to the direction corporate wanted to take.

[The trick was to be] very collaborative, and also taking something that is a good idea but not "their" idea, they're not going to accept it, and helping them come around to embracing the idea, accepting it and then running with it. So that's what a lot of my job was, and it was something that I enjoyed doing, because of the challenge and also because when you did something successfully with and for them and it worked, they were so appreciative.

While humility is most often understood as an impulse to deflect praise or credit and a stance of gratitude, J.P., Keith and Emily all exhibited what researchers have identified as other key features of humble behavior: an ability to honestly assess one's strengths and weaknesses and a recognition of the inherent value of others' perspectives. Humility is often associated with a sense of modesty, and this is fitting: Both are usually considered positive attributes, both are rooted in a mature sense of perspective and both serve important prosocial ends. In their study of modest behavior, Aiden Gregg and fellow psychologists found that "modest people emerged centrally as humble, shy, solicitous, and not boastful, and peripherally as honest, likeable, not arrogant, attention-avoiding, plain, and gracious. Everyday conceptions of modesty also spanned both mind and behavior, emphasized agreeableness and intro-version, and predictably incorporated an element of humility" (2008, p. 978). But humility most definitely is not equated with meekness. Truly humble people "demonstrate acceptance as well as resolve" (Morris et al., 2005, p. 1332). Jim Collins, a business researcher who advocates that humility is an essential yet often overlooked ingredient for excellence, said the ideal corporate leader is someone "who blends extreme personal humility with intense personal will" (2001, p. 138). French philosopher André Comte-Sponville (2001) argued that humility was "the science of the self" and that to exercise true humility, one must love the truth more than themselves, since all knowledge is a wound to the ego. One particu-larly useful definition of humility comes from Morris, Brotheridge and Urbanski (2005): "Humility can be thought of as that crest of human excellence between arrogance and lowliness" and "a personal orientation founded on a willingness to see the self accurately and a propensity to put oneself in perspective" (p. 1331). Their explication of the concept of humility notes three key features:

- Self-awareness: The ability to appraise one's strengths and limitations.
- Openness: In having an awareness of one's limitations and imperfections, one must be open to new ideas and new ways of knowing.
- Transcendence: "An acceptance of something greater than the self. Out of this acceptance comes an understanding of the small role that one plays in a vast universe, an appreciation of others, and a recognition that others have a positive worth. Transcendence brings about having a proper perspective on life" (p. 1331).

The media exemplars in this study repeatedly offered illustrations of each of these.

Self-awareness
Many of the exemplars frequently were able to refer to themselves in an objective sense and view themselves with clear-eyed appraisal. This

ability came in several different manifestations, including a frequently expressed concern about how they come across to others. Michelle, a younger journalist who has helped build digital services for local newspapers, talked often about constantly assessing herself:

> I think here—just being young—I think here it's a challenge between being ambitious and—I definitely could have sat back and just worked on the website. Because I worked on the website when I first got here, but I didn't just want to work on the website. I wanted to teach, and so I started teaching right away. I want to teach more but—I mean, there are other people who are about my age here, and I know that being ambitious and kind of pushing my bosses to look at me as a potential colleague probably affected those relationships, and so balancing that ambition with how others perceive me as being selfish or a climber, or, you know, all those things, which I know I'm not, but making sure I'm understanding why I want to do the things I do and that, um, it's not something that I'm just doing because I want to be ambitious. Because I'm an overachiever, and because I feel like it's an ego trip and it's really because that's where I'm feeling like I am contributing the most, or that's how I can best benefit the organization, and helping communicate that effectively, and um, not being too big for my britches, I guess.

Danielle, a Denver-based PR veteran, discussed how she strived to always perceive herself as a factor—ideally, a positive one—in the lives of others:

> In the world, you do the right thing for the people in the world, so that's the foundational element of how you live and take personal responsibility for yourself. That's not really religious, it's not really spiritual. I wish I could break it out well. This is where I wish I was smart—or smarter. I don't know how. I'm going to have a hard time articulating this. It's sort of the awareness of how you behave externally in the world with the people and the situations that you've come about, and how you think about your own internal being. That's not going to be described well—the awareness of how I am physically present in other peoples' worlds. So, what is it that I'm doing that creates cause and effect, or reaction? That's not described well, but that's sort of what I mean.

Dennis, a newspaper editor in the southeast part of the country, frequently invoked his humble beginnings in a family with little education to help understand his motivations later in life:

> People from my background do not become editors of major
> metropolitan newspapers. I have no children. I was always afraid
> I'd have somebody like me. [laugh] I think it's, you know, it's the
> cliché about the journey, not the destination. I've always been on
> this journey, always searching, always trying to do the right thing—
> failed more times than I like to recount, but that drive to excel and
> the drive to do the right thing has always been, always overridden
> everything in my life. Even when I mess up. I have to come back to
> think, OK, alright, I've screwed up again, and how am I going to
> fix this so I don't do it again? I think my whole life has been an
> attempt to overcome insecurity and lack of direction, and you
> know, it's been a battle.

Elaine, a Pulitzer-winning journalist, considered how her single-minded passion for her work was simultaneously narrow and expanding:

> Maybe it seems kind of one dimensional, but I don't have other
> passions so much, other than journalism and my kids. You
> know? My passion is just like, what is out there that I haven't
> discovered yet? What do I want to write about that I don't know
> anything about? What can I do—I know a little bit about so
> much, but I don't know a lot about anything. [laugh] You know,
> and I think that is just like that kind of curiosity. My friend,
> Kelly, was editing a story about pension funds, and she's like, "I
> don't know anything about pension funds." And I'm like, "That's
> awesome, because now you get to learn!" You know? "They are
> paying you to learn about something that maybe you don't think
> you care about. But do you have a pension fund? So, you ought
> to know something about a pension fund, and when you are
> done, can you tell me about pension funds because I would like
> to know." I'd like to think there was more to me than being a
> journalist but I don't know if there is. I think everything I am, is
> because of people I've met, and stories I've done, and situations
> I've been put in. I think my marriage, my friendships, my work
> with kids, my volunteering, has all been because of work.
> Something to do with journalism. But then, journalism is life.
> You know what I mean?

Openness

Starting from a healthy awareness of one's limitations and imperfections, true humility calls for us to be continually receptive to new knowledge and even different ways of knowing. This often involves not just passively receiving different perspectives but actively seeking out and engaging with opposing points of view and unfamiliar stances. This sense of active openness was repeatedly illustrated by the media exemplars. Mitchell, a Pulitzer-winning editor, referred several times to a practice of second-guessing himself as a secret to his ability to be a good manager:

> And I would say a couple of lessons I also learned, that I live by today. I remember one teacher I had saying, "If your microscope isn't working, remember gentlemen, it's usually the operator, not the equipment." Which is always something I think we should keep in mind—if the computer's not working or the system's not working, it's not the system that's screwed up, it's something you're not interacting with properly. And that's, I think, a key lesson. I think in terms of interacting with people, there are things I always am very conscious of. Have I completely discounted what somebody else is thinking? And so I try to be careful not to do that. That goes back to that early childhood, cocoon-intellectual, guy-oriented thing, to college, realizing, not everybody thinks like me. How inadequate they are! [laugh] To, "Hmm, maybe they don't think like me because I'm wrong!" [laugh] So, I always like to be careful of that.

Unlike Mitchell, who benefited from a high-quality, private education, Edward, a PR veteran, realized the shortcomings of his schooling. Yet, that realization shaped his interactions with colleagues in a similar way:

> I think the biggest challenge I had was the quality of education I had, which was awful. At both high school, and in college. Part of college was self-inflicted; I was not a very active student because I was too busy. And if I had to do it over again today, I'd be in every class. I'd be taking so much more general-ed and humanities and stuff that I avoided. And so, I think a life challenge is that I am not as smart as some of my peers and friends that I am in awe of. The fact that they really understand, you know, and can go into depth on the literature and stuff like that. I can't do it. Because back then—I was amazed I had friends that really enjoyed it. I'm like, "Are they nuts?" And now I look back like, "Oh, they were the smart ones."

James, a young digital media manager in Washington, D.C., said he was always fascinated by the inherent differences in perspective, and that we are all fated to continually struggle to bridge those differences:

> I'm no longer religious; I'm quite spiritual. I believe now, more than anything else, in the imperative of love. Khalil Gibran has this—one of his more famous sayings, "Your children are not your children, they are the sons and daughters of life's longing for itself." Uh, life's longing for itself, I think, is a particularly poetic way to put the imperatives of love and evolution. Just that we have this delightful and heartbreaking human problem, that we are social creatures, we love one another, we need one another, and yet we know, we're smart enough to know, or evolved enough to know that we'll never think the exact same thing. We'll never be able to see the exact same thing, to summon the exact same thing, for a particular concept. When I say "green," or "tree," these things could be completely different objects in your brain. Um, and I think that we have—we simply have three systems that we try to use to overcome them: religion, and art, and science. Each of them takes a totally different approach. And, I think it's a fascinating question. I think it's an inspiring one.

Jeff, a journalist who has built a career developing digital newsrooms, talked of the need to thrust himself in new environments:

> The only goal I go by is I want every job to be different than the one before. I don't want any job to be just—like, when I left the *Post,* I got a call from CNN.com, and they said, "Would you be interested in coming down and talking about this job?" And I just remember getting the call, and feeling like, "Wow, this is awesome." And the more I thought about it, it's like, that's the exact same job I have, it's just a bigger organization with the same problems, but it was going to be the same deal: it was going to be trying to convince the TV side that the Web was really important, and evangelizing and going and convincing the big personalities to do more on the Web, and I just felt like, change the name, and you pretty much have the same job. So every job I want it to be different, so I have to learn new things, and I want to be under pressure to learn new things. On this job, I'm having to go out on sales calls, and having to do the elevator pitch to

advertiser execs, and those are pretty high-pressure, trying to get people to spend money. So like that's the kind of thing I didn't have to do before. I like the fact that I have to keep learning different things; I like to be tested.

Transcendence

Self-awareness and openness cultivate clear-eyed perspective on the roles we play and of the roles of others. This transcendence of self-importance and of the tendency to see others in relatively narrow, utilitarian terms, is a critical feature of humility. This trait was suggested over and over in the interviews. Mick, a retired, Chicago-based corporate communications chief, talked about how gratifying it was to see protégés and younger colleagues succeeding him:

> I have no complaints. You'll never—again, luckiest guy in the world. I have no gripes. I've had a wonderful life. If I keel over this afternoon, I'm the luckiest guy in the world. If I have a hobby, it's watching the people that I worked with for a lot of years and a lot of people that worked in my area, grow and become big shots at other companies, and that has been tremendous. That's been one of the most gratifying things in my life, is seeing those young people become vice presidents of communication, senior vice presidents of communications, marketing, whatever, and that's—you know, the best feeling in the world.

Several other exemplars touched on the idea of transcendence in more philosophical, even religious, ways. Deb, a communications specialist in the nonprofit world, often pointed to religious principles:

> What I've tried to do is be gentler and kinder in my older age, and I have a couple of mantras: Be here now. That was from a leadership [mentor]—basically, they were grooming me to be a chapter manager, and I just thought that was valuable—you know, in this world of texting and everything else. The other thing, my other mantra, is to walk a mile in somebody else's shoes. You know, my staff will come in and say, "Oh, that doctor's so bitchy and he's—" And I'm like, "Hmm, I wonder if maybe he's had a surgery today and maybe it didn't go well." I'm always very good about trying to walk in others' shoes—because I think there is in me some anger, some emotion, and I squelch it—not to be a pacifist, but sort

of like, "Let's be more Christian about this," you know? Maybe something's going on with them that you aren't aware of.

Allen, a Pulitzer-winning syndicated columnist, discussed his struggles with religious conceptions of God and how it informed his global perspective:

My feeling is that there is a God, and we do a very poor job of understanding what that means. You know, maybe we are doomed to do a very poor job of understanding what that means and of serving that God. The thing about people believing in God, whatever their faith is, people will say I believe in God tend to then want two things: they want to create God in their own image, and then, whatever power they feel God has, God is not doing what they wanted him to do as they want him to do it, then they want to sort of step in and supplant God. That's what terrorism is. That's what terrorism is all about. That's what a lot of the stuff that goes on is all about. The Allah does not need your help, so I think there is a lot of, and there is a tendency to create God in our own image, and there's a tendency to want to step in and be God. My feeling is that if God is what you say God is, then you need to quit worrying about trying to account for or explain or understand everything of God or everything that happens in the world, because by definition, you can't. OK? If you are a child and your father does whatever, your father will be mysterious to you; your father will do things that you don't understand because you are six years old and he's forty-two. And that is just the way it is going to be. So, if God is infinitely above, you know, your human father, how can you pretend that you know—that you've got a handle on what he does? That is one of the things that frustrates me about fundamentalists—Christian, Islamic, whatever. You know, "God caused this to happen because of this, that or the other." Really? Are you sure, man? Where'd that come from? You know, what good is a God who is instantly understandable to us? What kind of God—it doesn't sound much like—that sounds like it is a bigger version of me. I think the first thing that you have to do in understanding God is to comprehend that you can't understand God. If there is a God, if you believe that there is a God, you can't understand God. I think that instills humility, which I don't think is a trait that we as human beings, is that natural for us. To be humble. I don't know.

Mitchell, the D.C. editor, discussed how he measured his success:

I believe an editor's worth is shown not by whether he was able
to take the most talented person and direct them, but whether he
was able to take the least talented person and direct them. And I
always look back and say, did I do the right thing by that person?
And there have been a few people that I look back on and think
I didn't do all I could have. The biggest professional failure in my
life was that I was not able to help the person who ultimately took
my job at [a southeast U.S. newspaper] and who got fired, because
I couldn't teach her how to stop elbowing everyone around her.
Finally the entire staff just revolted, and the editor was fired. I count
that as a failure on my part because in the years that I supervised this
editor, I was never able to bring the right wisdom to it, to help this
editor overcome this personality glitch that was just destructive. I'm
not sure what I would do differently.

Of course, there are countless, often subtle ways to self-enhance—
one of which is to recount a shortcoming or failure in a way that presents you in a redemptive light or that focuses attention on how smart
you were to learn so much from a mistake. It is possible to boast about
one's humbleness (we often refer to this as false modesty). It is probably
unavoidable, in a study such as this, to screen for such "false positives"
and social-desirability artifacts when analyzing expressions of humility,
pride, regret and other related responses to personal and professional
experiences. Yet, by and large, the exemplars' accounts suggested an
honesty and willingness to appraise the self that comports with previous exemplar research.

HUBRIS IN MORAL PSYCHOLOGY

"Nothing dies harder," T.S. Eliot wrote, "than the desire to think well of oneself" (1927, p. 8). Most of us tend to believe we are above average, and many
of us also harbor what psychologists call "self-superior" attitudes. "Most
people are average but few believe it," researchers have observed (Alicke &
Govorun, 2005, p. 85). Noting that quality-of-life surveys around the world
have shown people enjoy a "sense of relative superiority" in activities they
care about, Bruce Headey and Alex Wearing concluded that "a sense of relative superiority is the usual state for most people. The feeling 'above average'
is normal" (1988, p. 499). No doubt, this tendency to color our self-view
is a natural and often healthy response to interpersonal and environmental

challenges. And this tendency often leads to what psychologists call "self-enhancement" behavior: over-estimation of our achievements, deflecting responsibility for our failures, seeing our future as unrealistically bright and even going to great lengths to appear moral without necessarily being so. In short, self-enhancement is the opposite of genuine modesty (Sedikides, Gregg & Hart, 2007). Hubristic attitudes are simply more extreme manifestations of these and other self-enhancement strategies, stemming from a deep-seated sense of self-superiority. The curious thing about the concept of hubris, however, is that it is as much about perception as it is about actual self-regard. In their article, "The hubris hypothesis: You can self-enhance, but you better not show it," researcher Vera Hoorens and her colleagues suggested that, depending on how people express their self-superiority, they can actually reap social benefits. Boastfulness, of course, is a serious social turn-off. "Self-superiority beliefs are bound to reduce the quality of social relationships when they are expressed as claims," they concluded. "Others will feel demeaned and devalued" (2012, p. 1265). But when people express self-superiority claims in ways that don't promote themselves over others, or that are couched as expressions of self-improvement efforts, doing so not only boosts their well-being, but they also may "increase the holder's likeability and potential to respond to others' concerns" (Hoorens, Pandelaere, Oldersma & Sedikides, 2012, p. 1265).

HUBRIS AMONG MEDIA EXEMPLARS

As stated earlier, most of the media exemplars selected for this study are known stars in their fields, with resumes of privilege and opportunities seized. These veterans have not reached the pinnacles of their professions without some sharp elbows. Ambition and healthy egos don't necessarily equal hubristic behavior, but they certainly help set the stage. Egregious examples of hubris in the interviews were, of course, rare. Most were subtle, oblique references or claims. The line between socially acceptable self-assertion and outright hubris can be a fine one, and many of the exemplars, with impressive degrees of self-awareness, willingly explored it. Several recalled moments of brashness in their personal lives and early careers with healthy doses or regret, even humor. Many had stories that illustrated how self-esteem (or lack of it) and hubristic behavior are psychologically intertwined. For example, Allen, the Pulitzer-winning syndicated columnist, pondered how his younger, boastful self must have appeared to his coworkers during his stint as a staff writer at a national music-industry magazine:

> I worked there, I was a stringer there for, um, '76 until I graduated
> college in August of '77. And I started working there full-time,

and apparently I was an obnoxious kid. I never thought of myself as that, and I never was trying to be, but in talking to my friends from that time—you know, a few years ago they had a reunion, and there was a fairly general consensus that I was a fairly obnoxious kid, I think—a smart-ass kid is what it was, and you know, I think part of it was, I'm 18 years old, the youngest of them are in their twenties, and you know, most of them are like, late twenties or thirties, whatever, and I just remember trying to fit in. You know? I remember trying to fit in and just kind of having, you know, probably talked too much and had a smart mouth or whatever, but I was just trying to keep up with these guys. These guys were—they didn't know, but these guys were my heroes. It actually wasn't so bad. It might have been. I don't know. I really don't know. But I don't recall having that kind of response. I don't recall feeling there goes my head, in the sense that I am better than these folks. I felt, you know, I can hang in this environment, you know, I can compete in this environment. But they didn't, for obvious reasons, see it that way. I have a tendency to give people nicknames, which they didn't always appreciate. And I called myself "the Kid" for some reason, and I wasn't thinking like "the kid" in terms of being younger. I was like doing a Billy the Kid riff or something like that. And they didn't appreciate that either. I think it was reminding them, that I was coming in and that, you know, I had gotten this praise and I was significantly younger than all of them. So, I'm basically rubbing salt in wounds and exacerbating stuff, and having not a clue as to what is going on. I think the through-line on this now that I listen to this story is that there is a lot of obliviousness in my life story. (Laugh) But I had not a clue, you know, what was going on with folks.

Hubris and pride

It is a common conundrum, a hazardous workplace minefield: how to communicate authority, competence, expertise, success without alienating anyone. Psychology researchers have explored possible explanations for when people do this successfully and for when they fail dismally. A key factor seems to be how people manifest their self-esteem, or lack of it, and its connection with the notion of pride. Pridefulness, of course, is considered among the deadly sins, but it has enormous value, psychologically speaking. A healthy sense of pride is linked with "feelings of confidence, self-worth, and productivity, and [it is] positively related to a socially desirable personality profile characterized by extraversion, agreeableness, conscientiousness, emotional stability, and high implicit and explicit self-esteem" (Tracy & Prehn, 2012, p. 15). Psychologists call this "authentic" pride, and it is linked to genuine (e.g., actually deserved or hard-earned) self-esteem (Tracy, Cheng, Robins & Trzesniewski, 2009). This healthy pride is contrasted with "hubristic" pride, which is characterized by egotism and arrogance, and positively associated with disagreeableness, aggression, low implicit self-esteem, and shame" (Tracy & Prehn, 2012, p. 15). Both types of pride appear to function as a mechanism to attain social status—one through "hard work, the demonstration and sharing of socially valued skills, and resultant respect from others (i.e., *prestige*)," and the other "forcibly taken by intimidation, aggression, and others' resultant fear (i.e., *domination*)" [authors' emphasis] (Tracy & Prehn, 2012, p. 15). The two modes of prideful behavior can be distinguished both by features of individual expression and by the responses of others:

> Research suggests that the appearance of modesty and generosity promote a prestigious reputation, whereas the appearance of arrogance promotes perceptions of dominance. . . . Thus, causal attributions that make a proud individual appear modest, such as attributing one's own success to effort, may promote perceptions of authentic pride, whereas attributions that make the individual seem arrogant, such as attributing one's success to stable abilities like intelligence or talent, may promote perceptions of hubristic pride.
>
> (Tracy & Prehn, 2012, p. 16)

Authentic pride. Not surprisingly, analysis of the media exemplars' expressions of pride in their life stories found most were of the authentic version. They talk of their accomplishments and competencies not as results of their own intelligence but in terms of effort, of team support, of being in a position to serve a larger enterprise. Recounting memorable success stories of having a hand in turning around dysfunctional corporate communication teams, Bill, a veteran consultant in California said, "I like to think that's what I'm about, is trying to build world-class organizations." Keith, the foreign correspondent, described the pride he felt in his organization's coverage of the Iraqi insurgency:

> I've been in Iraq seven times. Twice before the invasion, and five times after. So in some ways that gave me a real leg up in—there was actually a small number of reporters, who were covering the aftermath, who actually had been there before. There were some

of us, but fewer than you would think. And I think our coverage, particularly early on, had a depth that was quite helpful and useful, and we were able to see things that others weren't and to anticipate some of the problems. I was writing about sectarian strife, and the fear of civil war, almost a year before it broke out, and actually six months before U.S. officials had decided it was a real threat. I was able to hear and see things, and the way people talked, to understand that this isn't the way they talked before; this isn't the way it's always been. This is something different. It was very satisfying—as a journalist, when you know the story, can recognize the signs, can—I didn't want to be right, but professionally it was very satisfying.

Martha, a veteran journalist who left her newspaper career to launch a successful metropolitan news Web site in the Midwest, similarly expressed pride in being able to provide "vision" for the organization:

So, we looked around, and we see these layoffs that are happening here and buyouts are happening on an even larger scale in most other places, and so that means the amount of professional reporting that's getting done is shrinking. The whole tenor— the resources are shrinking—the tenor of what's being done is changing. Various colleagues and we were upset about all of this, and finally it dawns on us, "Well, who can do this? You know, if we need more reporting, we need people who really understand their community, who really care about it and have deep roots in it"—You know, "Who can do this? Wait a minute! We can do this." So that opened up a whole new chapter, and really, what I now see as the most exciting part of my career, a tremendous opportunity, and I've switched from being in a sort of very depressed state of mind and negative about things to just being very excited about what can happen, and I feel like all of the valuable things I learned along the way—learned intentionally and sometimes unintentionally, some of the odd twists and turns in my life previously have all come together to make it possible to do what I'm doing now. But when I'm gone, somebody can easily step in and do those things, but I think what I can do is kind of keep my eye on the compass and be the person that keeps all the other people kind of moving efficiently together in the same direction, and trying to strike the right balance of letting people try things and keeping people organized and keeping people—not weighing them down with too much detail that they don't need to have about the whole operation, but still letting them understand enough so they can be creative in a good way. I think that kind of all goes back to that same sense of just sort of being able to focus on what's important.

Emily, a retired communications specialist in Denver, cited her ability to cultivate out-of-the box thinking in international corporate cultures:

And I had a great—one of the things I've been blessed with— I've really had pretty good teams of people. If there's been any—what's the word? Not "challenge," but they just needed someone to turn the light bulb on to give them a different way to look at things, and to know that someone had their back to try some things differently. And I think that's one of my biggest contributions. Now, some people will acknowledge it, and others, you know—and some people came kicking and screaming, because it's easy to stay right here in a little box, because thinking about things differently might mean a little more work. And criticism. And, boy, did I get pushback around that stuff, but at the end, we were doing different things.

Hubristic pride. If actual hubris rarely took the form of overweening pride among the media exemplars in the study, it more typically was couched in the guise of supreme self-confidence, or of outsized ambition. "There was this girl who came to our church, who used crutches, this girl on crutches and my father's funeral was the 31st of the last day of the year, the 31st of December of '75," recounted Allen, the Pulitzer-winning columnist:

And I remember after the funeral asking somebody, "Who was that girl, and could you bring her to church again? Because I'd like to talk to her." It amazes me, you know, when I look back on it—you know, hours after my father's funeral, and I'm making a date! (laugh) I'm making a date.

Bill, the California PR consultant, suggested a similar outsized confidence:

I'm supposed to go to Washington in a month, and I'm on the lunch panel in the afternoon, and it's talking about the Japan brand. The ambassador from Japan [will be there], and lots of CEOs, and I'm supposed to opine on Japan's global image and what they ought to do. A month ago, I was at the war college helping the professors there and the commandant think through strategic communications in the military, which is really fascinating. So I get exposed to these people, and do a lot of learning and research and have conversations, and it gets very sophisticated, but I don't know that it necessarily changes what I think, it just enriches what I think.

Derek, the CEO of an international PR firm, talked at length about his leadership style. "I lead from the front," he said:

I think that I'm recognized as a strong CEO, not just because of the growth of the business but also because people genuinely like working for the firm. They like working for me because I give them a lot of latitude. I'm not a micromanager. I'm not a paper manager. I go out and win business myself. Not interested in second-guessing. And if they perform, then they get a lot of rope. If they don't perform, then they go. But I think I'm a good boss that way, and you know, I work harder—as hard as anybody in the firm. I'm not a slacker.

Such instances of aggressive self-assertion routinely surfaced in the interviews. Larissa has her own PR boutique firm in the San Francisco Bay area:

I started to use some freelancers. But it's hard, because—this is going to sound awful, but I can do it so much better and faster. I mean, it's stunning to me. And these are not like entry-level people; these are people who have been doing this for 20 years. But what takes one person 15 hours, I can do in four and a half. And I don't know if it's just because I know the client so much better, so I don't have to ask the questions—that might be part of it. So, I keep thinking, "Well, I could just work more efficiently."

Faith, a communications specialist in Virginia, discussed how her drive for perfection can alienate coworkers and subordinates:

Everybody can do it, and in my mind's eye everybody should do, and that's been my challenge. I try to push people and bring them along—you see this, can we try, can we strive. And it created schisms a little bit. And it backfired a lot. People didn't always get on board and it created challenges in some respects. It did. And I never have figured out how to turn it off or turn the wick down some. But this conflict between these perfectionism tendencies and accepting people for who they are is where I am. This drive to be the best and to do the best is what has driven me to where I am today. My boss told me yesterday in a meeting, she says, "Faith, you are so great." At the time, I didn't receive it as a compliment, but as, "You are so great because you have the capacity to get a lot of things done, and you get them done well, and not everybody can do that." I've had people constantly tell me about my capacity, my capacity. I said, "This is like a broken record." Capacity. What is that? Everybody has a capacity. Right? What I try to do is demonstrate, look at what you have achieved based on me shepherding you even when you felt it was uncomfortable to get there.

Karen, a Boston-based PR veteran, discussed the outsized ambition that served her well on the job market early in her career:

So they asked me how much I wanted, and I just threw out a six-figure number. Never in a million years thinking that I'd get it, and then they gave it to me, and then I still didn't want it, and I said, "Maybe we should talk about a signing bonus." And then they gave me that. So I was like, "This is insane." So, I was pretty psyched, and I was like, "OK. And the VP title." It was a director job. They said, "No, it's a director job." I said, you know, "I'm really not interested unless it is a VP title, because that is the next jump for me." Which wasn't true. I was a supervisor, and in my mind; VP was next, but you know—and they gave it to me. So, there I was, like 28½, I think, and I was like, "Yeah!"

The hubris of youth

To a great extent, the media exemplars in this study were far more self-aware than to brazenly flaunt hubristic attitudes or even to exhibit overt self-superiority. Discussions of professional experiences that evoked pridefulness—even during more hubristic moments such as the passages above—were self-reflective to a large degree. But most of the exemplars were less guarded, and even eager, to recount examples of youthful hubristic pride: aggressive self-assertion, boundless self-regard and overweening ambition in childhood, early adolescence and young adulthood. These stories were most often recounted as humorous,

"I-can't-believe-I-did-that" narratives. These often served to underscore the more mature sense of self and humility that they exhibited. Elaine, the Pulitzer-winning writer, talked about her certainty about her career as a journalist even in grade school:

> So, in the fourth grade, I decided I wanted to be a newspaper writer, and we didn't have a newspaper at my elementary school, so my mom and my sister and I started one, and she would type it on the little electric typewriter. My dad would take it and Xerox it at his office. Maybe he shouldn't have done that. My sister and I would sit there and staple it, and so we did that. I wrote horoscopes and teacher profiles. So, we did that through sixth grade, and seventh grade—again, there was no paper, and I was like, "Oh, there has to be a paper." So, I bugged my favorite English teacher until she let us start one, and I—our school was called Wood, and it was the "Wood Log." [laugh] So we had the Wood Log. And, I wrote most of the stories, and my sister took most of the pictures, and my mom helped type it, so it was kind of like a family thing, but always, always something I wanted to do was write stories about the people around me. You know? Who is that weird teacher? Who is that janitor? Who is this kid that just moved here from Guatemala? You know. And that was something, a role that I wanted to play even as a little kid. I think I wanted to be Woodward and Bernstein even back then.

Ed, the Chicago-based PR veteran, talked about how outsize ambition and preternatural business acumen served him well in childhood and later, in college politics:

> Between the farm stand and lawn mowing service, I was doing 50 lawns a week, and so I'd get up early in the morning and my parents would not see me until nightfall. I started probably about fourth grade lawn mowing, but by my eighth grade or so I was up to 50 yards. People loved having a nicely mowed yard, and they all wanted their lawn mowed on Friday, which was rather difficult. So, you were taught negotiation skills—why it would really be better to have it done on Monday. [laugh] No one would buy it, but I'd try to work it out: "How about rotating, compromise? How about if I mow—if in May on Monday and then move you to Friday and move people around?" I had several others. I had a rabbit farm. I raised rabbits and we sold them, and I didn't know until probably

about two years into it—I said, "These people are buying lots of rabbits. They love pets." Well, I was selling them as pets and I had no idea until I went over to Ray Wagner's house and saw what he was doing to my five rabbits that he had just bought. I went out of that business quickly. I think the high point was when I was elected the State College Republican Chairman. There're like 50 chapters, and the county chairman and the district chairman all voted, meaning the adult county chairman, and we ran a statewide campaign for this. I must have been 18 at the time. This was in my sophomore year. I was way young, and we were running against the established candidate and the power. We sent out solicitation mailing to all of my family and friends, and we got money back. I mean, it was amazing that we were opening up envelopes with checks and money, and so we wondered how we would go to 12 different districts to meet with all of these people. How are we going to do it? And the incumbent was driving to all of them. We rented a plane. [Laugh] So, these two 18-year-olds in a plane flying from city to city, so we knocked out all 12 in two days, and this other guy is still driving probably, and so, we really were the underdog, and winning that was so much fun. I didn't think there was a chance that we could do it, but you know, you're dumb and young and figure what the heck, let's run a campaign, and I just think that we were brash enough to pull it off and no one thought it was possible.

Allen, the Pulitzer-winning syndicated columnist, recounted similar doses of chutzpah during his early years, both in grade school and later in college:

I was a writer, and I realized it at five. That's when I started sending stuff out. I had a little toy typewriter. When I was seven, I think is when I got my first real typewriter for seventy-five bucks. Bought it on layaway. When I was twelve years old, I was sending things out. From that point on, to magazines—it was always something that I knew that I was put here to do, and that sort of made a lot of the other stuff endurable. I sent them really awful stuff, and they sent it back. I specifically remember sending the story out to Playboy magazine when I am like twelve or thirteen years old on ants, because that was one of my favorite things to do, is dig up ants nests, and I had read everything there was about ants. (laugh) I was really fascinated about ants. You know—the head, the thorax, the abdomen, the soldier ant, the carpenter ant. I can tell you to this day more than you thought possible about ants. I remember writing up about four pages about ants, and sending it to Playboy. I had never seen Playboy. You know, but I think they were listed somewhere and they paid like a thousand, two thousand, whatever it was for an article. I just thought they wanted interesting articles. And I was interested in ants, so why shouldn't today's man be interested in ants? I remember college as being really a culture shock. I grew up in South LA, which at that time—South LA right now is probably better than 90 percent Hispanic, but at the time it was probably 95 to 98 percent African American, and I remember specifically thinking as a kid when I was eight years old that LA was a majority black city. You could not have told me that there were any white people in LA. White people lived on the Ponderosa or they lived in Mayberry—television. (laugh) So going to college that first year was just kind of a culture shock. I remember I had this roommate; this guy was a dead ringer for Howdy Doody. (laugh) We had some pretty interesting times together; we had some pretty good times together. He played Simon and Garfunkel and the theme from Camelot for some reason. I had the only record player, and I was playing the Temptations, the Isley Brothers, or whatever. I remember playing my music very loud, and I look back and I think it was more than just a kid playing his music loud. I realized, you know, later, that it was a "I'm here." Here I am. 'Cuz I'm playing music that is probably not music that they are playing.

HUMILITY AS A VIRTUE IN MEDIA

An ability to assess their own strengths and weaknesses; a habit of recognizing and seeking out the perspectives of others; a clear-eyed understanding of their station in the world and their duty to contribute to a larger enterprise—the media exemplars in this study repeatedly artic-ulated these key features of humility. In addition to echoing humility's dimensions of self-awareness, openness and transcendence (Morris et al., 2005), the exemplars' often humble outlook also corresponded with the humbleness that researchers have argued is an essential ingredient for successful leadership. Dusya Vera and Antonio Rodriquez-Lopez (2004) identified 13 characteristics of a successful and humble leader, most of which were underscored in the interviews with media exemplars:

- Is open to new paradigms;
- Is eager to learn from others;
- Acknowledges his or her own limitations and mistakes and attempts to correct them;
- Accepts failure with pragmatism;
- Asks for advice;
- Develops others;
- Has a genuine desire to serve;
- Respects others;
- Shares honors and recognition with collaborators;
- Accepts success with simplicity;
- In not narcissistic and repels adulation;
- Avoids self-complacency;
- Is frugal (p. 395).

"[T]he virtue of humility is valuable because it enhances the ability of firms to understand and respond to external threats and opportunities. Humility helps executives to avoid the problems of self-complacency and overconfidence" (Vera & Rodriguez-Lopez, 2004, p. 397). It is also important to emphasize how humility as a characteristic comports with high degrees of more fundamental personality traits; modesty is a key factor of Agreeableness (Sedikides et al., 2007), and all but eight of the 24 media exemplars in the study scored higher on this trait than their age cohort on the standard personality test. Feelings of authentic pride, in contrast to hubristic pride, are positively related "to a socially desirable personality profile characterized by extraversion, agreeableness, conscientiousness, emotional stability, and high implicit and explicit self-esteem" (Tracy & Prehn, 2012, p. 15). Humility is also linked to better academic and job performance (Exline & Hill, 2012).

In analyzing the media exemplars' stories, resolve or quiet determination becomes the axis on which they alternately pivot between humility and hubristic behavior. They repeatedly demur and deflect when it comes to claiming credit, but the passion they hold for their work translates into impressive degrees of perseverance and a keen focus on goals. This drive, combined with the exemplars' typically forceful personalities, can occasionally spill over into hubristic pridefulness.

REFERENCES

Alicke, M.D., & Govorun, O. (2005). The better-than-average effect. In *The self in social judgment* (M.D. Alicke, D.A. Dunning & J.I. Krueger, Eds.), 85–106. New York: Psychology Press.

Ashton, M.C., & Lee, K. (2005). Honesty-humility, the Big Five, and the Five-Factor Model. *Journal of Personality 73* (5), 1321–1353.

Colby, A., & Damon, W. (1992). *Some do care: Contemporary lives of moral commitment.* New York: Free Press.

Collins, J. (2001). Level 5 leadership: The triumph of humility and fierce resolve. (2001, July-August). *Harvard Business Review,* 136–139.

Comte-Sponville, A. (2001). *A small treatise on the great virtues: The uses of philosophy in everyday life.* New York: Henry Holt.

Cooper, D.E. (2002). *The measure of things: Humanism, humility and mystery.* Oxford: Oxford University Press.

Eliot, T.S. (1927). *Shakespeare and the stoicism of Seneca.* London: Oxford University Press.

Exline, J.J., & Hill, P.C. (2012). Humility: A consistent and robust predictor of generosity. *Journal of Positive Psychology 7* (3), 208–218.

Ford, R. (2006). Why we fail: How hubris, hamartia, and anagnosis shape organizational behavior. *Human Resource Development Quarterly 17* (4), 481–489.

Gregg, A.P., Hart, C.M., Sedikides, C., & Kumashiro, M. (2008). Everyday conceptions of modesty: A prototype analysis. *Personal and Social Psychology Bulletin 34* (7), 978–992.

Headey, B., & Wearing, A. (1988). The sense of relative superiority—central to well-being. *Social Indicators Research 20,* 497–516.

Hoorens, V. (2011). The social consequences of self-enhancement and self-protection. In *Handbook of self-enhancement and self-protection* (M.D. Alicke & C. Sedikides, Eds.), 235–257. New York: Guilford.

Hoorens, V., Pandelaere, M., Oldersma, F., & Sedikides, C. (2012). The hubris hypothesis: You can self-enhance, but you'd better not show it. *Journal of Personality 80* (5), 1237–1274.

Lebell, S. (1995). *The art of living: The classic manual on virtue, happiness and effectiveness. A new interpretation.* New York: HarperCollins.

Morris, J.A., Brotheridge, C.M., & Urbanski, J.C. (2005). Bringing humility to leadership: Antecedents and consequences of leader humility. *Human Relations 58* (10), 1323–1350.

Murdoch, I. (1997). The sovereignty of the good. New York: Routledge.

Nagel, T. (1986). *The view from nowhere.* New York: Oxford University Press.

Nehru, J. (1946). The discovery of India. Oxford: Oxford University Press.

Renard, J. (1964/2008). The Journal of Jules Renard. Portland, OR: Tin House Books.

Sedikides, C., Gregg, A.P., & Hart, C.M. (2007). The importance of being modest. In *The self: Frontiers in social psychology* (C. Sedikides & S. Spencer, Eds.), 163–184. New York: Psychology Press.

Tracy, J.L., Cheng, J.T., Robins, R.W., & Trzesniewski, K.H. (2009). Authentic and hubristic pride: The affective core of self-esteem and narcissism. *Self and Identity 8,* 196–213.

Tracy, J.L., & Prehn, C. (2012). Arrogant or self-confident? The use of contextual knowledge to differentiate hubristic and authentic pride from a single nonverbal expression. *Cognition and Emotion 26* (1), 14–24.

Trumbull, D. (2010). Hubris: A primal danger. *Psychiatry 73* (4), 341–351.

Vera, D., & Rodriguez-Lopez, A. (2004). Humility as a source of competitive advantage. *Organizational Dynamics 33* (4), 393–408.

CHAPTER 8

Crucibles of Experience

Character cannot be developed in ease and quiet. Only through experience of trial and suffering can the soul be strengthened, vision cleared, ambition inspired, and success achieved.

—Helen Keller, 1938

Experience is not what happens to a man. It is what a man does with what happens to him.

—Aldous Huxley, 1932

Elaine's phone rang around four in the morning of Christmas Day, nearly 15 years before she won a Pulitzer Prize for her storytelling. She was working in a newspaper bureau, writing about the happenings in small coastal communities. She had a 16-month-old son, was seven months pregnant with another, and her husband was away on tour with a band. A local firefighter was on the line. "I'm sorry to wake you up, but there has been an accident, and I know you'd want to know," he said. She bundled up, strapped her son in an infant carrier and headed out. The scene was grim: A car had gone off the road and into a canal. "This mom and dad and two little kids had been driving from Nashville, where the mom was a waitress, to go spend Christmas with her mom, and they were driving all night," Elaine recounted. "Mom fell asleep at the wheel. There's my friend the firefighter, and all of the rescue crew team, and the state highway patrol, and they are all out there and they are all crying on the side of the road. When they pulled the—went to pull the bodies out, the mom and dad were both turned over in their seats trying to unbuckle their kids from the car seats."

* * *

As a kid devoted to sports, it was natural that Michelle gravitated to sports journalism for her career. Yet, a traumatic sports-related experience in high school became a formative moment in other ways. Her father, she said, "always raised me to feel like I could always do whatever I really wanted to do," so when her high school's new football coach asked her to join the team, she didn't hesitate. "Even though I had always been there—all my best friends, we'd gone to school together since I was in kindergarten; I figured they knew me well enough that this wouldn't be surprising and this would be something that they would accept. And it was definitely not accepted." Michelle was quickly ostracized at her school for being the only girl on the football team. Her family received threats. "They'd throw stuff at me in class, and the teachers, they didn't want to do anything or say anything about it 'cause it was kind of—I was in the wrong for doing this, and they thought that, you know, I was kind of getting what I deserved. You know, I asked for it. And I believed it for a long time."

* * *

Long before Mick stumbled into his career in corporate communications, he served as a gung-ho member of the Army's special-forces unit at the height of the Vietnam War. He was a lieutenant leading a 20-man "strike recondo" team—a quick response squad sent to help units caught in firefights or ambushed. On one such mission, Mick said he jumped onto the lead helicopter to go. "And I go to get on that number one chopper, and there are seven or eight people on that chopper, then the crew—two door gunners, two pilots. As I jump on—I wanted to be on the first chopper, because when you're down on the ground, I wanted to be able to control things. I wanted to be the first one in so I could control things. Anyway, one of the pilots turns around, and he goes, 'Get off.' And I go, 'Let's go.' He says, 'We're overloaded. Get off, Lieutenant.' And then I said something obscene to him and I jumped off, and I went and jumped on number two chopper. To make a long story short, we're flying for about 11, 12 minutes into the AO, the area of operations where the team was in trouble. We're going in and land on a little hillside, and as we're going in, number one chopper, tail rotor—we're under fire, we're taking fire from the ground, from where they'd ambushed the team—that number one ship goes, veers just a little bit to the right; as it veers right, its tail rotor hits a tree, chopper flips upside down, crashes into the hillside, bursts into flames, everybody on board is killed. 12 minutes before that, OK, I had told the guy to go screw himself because he threw me off his chopper. Now, why did that happen?"

* * *

Every life features seminal events and watershed moments that leave indelible marks. Some burn enduring lessons into the consciousness. Others shape individuals' outlooks, priorities and life goals for years, even decades, afterward. This chapter recounts and examines the often gripping and sometimes traumatic experiences that the media exemplars in this study point to as pivotal in their life story narratives. While it is not intended to suggest that their exemplar stature was forged by specific experiences, the pivotal moments go a long way in helping reach an understanding of their motivations and values. The experiences explored here are both personal and professional. Some are broad, generalized experiences, such as the effect of growing up as a minority, which has forged an acute awareness of individuals' sense of otherness. Others are acute, pinpoint events that proved to be formative in some way, such as experiencing a childhood trauma or triumph. Many exemplars described the importance of experiences of failure in building strengths that later helped them succeed professionally. They also discussed what could be called defining moments of their professional lives that have been incorporated into their self-identities.

The psychology literature is rich with explorations of the significance and meanings of various types of momentous life events. For the last several decades, researchers have looked closely at the ways people deal with adversity, challenges and trauma. Do certain personality traits help some people develop better coping skills? How exactly do some people emerge from traumatic experiences not merely damaged but often empowered and thankful for a new perspective on the world? How might we explain the motivational factors that drive individuals who spend years in obscurity or who achieve success? And how might all this psychological research be brought to bear on the life stories of these media exemplars in ways that might help us to learn from them? Most of the exemplars who participated in this study were quite frank and open in their discussions of painful, even traumatic events in their lives because they felt the experiences were critical in being understood. For Elaine, the searing heartbreak of that Christmas Day auto tragedy scarred her, but it also ultimately strengthened her resolve to honor the subjects of her journalism by showcasing their innate dignity and always going the extra mile to understand the truth of their lives before writing about them. For Michelle, the injustice of her high school ostracism stamped in her consciousness a keen sensitivity to the notion of equality and to the discrimination suffered by others, ultimately driving her to complement her journalism career with a law degree. For Mick, his there-but-for-the-grace-of-God moment in Vietnam reinforced his determination to make the most of his life and never look back. This chapter endeavors to honor such openness—not by offering some speculative armchair psychologizing but by surveying relevant lines of psychology research as a context in which to understand themes of survivorship, of growth, of formative life lessons that run through their experiences.

Three areas of psychology research seem to be particularly relevant to the themes that run through the exemplars' formative life experiences. The first area of relevant psychology research is on what is known as adversarial, or posttraumatic, growth. Psychologists have long known that people are often transformed by traumatic events in positive as well as negative ways and that "tragedy is a substrate of experience from which wisdom can arise" (Birren & Fisher, 1990, p. 323). As two other researchers describe it:

> People may emerge from disruptive and even traumatic events with new skills for managing the external world or for managing their distress. The "skill" may be an actual skill, it may be an enhanced knowledge base, it may be enhanced social support. With new skills, people are better prepared to deal with an unpredictable world. With new pathways to get from one place to another, people are more flexible in confronting the unknown.
>
> (Carver & Scheier, 1988, p. 96)

A key feature among people who experience adversarial growth is resilience—the ability to resist being overwhelmed or defined by loss or negative experiences. Resilient people "are able to *assimilate* loss into their existing self-narratives in a way that it does not radically undermine the central themes of their life stores and, indeed, may even affirm them" [author's emphasis] (Neimeyer, 2006, p. 71). The second area of relevant psychology research focuses on the concept of *hardiness*—a trait described as "a pattern of attitudes and strategies that together facilitate turning stressful circumstances from potential disasters into growth opportunities" (Maddi, 2013, p. 8). Hardiness is also referred to as "existential courage." People who exhibit hardiness exhibit healthy coping strategies that enable them to deal with stress and challenges in ways that harness the experiences to their advantage. The third area of relevant psychology represents several distinct but related strands, referred to here as *motivation and flow*. Included in this area are psychological explorations of how people set goals and motivate themselves to achieve them, what kinds of predispositions help and hinder people in their efforts to reach their potential and some of the work in the field of positive psychology into the nature of human strengths such as self-efficacy, perseverance and the ability to extract wisdom from life events. This area also draws on the concept of "optimal experience," a state often referred to as being "in the zone," where one's concentration is perfectly matched with the task at hand and time seems to stand still. Such optimal experiences also are known as "flow" (Csikszentmihalyi, 1988, 1990).

"CRUCIBLES" IN EXEMPLARS' LIFE STORIES
The critical core lying at the center of all of these psychological theories and studies of personality characteristics is, as the quote from Huxley indicates, not experience itself but what a person does with experience. The media exemplars in this study discuss at length what they called pivotal moments in their personal and professional lives, but the aim of doing so is virtually always to illustrate how they came to be who they are rather than to marvel at the uniqueness or difficulty of the experience itself. How they survived a difficult childhood, how they incorporated a key lesson, how a setback was turned into an opportunity—they all framed formative moments, or times of struggle or crisis, as a setting for their own responses. In doing so, these media exemplars are not unique. Bookshelves are filled with accounts of rags-to-riches tales and stories of heroism that showcase this ability. Tom Wolfe's celebration of Chuck Yeager and a generation of early astronauts, *The Right Stuff,* is a classic example of this genre. Writers and researchers have undertaken numerous studies of what they perceived as groups of exceptional individuals and explored what makes them tick. In their 1998 book, *The Lessons of Experience: How Successful Executives Develop on the Job,* business researcher Morgan McCall and his colleagues sought to delve into the experiences and psyches of successful executives. They focused on "trials by fire" and other experiences of hardship and the executives' responses to them. They concluded that remarkable abilities of adaptation and extracting lessons from hardship constituted the key thread that defined their study subjects:

> What did seem to characterize the successful executives we studied
> was not their genetic endowment nor even their impressive array

of life experience. Rather, as a group, they seemed ready to grab or create opportunities for growth, wise enough not to believe that there's nothing more to learn, and courageous enough to look inside themselves and grapple with their frailties. . . . So if there is indeed a right stuff for executives, it may be this extraordinary tenacity in extracting something worthwhile from their experience and in seeking experiences rich in opportunities for growth. . . . In short, the closest thing to a prescription we could find was: Make the most of your experiences.

(McCall, Lombardo & Morrison, 1988, p. 122)

Other writers have found the same kind of driving values in their efforts to capture key elements of good leadership. Most recently, in their 2002 multigenerational leadership study, *Geeks & Geezers: How Era, Values and Defining Moments Shape Leaders*, Warren Bennis and Robert Thomas go so far as to urge businesses, organizations and training programs serious about developing leadership to actually create such trial-by-fire, or "crucible" experiences, as the best way to cultivate adaptive nimbleness and habits of learning from hardships and mistakes. The authors put forth a theory of leadership as a process that involves testing designed as opportunities to grow from adverse events. "It is a model that explains how individuals make meaning out of often difficult events—we call them crucibles—and how that process of 'meaning-making' both galvanizes individuals and gives them their distinctive voice," they wrote (p. 4). They described their rationale:

Whether the crucible experience is an apprenticeship, an ordeal, or some combination of both, we came to think of it much like the hero's journey that lies at the heart of every myth, from *The Odyssey* to *Erin Brockovich*. It is both an opportunity and a test. It is a defining moment that unleashes abilities, forces crucial choices, and sharpens focus. It teaches a person who he or she is. People can be destroyed by such an experience. But those who are not emerge from it aware of their gifts and goals, ready to seize opportunities and make their future. Whether the crucible was harrowing or not, it is seen by the individual as the turning point that set him or her on the desired, even inevitable, course. . . . [P]eople with ample adaptive capacity may struggle in the crucibles they encounter, but they don't become stuck in or defined by them. They learn important lessons, including new skills that allow them to move on to new levels of achievement and new levels of learning. This ongoing process of challenge, adaptation, and learning prepares the individual for the next crucible, where the process is repeated. The extraction of wisdom from the crucible experience is what distinguishes our successful leaders from those who are broken or burnt out by comparable experiences. In every instance, our leaders carried the gold of meaning away from their crucibles. And they emerged with new tools as well.

(Bennis & Thomas, 2002, pp. 16, 93–94)

This chapter draws on Bennis and Thomas's use of the term to refer to the experiences that the media exemplars discuss as critical or formative in their lives as well as their responses to them.

ADVERSARIAL GROWTH AND RESILIENCE

Both Linda and her husband were veteran journalists at the *Rocky Mountain News*, Denver's oldest daily newspaper, when it was shut down permanently in 2009. Not only did the traumatic experience throw her family into turmoil in the middle of an economic recession, but it sparked a bit of an identity crisis for her as well.

> I can remember being up in our bathroom crying, because I didn't want the kids to see me. Just thinking, "Am I no longer a journalist?" Because I didn't realize how intertwined my understanding of my—my identity, how strongly attached it was to being a journalist. I mean, my god, I've been a journalist since—you know, my grandmother made me write that story. Right? Since I got my first assignment from my grandmother editor. And it was just—well, who am I if I'm not a journalist? And, how the hell are we going to feed the kids if we don't have jobs?

And yet Linda emerged from that upheaval about a year later and ended up opening what may prove to be the most significant period of her professional life by spearheading the establishment of an online investigative news cooperative, similar to others sprouting up around the country.

> But as dramatic as it was for Colorado to lose the *Rocky*, I knew that every other newsroom in the state was half the size it had been five years before. And that everybody had stories they knew about that they couldn't get to, which is torture. Torture. You

know the stories out there. So, I wanted to create a way to leverage all of these newsrooms to get at some of these stories that would have otherwise never be told, and because of my background, in computer-assisted reporting, I knew if I focused on those kinds of stories, that I wouldn't be competing with those other newsrooms, because they couldn't do that.

Jeff, now president of a digital news organization in Washington, D.C., talked about memories of watching his mother struggle with depression when he was a child:

And I didn't understand what clinical depression was, and I didn't understand why she wasn't getting out of bed in the morning, and I think my father knew, but couldn't try to explain it to a 13-year-old, or 12-year-old, and 9-year-old kid. So we just didn't know. It was scary, because you didn't know if it was a health thing, or what. Getting myself up for school when my mother was sick, because she was depressed. Having to get up, going by that closed door every morning wondering what was going on, hoping she was OK. You know, I had to be self-sufficient growing up because of my mother's thing—like I had to learn to get myself up and out of the house in the morning without anybody waking me up or anybody driving me to the bus stop. If I missed the bus, I didn't wake my mother up, I figured out how to get to school some other way. Not that there were a lot of them, but I could walk—it was a two-mile walk, so I might walk and would miss my first class. But I just felt I was not going to put this on her; she just can't—it was my fault I missed the bus, so I'll pay the consequences.

While Jeff links that experience with the value he places on being self-sufficient, he also talked about how it helped make him cautious about coming to any judgments about the behavior of other people and how similar scars might have affected them, which in turn has largely determined his management approach.

Like, I'm just not going to—I have no reason to blame anybody else for anything that happens in my life; I've been handed a pretty good setup. And not everybody's been handed this good of a setup—I acknowledge that—that's why I'm not going to be one of these people who sits and who thinks it's all about personal accountability—that no matter what crappy circumstances you were born in, you can fix it. Sometimes it's hard. People were born into much worse situations, by degrees, than I was ever put in, so I can't really. . . . So to me, that personal responsibility thing extends to the fact that, uh, I have no preconceived judgments in any way, shape or form. I have my own opinions, and I believe that everybody gets to where they are politically, honestly.

The sea of research on the many emotional and psychological scars left by trauma and hardship might invite some sort of psychoanalytic approach to the life stories of the media exemplars in this study. But more appropriate, and more useful, is the context provided by work that has focused on the brighter side of the effects of life's bumps and jolts: the phenomenon that psychologists have termed "adversarial" or posttraumatic growth, suggested by the accounts from Linda and Jeff. "The view that individuals can be changed, sometimes in radically good ways, by their struggle with trauma is ancient and widespread," noted two prominent theorists in this field (Calhoun & Tedeschi, 2006, p. ix). Researchers have looked closely at how people respond in positive ways when bad things happen—what coping mechanisms they recognize as needed and proceed to develop; what methods of introspection or rumination occur to enable them to reflect on not only what has been lost but what has been gained; how their worldviews and self-perceptions are changed. "As a burgeoning field of research documents, whether the challenges to the fundamental schemas of survivors' lives result from encounters with tragic bereavement, catastrophic illness, interpersonal violence, or political oppression, a great many experience growth as well as grief, being prompted by highly distressing circumstances to higher levels of posttraumatic adaptation," according to one theorist (Neimeyer, 2006, p. 69).

Of course, only a handful of exemplars in this study discussed experiencing these sorts of trauma; most involved less disturbing yet still significant narratives of loss, hardship and failure. But the psychology of rumination and adaptation remains instructive. Further, researchers who have studied cases of people exhibiting adversarial growth noted patterns among those with personality traits similar to those of the exemplars in this study: One's personality traits not only appear to predict whether people will be likely to experience crisis-related growth but also predict the types of benefits people will say they derived from their negative experiences. As discussed in Chapter 3, as a group, the media exemplars in this study scored significantly lower than their age cohorts for Neuroticism and significantly higher than their cohorts for Extraversion and Openness to experience. Psychologists have found that people with the same trait pattern who experienced trauma were more likely to perceive ways that they have actually benefited from hardship or crisis. They also tended to rely to a greater extent on drawing strength from adversity as a style of coping with threat:

> Those scoring higher on measures of extraversion, who are more gregarious, cheerful, and seekers of social contact, might be especially likely to cite positive consequences of adversity for social relationships. The individual who is more open to experience—imaginative, emotionally responsive, and intellectually curious—might be particularly likely to meet the challenge of adversity through a philosophical re-orientation and a new direction in life plans.
>
> (McCrae & Costa, 1986, pp. 72–73)

The exemplars in this study repeatedly illustrated this, usually unaware that they were actually doing so. Bill, a corporate communications veteran in the San Francisco area, talked about how his "otherness" as an Asian minority growing up in the Midwest underscored the value of being challenged that served him well throughout his career:

> I think what's important is that I'm Japanese-American. As far as I know, we were the only Asian family in our community. And to be Japanese-American after World War II, we certainly encountered our share of racism and prejudice. So my whole life I've sort of been in the role of "other." So, you know, we grew up with sometimes that amount of emotional sort of negative vibes. So you're either going to be really strong and just tough it out, or you were going to crumple under the weight of that. Either you're going to get tough and have a thick skin and a lot of determination, or you're not.

Deb talked about the role that the chronic issue of weight gain played in the development of her professional self. She recalled being taunted for her size as a child and how she responded by burrowing into every possible activity to master it. That drive to continually seek new challenges later in her career as a PR specialist helped her set aside her body insecurity.

> And so I'll never forget—we were playing Red Rover, and I would be the last to be picked, and people called me names. The name-calling had a profound effect on me. So I think my mother realized to cope I should focus on the positives. She saw I had this great

imagination, she was so smart and talked to me, she said, "You can do anything you want—you can put yourself out there—" So I got involved in everything—4-H—Not the typical farm experience but what's called demonstrations and public speaking, and I won every purple ribbon. I got into Voice of America. I think I became very driven, very focused at that early age. She was the one that said I could do anything, and she pushed me. As I got older I tried to understand more about myself. I did some therapy when I was in D.C. around why I would lose weight and gain it back and the whole thing maybe being a self-defense mechanism. My Mom often thought she drove me too hard. But what I realized and what I would say to her, "Look where I am? You know, how can I regret that you pushed me? I found my niche."

The kinds of personal responses illustrated by Bill's and Deb's narratives—the ability to cope effectively and not be debilitated by adversity or hardship, the ability to perceive benefits derived from difficult experiences, the ability to respond to harsh realities with flexibility and adaptation rather than with bitterness and belligerence—constitute what psychologists call the quality of *resilience*. "The key difference here is that resilient individuals are able to manage these difficult experiences in such a manner that they do not interfere with their ability to maintain functioning," according to researchers who have studied this issue (Mancini & Bonanno, 2009, p. 1808).

Resilience

James grew up in a happy household in Florida, went on to attend Harvard and started a career in digital news. As a young prodigy in a burgeoning field, he was comfortable with his identity as an openly gay man—in most ways. But coming out to his family was a different, painful matter.

I had actually concocted this whole plan, and it began with me coming out to my sister. This was something I knew was going to have to happen eventually. And I put off coming out to anyone in my family for years, because I just didn't need to—logically, I could live my whole life—I could date who I wanted, I was out at work, I was out to my friends. I was living the life of a fully out person, except for my parents, who were living in a totally different state. But my mom started getting suspicious. I told my sister. And first she said everything you're not supposed to say to someone that

comes out. You know, "Were you abused as a child somehow?"
Later, she and I had a conversation that was just—it was sad, that
all of a sudden, talking about Leviticus, and I'd thought we'd been
over all of this, and the next thing I knew, I get a call from my
mom, and she said, "Son, what's going on in your life? Are you
gay?" And I said, "Yes." And she just broke down wailing, and she
didn't say anymore, and she hands the phone to my sister, and my
sister starts telling me that she thinks this is wrong, that I've fallen
from the path of righteousness, and I was just shocked. Two weeks
later, they both come fly to visit me, and the two of them carrying
bulletin boards with photos of me as a child. And my sister has in
her hand sheaves of research reports from the National Association
for the Research and Treatment of Homosexuality. I mean, all this
stuff, I had long since grown sort of an intellectual immunity to it.
But they came in, and for the next couple of hours, started reading
me the most ridiculous, hateful literature about the true nature of
gay men, and all that sort of stuff. I stepped out for a moment. I
couldn't take it anymore. Went to my car got in my car, closed the
doors, locked the doors, and called my friend, and told her what
was happening. Later, I went back to my house. And I asked them
for 15 minutes. I said, "I listened to you guys for about two and
a half hours, and so all I ask is for 15 minutes, just to make a few
points. I love you so much, I love you both so much, and I'm so
happy that you're here. I think we could have a lovely and beautiful
weekend together. But I need you to know three things. One, I love
and respect you more than any other women. Two, I will always
love you, no matter what happens, and three, I will always be gay.
And, if you can accept that, and we can have a weekend together,
I'm happy to tell you anything you need to hear from me, answer
any questions you might have, but if you can't, and if you keep on
saying things that hurt me and strike at the core of who I am, I'm
not going to stay. Not going to listen." And they chose that second,
and kept on reading their tracts, and so I got my coat and I left. I
said what I said, and it was the right thing to say, and it felt—even
now, that it was the right thing to say, that I meant it—implicit in
that moment was a sort of forgiveness, even then. And it felt like
I've discharged this problem, I've done this right, and my role in
this doesn't need to hide.

Resilient people, such as Bill, Deb and James, often share a variety of
traits that enable them to endure hardship, handle challenges and even

perceive benefits from experiences of loss better than those without these traits. Resilience is the result of "dynamic processes that lead to adaptive outcomes in the face of adversity," according to psychologists (Lepore & Revenson, 2006, p. 29). Resilient people often feature what psychologists call "dispositional optimism": that is, they have a sense of confidence in their identities, a confidence that cultivates a general expectation that things will work out for the best, which in turn makes them more likely to be able to experience some sort of growth or perceive some benefit during experiences of loss or hardship. "There is also good reason to believe that optimistic individuals might be more inclined than pessimists to extract a sense of benefit or gain from adversity: Their hopeful view of the future may well stem from a positive interpretation of the present," according to two theorists in the field (Tennen & Affleck, 1998, p. 68). There could be several reasons why optimism is a common trait among people with a strong sense of resilience. For one, they may try harder. Psychologists Stephen Lepore and Tracey Revenson argued that "they may use more coping efforts, particularly approach-oriented, problem-focused strategies" (2006, p. 31). For another, optimists may "reframe" stressful experiences in a positive way, thereby actively imposing meaning. Also, optimists have been found to be more "forward-thinking" about their negative experiences, anticipating and often expecting to reap benefits from adversity. "Optimists do not simply report greater benefits from adversity, but actively remind themselves of the benefits they have found" (Lepore & Revenson, 2006, p. 31). Researchers also have found that optimists seem to know when to disengage from unachievable goals and to shift their efforts to other aspirations. "The idea of being able to shift attention from maladaptive to adaptive thought processes resonates with other work, which suggest that importance of disengaging or not ruminating on unproductive thoughts" (2006, p. 31). And finally, researchers say that optimists are likely to have better quality relationships with others and thus have greater social resources to draw upon. "Optimists may signal to others that they have positive expectancies about recovering from stressors, so other may feel that any efforts they take to help an optimist are likely to be fruitful" (2006, pp. 31–32).

HARDINESS

The tendency to view the world with a glass-half-full attitude also is tied to a related characteristic that has gotten the attention of psychologists over the last two decades: hardiness. Some have called this "existential courage": a pattern of attitudes and strategies that enable individuals to transform stressful circumstances and potential disasters into growth opportunities (Maddi, 2013). Hardiness is exemplified by what Salvatore Maddi refers to as the three "Cs": challenge, commitment and control:

- People who embrace life as fundamentally *challenging* accept that life is stressful, yet see stressful change as growth opportunities. They are aware of the value of learning through failure and do not seek to avoid adversity or feel entitled to easy comfort and security.
- People with a strong sense of *control* are not necessarily "control freaks" who must micromanage everyone and everything, but they are driven by a sense of purposefulness and the idea that they often have the capacity to influence outcomes. They eschew attitudes of powerlessness and passivity.
- People with high levels of *commitment* believe that no matter how bad things get, perseverance is critical, as is avoiding a sense of detachment or alienation. They realize the value of being engaged in life interests and do not find boredom or negativity to be acceptable responses.

While most people may exhibit one or more of the three Cs, only the combination of them can result in hardiness. For example, an individual high in control yet little in the way of commitment and challenge would desire to determine outcomes but would not be inclined to spend effort to learn from experience or engage with people. Or someone high in only a sense of commitment would be completely involved with other people to the extent that they might have little faith in their own ability to influence things, defining themselves through others. "People who are simultaneously strong in all of the three Cs tend to 1) see life as a continually changing phenomenon that provokes them to learn and change (challenge), 2) think that through this developmental process, they can work on the changes in a fashion that turns them into fulfilling experiences (control), and 3) share this effort and learning in a supportive way with the significant others and institutions in their lives (commitment)" (Maddi, 2013, p. 9).

The media exemplars in this study offered up a range of stories and anecdotes from their personal and professional lives that illustrated manifestations of the first C, challenge. Faith, a corporate communications veteran in Virginia, talked about the difficulty of accepting a position with a large Midwest manufacturer early in her career and working as a young black woman in an overwhelmingly white business culture:

I was somewhat isolated, because, just think about Peoria. I'm 22. African American, and there is not one—and this is the analogy

I use to kind of demonstrate how strange it seemed. There's not one African American radio station in Peoria. Not one. And I just use that as my example to say how different an environment it is. And then it was a little bit racist. So I was also a loaned executive to United Way, and this one gentleman, who was extremely racist—and I just remember he gave me the hardest time—and see, my attitude is, "I'm going to fix this. I'm going to work on him. I'm going to handle it." It never occurred to me to go report it, but I just remember him; he said some pretty harsh things, and one thing in particular, we were talking about Reba McIntyre, who's a country singer. I really like her, and I was talking to this friend, who was also a loaned executive, about Reba, and I said, "I love that name. Isn't that a great name?" And he said, "Reba. I think that's a nigger's name." I mean, I just looked at him. I don't know what I said. The retort I gave him, I thought handled it. I just found it odd sometimes to work in this environment.

Mitchell, a Pulitzer-winning editor in Washington, D.C., talked about what he saw as a constant challenge posed by the ability of words to obscure meaning. As a journalist, he said this has served him well:

The other thing I learned from an English teacher, who again—probably my sophomore year—who began the year with a game called Propaganda. And what his message was, that words are used to hide things, not to illuminate them. And I can always tell people here, "When you get a document, read it, but read it not for what it says, but for what it doesn't say." And it often—for example, we just did this exercise with a Pentagon release they put out that talks about the things they've done since the Fort Hood shooting. They never released their own investigation, but by reading the report of what they'd done, you could then tell what their investigation had found. For example, they were instituting a new way of tracking complaints about suspicious activity by military people. That's because they didn't have that sort of system. So you know their conclusion was, there was no way to report Maj. Hasan. They didn't have such a system. So, that's really a lesson I got in high school.

As Maddi (2013) and others note, the attitude of seeing life challenges as learning opportunities, even through failure, is a critical attribute of hardiness. The exemplars offered many stories of learning through failure. Emily recounted an embarrassing experience as the communications chief for the executive of an international auto manufacturer:

> This is in terms of a career lesson. We had a new president, and he did not want to be interviewed by the media. And we were at the Automotive Dealer Association conference in New Orleans, and there was one reporter, and he was bound and determined he was going to interview the new president. And one of my colleagues, who was from D.C. and knew this guy well, was at the conference. I asked my colleague to intervene and to call him off, because it's just going to be awkward. But my colleague couldn't dissuade the reporter. So the next day, we're at a panel discussion, I think, and the reporter is in the room. My president was on the panel. And I don't know what I was thinking, and I said, "We've got to spirit him out of here because the president doesn't want to be interviewed." Well, it became a kerfuffle. You know, this guy is chasing him down the hallway yelling at him and corners him, and it's awkward, and I'm as embarrassed as hell, because I've totally mismanaged this. The reporter ambushed him, but we knew the ambush was coming. If we had just said to the president, "Just give the guy five minutes, if there are questions you don't want to answer, you can just say I'll get back to you or whatever." I totally mismanaged it. I was so humiliated, and I felt like I put the president of the company in a terrifically humiliating, awkward position. And that evening, we were at a cocktail party with my colleague who knew this guy, and this reporter, he came up to me, and he said, "I really put you in a bad position," and I said, "Ha ha! You really did, but I didn't handle it well either." He had to get his story, and I knew that, but I tried to be too smart for words.

The second C of hardiness, control, was illustrated by the exemplars in many different ways. Michelle, a digital media specialist, said a key moment was her decision to turn down a job offer at the *Washington Post* early in her career—an offer that came from a former boss:

> He said, "Well, you know, you could always come and work at the *Post,* and you could do a podcast with Tony Kornheiser." And it was like that turning point where I kind of took ownership of my journalism career, and I realized that, you know, there were so many challenges that we had to go through with him [at the former

job], and me just being a woman, and I felt like, kind of objectified a little bit in this project and, um, I just felt like I wasn't really respected. I had heard other people say that sometimes that he kind of breeds that frat house environment, and I kind of felt like that was a turning point where I decided that journalism—I'm sure good journalism could be done in a frat house environment, but I was kind of ready to grow up. I was kind of ready to take ownership of my own ideas and my own journalism career.

A sense of purposefulness is critical for those who exhibit hardiness; Mitchell, the prize-winning Washington editor, recounted an example early in his career, during the burgeoning civil war in El Salvador in the 1980s:

My favorite memory as an adult, it's the Romero assassination. I was a correspondent in Mexico City, it was 30 years ago, so I was 26 years old, kind of a neophyte in a new place, and I just happened to arrive in El Salvador on my initial reporting trip, in the days before the archbishop in San Salvador was murdered. And I really didn't know the country that well. I'd been sort of familiarizing myself with what the situation was, and the archbishop, I'd talked with him, I'd met him previously—the American news media at that point wasn't paying a lot of attention. But it wasn't really a story in the U.S. So I'm going to a going-away party for the public-affairs officer at the U.S. embassy that they're having at the ambassador's house. And here—especially in hindsight, I'm trying to fit in, and I see the public affairs officer's secretary talking on the telephone, and I see her trembling, shaking. And I hear her say, "They've killed the archbishop." And I didn't say a word to anybody; I just walked out of the house, I hailed a cab, and I went back to the hotel, and I grabbed two other foreign TV reporters I knew, and I said, "We've got to go to the hospital; they've killed Archbishop Romero." And so we go to the hospital—and it's such a strange memory for me, but we somehow end up in the same room with the archbishop's body, and the nuns. And they had undressed the archbishop's body. And in my memory, I remember the only light being Fredo's camera light, and I don't know if that's true or not. And I remember a tiny hole, here, in the archbishop's chest, and—when I think about it, it was really extraordinary—you would never find yourself today in that situation—when a president gets assassinated—but it also speaks to the situation there, which was that of course the archbishop was an outsider. There was no security provided for that—the nuns weren't trying to keep us out, they were grief-stricken, and we got into that room. And as a professional, it also allowed me to be the only American reporter to report what his wound was. Because I saw it—everybody else was saying he was gunned down, it was a machine gun—no, it was a single shot, through the heart, from a small-caliber weapon. And it turned out to be a .22, I think.

Control, however, can take many forms. Ava, a corporate communications director in New York, also hinted at this aspect of hardiness in her story about preparing her corporate executive for his appearance on a segment of the reality television show "Undercover Boss."

We were able to get our president on "Undercover Boss." That was one of the biggest challenges that I have ever had in my life. Fourteen million people during prime time. It was one of the most challenging pitches, one of the most strategic placements that I've ever done in my entire career. It was so challenging because it was a shift in how communications is today. It's reality TV. And as a consumer company, you're afraid as a PR person to invite people to see the back of the house, because *anything* could happen in the back of the house. I mean, you know, even in our personal lives—anything can happen in my house! So how do you prepare your executive for that? And probably one of the best things I said to Chris was—he goes, "Any last-minute advice?" And I said, "Yes, actually, there is. Chris, this is reality TV, which means that you have an incredible opportunity that if you see something that's not great, fix it on the spot, because it's normally what you would do. Be who you are. If you walked into the factory and you saw something that wasn't right, you would address it. Just because this is television doesn't mean you should do different. Address it. Because at the end of the day, consumers know companies make mistakes all of the time, but it is the way you respond that resonates with the consumer." And he remembers that.

The third C of hardiness, commitment, connotes an outlook of proactive engagement and a belief that detachment is not a responsible answer to difficulty or adversity. Once more, the exemplars in this study provided plenty of inspiring examples of commitment, in both personal and professional contexts. Ed, a successful public relations practitioner in Chicago, talked about the entrepreneurial spirit that animated him since childhood and that served him well as a communications professional:

> While I was in high school, I worked many jobs. Actually, starting in grade school. I was an entrepreneur in the fact that I started a lawn service. I raised vegetables. I sharecropped all of the old ladies' gardens in town, and they could help themselves. I made sure that the woman—that the little old lady was old, that she wasn't going to eat a lot, and then I would agree to farm her garden. I learned the hard way because I used to sharecrop for people who harvested all of my vegetables, and gave them to their relatives, so then I made sure that they didn't have a big family. And I sold them at a farm stand in front of my parent's house. And how they tolerated that, I'll never know. Because it was tacky as could be. Between the farm stand and lawn-mowing service, I was doing 50 lawns a week, and so I'd get up early in the morning and my parents would not see me until nightfall. I started probably about fourth grade lawn mowing, but by my eighth grade or so I was up to 50 yards. I think the experiences taught me, certainly taught me the work ethic because my father worked hard.

Keith, a foreign-affairs journalist in Washington, said his interest in world events was galvanized by experiences growing up in Europe:

> I still remember standing—I don't remember which date it was, but around November 1st or 2nd of 1989, standing in an eerily quiet East Berlin, and it was—there had been protests the day before, my parents and I were on vacation, monitoring the news, and there were questions about whether the East Germans were going to shoot the demonstrators. It didn't happen, and Sunday was eerily quiet, and we decided to cross, to go in, and poke around for the day, and got back, and after that trip, 10 days later, the wall came down. That, to me, was one of those moments, when I was like, "God, I wish I was there." That was, I think—I've still thought back on that moment as just one of those realizations of—even if I didn't know it yet, that was where I started to figure out what I wanted to do with my life. I don't know that I ended up covering a Berlin Wall falling per se, but being there and experiencing and trying to understand it, and then trying to explain it—it's kind of all grown out of that.

Larissa, a PR veteran in California's Bay Area, discussed experiences during her career that taught her the need to often make difficult choices that allow you to remain positively engaged rather than professionally and emotionally drained:

> Then I got a gig working for Microsoft for about nine months, which was interesting. I'm not surprised to see the decline and fall of Microsoft. It became a culture where everything was solved with a meeting. I spent 75 percent of my time going to meetings that endlessly discussed the same thing over and over. "What will the fall promotion be? How will we execute it? What PR can we get?" And they never made a decision. It was unbelievable. And I was driving 55 miles each way—again, with young children. And the morning that I got in my car to drive to Silicon Valley for work and heard the twin towers go down, was the morning I said, "I can't do this anymore." So I went in and quit Microsoft, and went back to working with the other clients that I had. And the minute that I quit Microsoft, more business poured in. And that is actually one of the lessons I have learned. Never pour your energy into something that's negative. Because all it does is drive away the positive energy in your life. So, the minute I've gotten rid of bad clients, it's just been wonderful to learn that. Let go of the bad things, because it opens the door for fresh air to come in.

MOTIVATION AND FLOW

Ed, the corporate communications veteran in Chicago, recounted how he traveled alone from Indiana to Washington, D.C. when he was 15 years old:

> I applied for some scholarship to some right-wing conference in Washington, D.C., when I was 15. And I won it. And so, you had to go out and claim the money, and then you could go to this conference. And so I was put on a bus by my parents and I went out to Washington. I get off the bus, the seedy bus station, and I'm walking to the hotel because it takes too much money for a cab, and derelicts are stopping and asking me if I want a ride, and I'm like, "Oh no, my brother is coming by to pick me up." I go into 7–11 and I'm like, "Oh God, I'd better take a cab after all." So, I get to the hotel, where my parents thinking I'm going to be staying and I said, "How much are the rooms? I've got my check." And they tell me, and

I say that's ridiculous. That's going to take most of this money, so I went out and looked for another hotel and I found The Washington Inn, which was almost a flop house, but it was half the price of the International, but knowing I better tell my parents, I sent them a postcard. [Laugh] And so, they are calling the hotel wondering where I am and because there has been no response from me, and four days later they get a postcard. It was an interesting conference. One of the speakers was Ayn Rand, who was pretty amazing. It was pretty cool to hear her and I since read all of her books. So, when the conference was over, two of the guys from Flint, Michigan, were driving back and they said, "Don't take the bus. Come with us. We'll drop you off at the bus stop in South Bend before your parents get there. We go right through Indiana." I didn't tell my parents that I was now switching from the bus. So, of course, the bus gets there about a half an hour before we arrive. [Laugh] So, they're sitting there worried like hell when we pull in, in my new friend's convertible, and I get out, "Hi, Mom and Dad." They're ready to kill me. But relief quickly took over and they were happy to have me home, but admitted they were crazy to allow a 15-year-old to make such a trip on his own.

Ed's tale is emblematic of the notions of determination, perseverance, goal-setting and self-efficacy that psychologists say are key characteristics of successful people. The idea of striving, of having a keen awareness of the value of challenge and seeking opportunities to replicate such experiences, which in turn reinforce self-efficacy, often leads to experiences of "flow"—and this process becomes a cycle, a behavioral loop, that comes to define the individual. Some research even suggests that knowing what goals a person has can serve as a better predictor of behavior than knowing the person's personality traits (Locke & Latham, 2002, p. 713). This emphasis on the value of motivation, and the various factors that cultivate it, is rooted in work done back in the early 1900s that rejected behaviorism, most notably that of William McDougall:

We foresee a particular event as a possibility; we desire to see this possibility realized; we take action in accordance with one desire, and we seem to guide the course of events in such a way that the foreseen and desired event results. To explain an event as caused in this way was to invoke teleological causation, a causal activity thoroughly familiar to each man through his own repeated experiences of successful action for the attainment of desired goals.

(1930, p. 5)

Motivation, of course, is a concept that has preoccupied researchers for decades and has been defined differently in a range of settings (e.g., Brunstein, Schultheiss & Grässman, 1998; Madsen, 1974; Trope & Liberman, 1996). Much research suggests that "the successful pursuit of personally meaningful goals represents a major source of psychological well-being. . . . [M]otivated behavior is triggered by environmental cues that signal the availability of a motive-specific incentive. This gives rise to an anticipatory motivational state that energizes, selects, and orients a person's behavior toward the attainment of the desired incentive. The incentive made available by the instrumental behavior then leads to a pleasant affect that in turn reinforces the (learned) behavior" (Brunstein et al., pp. 494–495).

Don, a veteran computer-assisted reporting editor in Washington, D.C., talked about the long road he took before his career came into focus. He spent years selling outdoor equipment, then returned to school late in life thinking journalism might fill an ill-defined need for more focus:

> Actually, while I was in grad school near the end of my term, and I can still remember how that came about. And I was in their big library, their big 12-story research library, at Kent State, and what I like to do sometimes—I don't do it as much as I used to—would be to go to the shelves that were a specific subject area I was interested in and then just look through titles, not have something specific in mind. And so, I was going through the journalism section at the library, and I came across to me what sounded like the, the strangest title in the journalism section, it was called *The New Precision Journalism*. It's a book that so many people have gone to by Phil Meyer. And, I can remember getting that down off the shelf—not even going to a desk but just standing in the stacks reading this going, "This is amazing." So obviously it hit the right chord.

In discussing the profile that emerges from the exemplars' quantitative data, Chapter 3 referred to Abraham Maslow's notion of "self-actualizing people": "They are devoted, working at something, something which is very precious to them—some calling or vocation in the old sense, the priestly sense" (1971, p. 43). The media exemplars in this study repeatedly talked about how their motivations evolved or morphed into professional passions—some clear trajectories, some with nothing of the kind. But most all exhibited the characteristics of perseverance and awareness of the potential for growth that psychologists have long known are key features of successful lives. When these characteristics are routinized, we can increase the likelihood that we experience "flow"—moments when we are wholly living in the moment, when time seems to stand still, when our abilities are perfectly matched with the challenge before us. In his research establishing the concept, researcher Mihaly Csikszentmihalyi (1988, 1990) also called it "optimal experience," which individuals seek to replicate:

> [Flow] obtains when all the contents of consciousness are in harmony with each other, and with the goals that define the person's self. These are the subjective conditions we call pleasure, happiness, satisfaction, enjoyment. Because the tendency of the self is to reproduce itself, and because the self is most congruent with its own goal-directed structure during these episodes of optimal experience, to keep on experiencing flow becomes one of the central goals of the self. This is the teleonomy of the self, that is, the goal-seeking tendency that shapes the choices we make among alternatives.
>
> (1988, p. 24)

Other researchers have found that people identified as high achievers, compared with low achievers, report a greater frequency of flow during work (Lefevre, 1988), and the ability to experience flow is related to perceived psychological strengths such as self-discipline, perseverance and a sense of when *not* to spend energy on unrewarding endeavors (Carver & Scheier, 1988). Csikszentmihalyi stressed that flow is primarily about the ability to impose order onto the awareness of one's environment, or consciousness:

> When a person is able to organize his or her consciousness so as to experience flow as often as possible, the quality of life is inevitably going to improve. . . . In flow we are in control of our psychic energy, and everything we do adds order to consciousness. One of our respondents, a well-known West Coast rock climber, explains concisely the tie between the avocation that gives him a profound sense of flow and the rest of his life: "It's exhilarating to come closer and closer to self-discipline. You make your body go and everything hurts; then you look back in awe at the self, at what you've done it just blows your mind. It leads to ecstasy, to self-fulfillment. If you win these battles enough, that battle against yourself, at least for a moment, it becomes easier to win the battles in the world." The "battle" is not really *against* the self, but against the entropy

that brings disorder to consciousness. It is really a battle *for* the self; it is a struggle for establishing control over attention. The struggle does not necessarily have to be physical, as in the case of the climber. But anyone who has experienced flow knows that the deep enjoyment it provides requires an equal degree of disciplined concentration [author's emphasis].

(1990, pp. 40–41)

The media exemplars of this study repeatedly recounted what they felt were telling, indelible "optimal experiences" of their own. Many such stories were formative in nature, describing how their personal values or professional motivations came into focus. None of them explicitly talked about experiencing flow, but their stories suggested they did just that. Other accounts, while difficult to categorize as experiences of flow, certainly proved to be pivotal experiences that were fortuitous, serendipitous or simply of much-appreciated instances of some sort of celestial alignment. Elaine, the Pulitzer-winning feature writer, recounted how her personal and professional lives intersected when she spent time with the unofficial leader of the fishing community she covered years ago:

Omie led the fishing fleet; they would go in like a "V" formation out of the fishing docks through Oregon inlet, and Omie, every morning, he'd get on the radio and he'd say a prayer. And he would lead the fishing boats out to the Gulf Stream with a prayer. I kept hearing him when I was on the shark boat and the blue fin tuna boat. I'd be like, "Who is that old guy on the radio?" So, finally I was like, I need to write about Omie. I knew who he was; he was really kind of curmudgeony. So, one morning I asked him, and I just remember that scene—being on the deck of that boat and climbing up on the bridge so I could hear him and talk to him, and watch the sun crawl out of the sea, real, real slow. It was January or February, so it's cold, but it wasn't freezing, so it was like gray, mist, and he was just praying over the microphone, and all the other boats sort of followed up behind. And they gave me an A1 story with this huge picture. You know how you get that feeling like you are experiencing something, and you're like, "Am I ever going to be able to recreate this?" And then I sat down and I did and it was like—usually, I'm like, "I suck! This is not good. I'm not worthy." You know? I do that to myself a hundred times a story. This time, I was like, "I've got this." But when I was interviewing him up there on the bridge, I started throwing up. And I'd never gotten seasick, I mean, in like, five years I'd been covering commercial fishing, and I'd never gotten seasick. He didn't want me there, but as soon as I got sick, he became a grandfather. Put his arm around me. He brought me a bucket to puke in. Brought me a handkerchief. [Laugh] You know, he was taking care of me, and I kept saying, "I never get sick. I'm sorry. I'm sorry. I never get sick." And I found out a month later, I was pregnant. That was why I was throwing up. So that was the first time in probably like 10 years that I felt any kind of presence of the Lord, was that morning on the boat with Omie and watching the sun come out of the ocean. And it was really a simple fisherman prayer, but, like, there can't *not* be a God with a moment like that. You know? One of those things you're like, "They pay me to do this?"

Martha, a veteran journalist who runs an online community news site in the Midwest, talked fondly of her formative experience as editor of her college newspaper in the tumultuous 1960s:

But really, my best experience there in terms of journalism was working on the *Daily*, because that was serious journalism at that point. I mean, every spring there were riots on campus, there were demonstrations, there was discussion year-round of Vietnam and various other issues, and it was a very good training ground for journalists, because if you got something wrong, people would be there in your face the next day, saying, "Why did you do that?" and "Look what you've done." That was the kind of thing—this wasn't a theoretical public; this was a public that felt perfectly comfortable walking in the door and demanding whatever it is they wanted to demand. And the faculty too. So that was really good, and it's interesting that of the people that were kind of the core of the *Stanford Daily* when we were there, many of them went into journalism as a career. I think we weren't fit for anything else after that. First of all, it was really exciting, and secondly, we were spending so much time doing that that we weren't really doing anything else, but it was a great way to learn the consequences of what you're doing.

Finally, Dennis, editor of a metropolitan newspaper in the southeast United States, talked about his circuitous path into newspaper journalism that required him to take a leap of faith in his abilities as a budding photographer after having worked in a series of South Florida restaurants:

I mean, I was at a crossroads—really, truly, at a crossroads. I was either going to keep doing what I had always been doing, which would have led nowhere, or I was going to make a major change and try to find a new path and try to be successful at it. Now, I didn't believe I would be successful. I thought this is crazy but I've got to do it. I'm going to do it and I'm going to give it a shot. So, I think that probably is the wisest decision I made. Went back and then set about trying to figure out how to become a photographer. That's what I wanted to do, and then I decided that the best way to do it is newspaper photography. Because you get to do it every day. And I admired the documentary photographers, mostly from the Farm Security Administration period. People like Walker Evans and Dorothea Lange and Arthur Rothstein. I loved their work, and that most closely resembled newspaper work of the '70s and '80s that I admired. So, after, it took me about a year to figure it out.

CRUCIBLE EXPERIENCES AND VIRTUE IN MEDIA

As this chapter shows, crucible experiences can take many different forms. They can be personal or professional in nature. The lessons derived from such pivotal or formative experiences are largely dependent upon individual dispositions—degree of optimism, resilience, hardiness, the tendency to engage in or avoid self-reflection, attitude toward challenge, among others. The media exemplars in this study strongly, sometimes passionately, identify not only with their work but with the moral principles associated with the best work in journalism and public relations: a concern for justice, the imperative of public service, of individual and organizational accountability. While this chapter does not intend to suggest that they might owe their exemplary status to the way they have handled difficulty or challenge, their experiences are indicative of what psychologists have pointed to as successful coping and adaptive strategies that, in turn, increases the likelihood of flourishing in the Aristotelian sense.

REFERENCES

Bennis, W.G., & Thomas, R.J. (2002). *Geeks and geezers: How era, values and defining moments shape leaders*. Boston: Harvard Business School Press.

Birren, J.E., & Fisher, L.M. (1990). The elements of wisdom: Overview and integration. In *Wisdom: Its nature, origins and development* (R.J. Sternberg, Ed.), 317–332. Cambridge: Cambridge University Press.

Brunstein, J.C., Schultheiss, O.C., & Grässman, R. (1998). Personal goals and emotional well-being: The moderating role of motive dispositions. *Journal of Personality and Social Psychology 75* (2), 494–508.

Calhoun, L.G., & Tedeschi, R.G. (Eds.) (2006). *Handbook of posttraumatic growth: Research and practice*. Mahwah, NJ: Lawrence Erlbaum Associates.

Carver, C.S., & Scheier, M.F. (1988). Three human strengths. In *Optimal experience: Psychological studies of flow in consciousness* (M. Csikszentmihalyi & I.S. Csikszentmihalyi, Eds.), 87–102. New York: Cambridge University Press.

Csikszentmihalyi, M. (1988). Introduction. In *Optimal experience: Psychological studies of flow in consciousness* (M. Csikszentmihalyi & I.S. Csikszentmihalyi, Eds.), 3–24. New York: Cambridge University Press.

Csikszentmihalyi, M. (1990). *Flow: The psychology of optimal experience.* New York: Harper & Row.

Huxley, A. (1932/1976). *Texts and pretexts: An anthology with commentaries.* Westport, CT: Greenwood Press. [Cited passage from page 5.]

Keller, H. (1938). *Helen Keller's Journal: 1936–1937.* New York: Doubleday, Doran, 60.

Lefevre, J. (1988). Flow and the quality of experience during work and leisure. In *Optimal experience: Psychological studies of flow in consciousness* (M. Csikszentmihalyi & I.S. Csikszentmihalyi, Eds.), 307–318. New York: Cambridge University Press.

Lepore, S.J., & Revenson, T.A. (2006). Resilience and posttraumatic growth: Recovery, resistance and reconfiguration. In *Handbook of posttraumatic growth: Resesarch and practice* (L.G. Calhoun & R.G. Tedeschi, Eds.), 24–46. Mahwah, NJ: Lawrence Erlbaum Associates.

Locke, E.A., & Latham, G.P. (2002). Building a practically useful theory of goal setting and task motivation: A 35-year odyssey. *American Psychology 57* (9), 705–717.

Maddi, S.R. (2013). *Hardiness.* New York: Springer.

Madsen, K.B. (1974). *Modern theories of motivation: A comparative metascientific study.* New York: John Wiley & Sons.

Mancini, A.D., & Bonanno, G.A. (2009). Predictors and parameters of resilience to loss: Toward an individual differences model. *Journal of Personality 77* (6), 1805–1831.

Maslow, A. (1971). *The farther reaches of human nature.* New York: Viking Press.

McCall, M.W., Lombardo, M.M., & Morrison, A.M. (1988). *The lessons of experience: How successful executives develop on the job.* Lexington, MA: Lexington Books.

McCrae, R.R., & Costa, P.T. (1986). Personality, coping, and coping effectiveness. *Journal of Personality 54,* 385–405.

McDougall, W. (1930). Autobiography. In *A history of psychology in autobiography* (C. Murchison, Ed.), Worcester, MA: Clark University Press.

Neimeyer, R.A. (2006). Re-storying loss: Fostering growth in the posttraumatic narrative. In *Handbook of posttraumatic growth: Research and practice* (L.G. Calhoun & R.G. Tedeschi, Eds.), 68–80. Mahwah, NJ: Lawrence Erlbaum Associates.

Tennen, H., & Affleck, G. (1998). Personality and transformation in the face of adversity. In *Posttraumatic growth: Positive chances in the aftermath of crisis* (R.G. Tedeschi, C.L. Park & L.G. Calhoun, Eds.), 65–98. Mahwah, NJ: Lawrence Erlbaum Associates.

Trope, Y., & Liberman, A. (1996). Social hypothesis testing: Cognitive and motivational mechanisms. In *Social psychology: A handbook of basic principles* (E. Higgins & A. Kruglanski, Eds.), 239–270. New York: Guilford Press.

Lessons for Media Ethics Theory

A more empirically minded response to the disconnect between moral theory and practice would be to claim that our theories must do a better job of representing the individual character of our moral practice; in other words, we should work toward ethical theories that reflect the concreteness and particularity of moral practice.

—Gregory Pappas, 2008, p. 44

This book began with the statement that in studying media professionals known for their ethical leadership and in analyzing the profile of their moral orientations that emerged, we may deepen our understanding of morality in media practice. It also began with the claim that the maturation of media ethics as a discipline depended, in part, on our ability to draw on the theories and methodologies of moral psychology. Looking at both the quantitative analysis of the survey data and the thematic analysis of the "life story" interviews does indeed suggest a profile of moral identity that holds across the group—a profile in which there are clear "clusterings" of features and a compelling consensus on a range of moral concerns. The results also suggest an exciting path for future moral psychology projects of inquiry that may broaden or even complicate this profile, drawing on theories of moral development, moral identity, professional agency and virtue ethics that use a host of methods now just beginning to be applied in media ethics research. The inductive thrust of this study, rather than relying on popular deontological assumptions about the duties of media practitioners, identifies features of cognition, environment and behavior and traces their links with moral virtues. Rather than deductively asserting the "fact" of moral realism that entails a roster of moral duties regardless of substantive cultural and environmental distinctions, the approach here advocates a different starting point. This study does not unreservedly embrace the radical empiricism for ethics that John Dewey called for, but it is sympathetic to his well-articulated disdain for philosophical proclamations of abstract norms masquerading as the work of ethics: "What passes for 'ethics' oscillates between sermonizing, moralizing of an edifying emotional type, and somewhat remote dialectics on abstract theoretical points," he wrote (1991a, p. 398). Similarly, Alasdair MacIntyre argued we must "avoid the error of supposing that there are facts of the moral life completely independent of and apart from theory-laden characterization of those facts," (1990, p. 371). This error stems largely from top-down theorizing that prioritizes the "right" over the "good." "It is only because theorists have favored the detached theoretical standpoint that their descriptions of the moral life are at odds with how we experience moral life," Pappas noted (2008, p. 36). Echoing MacIntyre, Nick Couldry wrote, "A neo-Aristotelian virtue ethics, applied to media, would ask what virtuous dispositions can be expected to contribute to our living well together with and through media" (2013a, p. 47). The model of inquiry put forth by this study offers a way to begin identifying those dispositions. It calls for rigorous efforts to identify facets that constitute the complex notion of human moral identity and to uncover related variables that may promote or hinder moral action. The virtue ethicist Rosalind Hursthouse argued that the virtues "are not excellences of character, not traits that, by their very nature, make their possessor good and issue in good conduct." We must remember the "Aristotelian idea that each of the virtues involves practical wisdom, the ability to reason correctly about practical matters" (1999, p. 154). Focusing on the moral lives of individuals using this approach—truly *attending to* myriad individual manifestations of virtue—grounds our normative claims in a way that is critically needed if media ethics theorizing is to mature. It also opens portals through which we might glimpse the universal: Such research opens opportunities to more formally explore these manifestations across political, economic and cultural environments, to better explain relationships among variables and clarify potentially important distinctions.

This book builds on earlier works that suggested moral psychology approaches ought to be brought to bear on media practice—*Custodians of Conscience* by James Ettema and Ted Glasser (1989), *Good Work: When Excellence and Ethics Meet* by Howard Gardner, Mihaly Csikszentmihalyi and William Damon (2001) and *The Moral Media: How Journalists Reason about Ethics* by Lee Wilkins and Renita Coleman (2005). None of these explicitly acknowledge their genetic roots in the field of moral psychology but all, in distinct ways, helped begin the conversation about how the theories and methodologies of moral psychology can and should be brought to bear in media ethics research. As the first extended book to make such a claim a central part of its premise, this study offers a modest step toward a more comprehensive theory of moral action in media. Based on the results of this study's dual-method approach, we can make some useful observations about the moral psychology profile that emerges from the media exemplars. At the core of this profile is morally motivated self-identity, an achievement among the media exemplars to marry their conception of the self with external moral principles. In representing an authentic form of moral agency, the exemplars seem to have transformed "objective" virtue in a key part of how they are motivated to live their lives. This moral identity, or successful integration of issues of morality into the self, echoes the theories of moral identity developed by Abraham Maslow (1971), Augusto Blasi (1984), Daniel Lapsley (2008) and others. It also echoes the conclusions of Anne Colby and William Damon in their 1992 landmark study of moral exemplars, *Some Do Care:*

> The great difference between moral exemplars and most people is that exemplars act without equivocation about matters that go well beyond the boundaries of everyday moral engagement. . . . It is not so much that the exemplars' orientation to moral concerns is unusual but that the range of their concerns and the extensiveness of their engagement is exceptionally broad. . . . The exemplars' expansive moral concerns, and their steadfast moral commitments, are extensions in scope, intensity, and breadth of normal moral experiences. Their moral concerns and commitments are continuous with that of most people but are greater in degree. It is the remarkable extensiveness of their concerns and commitments that must be explained.
>
> (1992, p. 303)

Colby and Damon (1992) described this sort of integration as "sustained commitment to moral ideas" (p. 29), though the idea of consistency, to the extent that it describes human behavior, may itself be relative. More often, notable moral commitment is rooted in the skill of discrimination: the ability to make fine-grained distinctions among similar situations and to thoughtfully respond with just the right mix of appraisals, beliefs, emotions and behavioral scripts that still reflect one's broader moral commitments. This integration of the moral self aligns with descriptions of the virtuous agent by Hursthouse: "Built into the theory is the claim that part of the virtuous person's practical wisdom is her knowledge, her correct appreciation, of what is truly good, and, indeed, of what is truly pleasant, truly advantageous, truly worthwhile, truly important, truly serious (and, correspondingly, of what is truly bad, unpleasant, or painful, disadvantageous, worthless, unimportant, and trivial)" (2012, p. 73). Considering both the quantitative and qualitative results of this study, the emerging morally motivated self-identity of the media exemplars appears to be largely shaped by features of 1) their moral development, 2) their ethical ideology, 3) their personality traits and 4) their professional environment, or moral ecology. The emerging model also corresponds to the description of identity "as source of moral motivation" by Sam Hardy and Gustavo Carlo (2005). This morally motivated construction of the self, in turn, emphasizes a constellation of morally driven principles, as illustrated in Figure 1. Several of

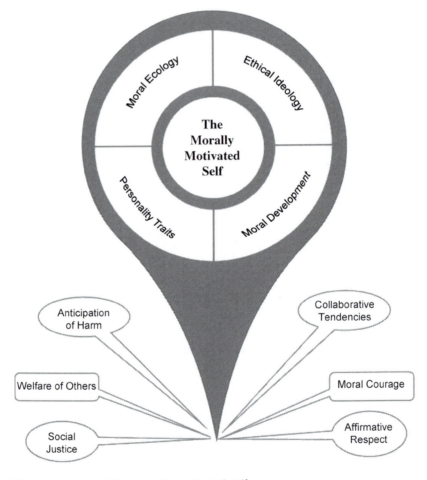

Figure 1 Model of the morally motivated self

these principles, such as social justice, concern for the welfare of others and moral courage, are directly linked to moral development theory: Individuals in Lawrence Kohlberg's higher "postconventional" stages have achieved a broadened scope of concern for impacts on others and a philosophy of proactive social engagement. Others, such as exemplars' emphasis on the value of professional collaboration, are more closely linked to personality traits of Agreeableness and Openness to new experience. Still others, such as the priority they place on affirmative respect, appear closely tied to their high levels of idealism and rejection of relativistic thinking. The notion of affirmative respect is rooted in discourse ethics, which insists on a mode of exchange that is not only rational but that balances an active respect for individual moral autonomy with a recognition that moral deliberation is, at bottom, a communal enterprise (Habermas, 1996). While personality traits have long been considered largely immutable, recent personality research has suggested that our social environment—the roles we fulfill, the influence of peers, the expectations under which we perform—has a profound influence on our personality traits and can actually produce changes in our characteristics (Roberts, Walton & Viechtbauer, 2006).

Colby and Damon's research on moral exemplars found a similar melding of identity and moral action:

> Just as there is little separation between moral and personal goals among our moral exemplars, so, too, is there little divergence between judgment and conduct. The unity of goals provides a compelling call to engagement as well as a sense of certainty about one's course of action. Where one's personal choice seems predetermined by one's sense of self, there is little room for hesitation or doubt. Hence the "automatic pilot" quality of the exemplars' moral actions.
>
> (1992, p. 307)

This profile of exemplars' moral psychology shares several features of the "model of sustained moral action" proposed by Chuck Huff and colleagues (2008a, 2008b) in their study of computer science exemplars. Their model "grounds moral action in relatively stable personality characteristics, guides moral action by the context of the surrounding [moral ecology], and facilitates moral action with morally relevant skills and knowledge" (2008a, p. 253). They then locate these four components on dimensions of malleability and personal control (Figure 2).

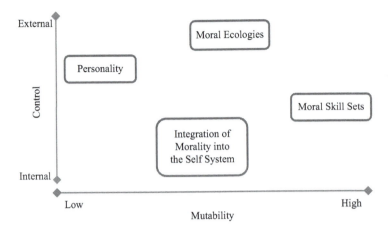

Figure 2   Model of sustained moral action (Huff et al., 2008a)

The profile of media exemplars that emerges here, like the work of Huff and colleagues, challenges conventional, one-dimensional perceptions of ethical behavior that emphasize either deontological reasoning or simplistic claims of personal integrity and grounds its approach in a more complex—and more useful—neo-Aristotelian framework of contextualized virtues. Their model, Huff and colleagues wrote, "seeks to explain the daily performance of moral action of computing professionals and to illuminate the way that computing professionals might be trained to be more active, ethically committed, and ethically effective in their daily performance, across the lifespan of their careers" (2008a, p. 253). Similarly, it is hoped that the emerging profile of moral action among media exemplars might strengthen the basis of pedagogical efforts to cultivate morally motivated practitioners and to lend empirical heft to normative theorizing for media practice.

VIRTUE ETHICS AND MEDIA PRACTICE

"One cause for the inefficacy of moral philosophies," theorist John Dewey argued, "has been that in their zeal for a unitary view they have oversimplified the moral life" (1991b, p. 288). Claims about conscientiousness, about commitment, about care all can easily be inferred from moral psychology findings. And it is tempting to interpret these claims as moral duties. But efforts to impose a deontological framework on, for instance, the profile of the morally motivated self that emerges from this study of exemplars, runs aground on several important points. Surely there is no single constellation of personality traits that is required to constitute the "moral" person. We know that our abilities of moral assessment are fluid, not static: Moral development is a lifelong process. And any number of responses we might have to our environment will be considered admirable and morally defensible, contingent on the professional roles we claim to be performing. The claims of this study on media exemplars mirror the shift away from a one-dimensional focus on moral reasoning and the cognitive-developmental perspective of Kohlberg (1984) to a broader view that includes moral personality and moral emotions (e.g., Osswald, Greitemeyer, Fischer & Frey, 2010). "The origins of this conceptual skew can be traced to the formalist moral philosophers of the Enlightenment (e.g., Immanuel Kant)," wrote Walker & Hennig (2004, p. 629). This shift calls for precisely the kind of multidimensional, mixed-method approach to media ethics research demonstrated here. The shift also suggests why the virtue ethics of neo-Aristotelian philosophers of Philippa Foot, Rosalind Hursthouse, Martha Nussbaum, Alasdair MacIntyre and others provides a much more compelling philosophical framework for moral psychology approaches. Most recently, Nick Couldry reiterated this claim, arguing that "by building . . . from our appreciation of 'particular facts' about how media operate in the contemporary world, we have a more useful starting point for the tangled problems of media ethics than by relying on supposedly consensual norms, rights, or obligations" (2013a, p. 42). Imposing a deontological framework requires more intuitive leaps and assumptions about the right than the approach of moral psychology permits in its call for rigorous inquiry. It has long been a common criticism of virtue ethics that it does not aim to produce a set of rules or an attempt to "codify" morality as utilitarian, and deontological theorists assume it should, that its goal is not universalism. Why shouldn't we accept that a deontology should be what we aspire to achieve—that if only we could properly cultivate these values and internalize them, that we could say we have attained the right motives and duties in the Kantian sense? On the surface, this is a fair question. And yet, moral psychology research shows us again and again that a Kantian framework does not necessarily reflect the nature of moral functioning. "Ethical theorists," Pappas argued, "have neglected the non-cognitive, pluralistic, and incommensurable aspects of moral life because they are of no use in constructing a theoretically coherent system that can presumably provide solutions to moral problems" (2008, pp. 29–30). The constellation of personality dispositions, experiences, moral ecologies and moral schemas all fit better with virtue ethics theory, which not only emphasizes the process of interpreting and selecting inputs, the internalization of values and development of perceptions of virtuous motivations but direct our focus on what is essential for human flourishing. This framework also helps ensure that our theory-building in media ethics does not slip into a form of theological moralism. Hursthouse's response to the common attack on virtue ethics is worth quoting at length:

> If we thought that we were living in a world created by a good God, a God who wanted us to live well and who had organized the world and us in such a way that our reason could discover how to live well, then we might indeed expect our moral theory to consist of codifiable rules and principles. But a genuinely secular morality must be more than a morality that does not happen to mention God explicitly; and more than a morality espoused by people who make a point of claiming proudly that they have thrown off the shackles of Judeao-Christian tradition. It must be one which does not, even implicitly, presuppose the existence of a God. But then it is quite unclear what could entitle it to presuppose that every aspect of the world will fall within the realm of rational understanding; and, in particular that our categories of right-wrong, good-bad, permitted-required, etc., are guaranteed to fit on to the world neatly. . . . Why should it be a condition of adequacy on a moral theory that it should provide an algorithm for life? Rather than criticizing a secular theory for failing to come up with rules that settle difficult cases, we might say that it is entirely to its credit that it does not do so.
>
> (1995, p. 61)

Couldry articulated how the neo-Aristotelian approach is brought to bear on questions of media:

> The basic question for media ethics flows quite readily: How should we act in relation to media, so that we contribute to lives that, both individually and together, we would value on all scales, up to and including the global?. . . . Far from claiming to start out from some accepted and already authoritative norm by which contemporary journalists can be judged, media ethics in the neo-Aristotelian tradition asks what, in today's factual conditions, can we expect that media as a practice *might* contribute to our possibilities of living well together [author's emphasis].
>
> (2013b, pp. 25–26)

The power of moral psychology approaches' contribution to ethics theory lies in the reinforcement of an *ethical naturalism*. In identifying features of the morally motivated self and exploring their relationships among each other, we may move forward the discourse begun with Aristotle's notion of virtue and continued by Hursthouse, Foot and others: to frame moral and normative claims as straightforward matters of natural fact, or at least to ground ethics in human nature and in what is involved in being a good human being. This is not to suggest that a neo-Aristotelian approach presumes to offer any sort of "foundational" claim about virtue— that is, arguing that moral behavior is an objective manifestation of, say, evolutionary biology. Hursthouse, in her "Naturalism" chapter (1999), as well as Nussbaum (1995), effectively dispense with this common attack. Virtue ethics does not assert the nature of virtue with scientific claims, or that virtue can be discerned from any neutral perspective. Ethical naturalism, Hursthouse wrote, helps us examine "whether my beliefs about which character traits are the virtues can survive my reflective scrutiny and be given some rational justification" (1999, p. 194). Such a naturalist agenda, she suggested, does not assert a singular—and thus suspicious— notion of the right, but encourages us "to think about what empirical assumptions we make about ourselves as a kind of animal with a contingent nature when we talk about ethics" (2012, p. 179). While a full account of virtue ethics and its naturalistic approach will not be explored here, Foot, in her landmark book *Natural Goodness*, made a compelling case that we do indeed have objective reasons for acting in ways we call virtuous, quite apart from any claim that, as Kant argued, we are morally obligated to do something when we properly understand what is "right." Rather than focusing on abstract concepts such as sacredness of life, goodness and duty, Foot argued we must concentrate on traditional virtues and vices, and by doing so, we can see the concrete connections between the conditions of human life and the objective reasons for acting morally. She rejected the longstanding distinction insisted by philosophers between the nature of a fact and the nature of a value. The "negative value" of vice, she argued, is a defect in humans the same way that poor roots are a defect in an oak tree, or poor vision a defect in an owl: The two assessments have clear normative implications, yet are also entirely factual.

> [V]irtues play a necessary part in the life of human beings as do stings in the life of the bee. . . . In spite of the diversity of human goods—the elements that can make up human lives—it is therefore possible that the concept of a good human life plays the same part in determining goodness of human characteristics and operations that the concept of flourishing plays in the determination of goodness in plants and animals.
>
> (Foot, 2001, pp. 35, 44)

The constellation of values, traits and moral skills exhibited by the media exemplars in this study suggests an illustration of virtue ethics articulated by Foot, Hursthouse and others.

At first glance, it may seem incoherent to claim that the emerging profile of the morally motivated self, with its foundational components and its catalogue of resultant driving values, is compatible with virtue ethics theory. After all, the very term "moral motivation" (or inclination) has long been considered the property of Kantian deontology, wherein the German philosopher specifically articulates its roots in the notion of our moral *duty* in his *Groundwork*. The response has been that the Aristotelian notion of virtue is quickly drained of its force if one concedes being morally motivated is taken only to mean one should feel (morally) obligated to do something. However, Hursthouse compellingly rejected this dichotomy, saying those same ethicists "have misidentified [the *Groundwork*'s claim] as an issue about motivation instead of an issue about the nature of full virtue" (1999, p. 122). She continued:

> [B]eing "morally motivated" is not solely a matter of acting, on a particular occasion, for a special kind of reason, let alone one that is vitally different from other kinds of reasons . . . but, primarily, acting *from virtue*—from a settled state of good character. . . .
> "[B]ecause she thought she was right" ("from (a sense of) duty", etc.) is an ascription that goes far beyond the moment of action. It is not merely, as grammatically it might appear to be, a claim about how things are with the agent and her reasons at the moment. It is also a substantial claim about the future (with respect to reliability) and, most importantly, a claim about what sort of person the agent is—a claim that goes "all the way down". . . . [W]e are not insisting that she have explicit thoughts about right action, duty or principle. . . . Such explicit thoughts are not a necessary condition for being morally motivated [author's emphasis].
>
> (1999, pp. 123, 140)

Hursthouse further argued that the truly virtuous person, when acting virtuously, "sets the standard for 'moral motivation'" (p. 141). Hers is a subtle but critical distinction that underscores how the profile of the morally motivated self offered here meshes to a remarkable degree with the power of virtue ethics in its ability to account for moral action in professional life. Nussbaum, too, reinforced the basis for the connection between the morally motivated self and virtue ethics in her rejection of claims that human nature—and by extension our understanding of morality—is "internal" rather than "external": that personal identity and notions of the self provide an objective foundation for moral thought that need not require independent validation beyond morality itself. "Human nature cannot, and need not, be validated from the outside, because human nature just *is* an inside perspective, not a *thing* at all, but rather the most fundamental and broadly shared experiences of human beings living and reasoning together" [author's emphasis] (1995, p. 121). This claim echoed Hilary Putnam's insistence that "truth" be understood as an "ideal coherence of our beliefs with each other and with our experiences *as those experiences are themselves represented in our belief system*—and not correspondences with mind-independent or discourse-independent 'states of affairs' " [author's emphasis] (1981, pp. 49–50).

FUTURE MEDIA ETHICS RESEARCH

This project certainly is not alone in advocating for virtue ethics as a more useful framework than the deontological and quasi-theological approaches that have dominated media ethics theorizing for the last couple of decades. The call here is simply the latest addition to a growing chorus of compelling scholarly voices that articulates how a neo-Aristotelian ethics provides a better way to connect moral deliberation with media practice. Stephen Klaidman and Tom Beauchamp (1987) first articulated how virtue ethics should inform journalistic professional norms and behavior. Aaron Quinn echoed this effort, arguing journalists' cultivation of "internal" values was an essential complement to external ethical standards (2007). In her landmark work published that same year, Sandra Borden elegantly argued for a conceptualization of journalism as a virtue-based *practice* in MacIntyre's sense of that term. Sherry Baker provided a similar virtue ethics-driven framework for the work of public relations and advertising (2008). Couldry has emerged as a central voice championing the value of neo-Aristotelian ethics for media (2010, 2013a, 2013b). All of these scholars helped inspire the introduction of the groundbreaking "ethical naturalism" of Philippa Foot to media ethics theory and digital media use (Plaisance, 2013). The need for further elaboration of virtue ethics as a useful framework for media practice is considerable. Explication of morally motivated behavior regarding technology-driven discourse is one example of an area ripe for more theoretical development. More sophisticated mapping of persuasive communication as MacIntyrean *practices* that contribute to human flourishing is another.

This study's emphasis on virtue ethics aside, the field of moral psychology in general offers exciting methodological tools for media ethics research. While this study attempted to explore a detailed profile of the morally motivated self using an array of qualitative and quantitative instruments, the list of tools used here is by no means definitive. Other psychology-based assessments, used in tandem with those of this study or in other combinations, promise to open up exciting new lines of inquiry. They include:

- The "Moral Sense Test" developed by Fiery Cushman and Donal Cahill (http://wjh1.wjh.harvard.edu/~moral/index. html), an online set of scenarios that can be used to explore a host of patterns among moral judgments, ethical orientations, demographic data and other potential factors (e.g., Cushman, Young & Hauser, 2006).
- The "Self-Understanding Interview, Transmogrified," developed by Frimer & Walker (2009), is a structured interview format that allows subjects' narratives to be quantitatively coded to produce a "moral centrality index" as a way to explore morality-related themes embedded in the stories people tell about themselves.
- Value theory, which is based on assessment of peoples' "circumplex" of value rankings as developed by Shalom Schwartz and colleagues (1990, 1992, 2004).
- "Personal Projects Analysis" (Little, 1983), which enables assessments of individual goal characteristics with other relevant features such as integrity and self-efficacy (McGregor & Little, 1998).
- The "Personal Strivings List" developed by Robert Emmons (1999), which links peoples' goals or strivings to moral desires, priorities and autonomous agency. Elsewhere the author compellingly constructs a framework that melds virtue ethics with spiritual agency (2003).

This study has tried to embody the multidisciplinary approach that moral psychology theorist Owen Flanagan and his colleagues emphasized in describing their view of theories that bear on moral action. They suggested that "instead of *conceptual truths* concerning morality, we have an evolving *theory* of morality, and that the proper way to investigate and evaluate this theory is to see how it coheres with other theories in the empirical and social sciences and with our experience of morality as found in history, literature and phenomenology" [authors' emphasis] (Flanagan, Sarkissian & Wong, 2008, p. 46). Virtue ethics, married with moral psychology approaches, opens a clear path to useful and rigorous theory-building for the media ethics field, leading to a more enduring foundation for the normative claims we might make in our future scholarship. Such scholarship may well usher a more interpretive ethics, complementing and reinforcing our normative theory by providing avenues to better understand and account for moral action in media.

REFERENCES

Baker, S. (2008). The model of the Principled Advocate and the Pathological Partisan: A virtue ethics construct of opposing archetypes of public relations and advertising practitioners. *Journal of Mass Media Ethics 23*, 235–253.

Blasi, A. (1984). Moral identity: Its role in moral functioning. In *Morality, moral behavior, and moral development* (W.M. Kurtines & J.L. Gewirtz, Eds.), 129–139. New York: Wiley.

Blasi, A. (2005). Moral character: A psychological approach. In *Character psychology and character education* (D.K. Lapsley & F.C. Power, Eds.), 67–100. Notre Dame, IN: University of Notre Dame Press.

Borden, S.L. (2007). *Journalism as practice: MacIntyre, virtue ethics and the press*. Burlington, VT: Ashgate.

Colby, A., & Damon, W. (1992). *Some do care: Contemporary lives of moral commitment*. New York: Free Press.

Couldry, N. (2010). Media ethics: Towards a framework for media producers and media consumers. In *Media ethics beyond borders: A global perspective* (S.J.A. Ward & H. Wasserman, Eds.), 59–72. New York: Routledge.

Couldry, N. (2013a). Living well with and through media. In *Ethics of media* (N. Couldry, M. Madianou, & A. Pinchevski, Eds.), 39–56. Basingstoke, UK: Palgrave Macmillan.

Couldry, N. (2013b). Why media ethics still matters. In *Global media ethics: Problems and perspectives* (S.J.A. Ward, Ed.), 13–29. Malden, MA: Wiley-Blackwell.

Cushman, F., Young, L., & Hauser, M. (2006). The role of conscious reasoning and intuition in moral judgment. *Psychological Science 17* (12), 1082–1089.

Dewey, J. (1991a). *The later works of John Dewey, 1925–1953*, vol. 2 (J.A. Boydston, Ed.). Carbondale: Southern Illinois University Press.

Dewey, J. (1991b). *The later works of John Dewey, 1925–1953*, vol. 5 (J.A. Boydston, Ed.). Carbondale: Southern Illinois University Press.

Emmons, R.A. (1999). *The psychology of ultimate concerns: Motivation and spirituality in personality*. New York: Guilford Press.

Emmons, R.A. (2003). Personal goals, life meaning, and virtue: Wellsprings of a positive life. In *Flourishing: Positive psychology and the life well-lived* (C.L.M. Keyes & J. Haidt, Eds.), 105–128. Washington, D.C.: American Psychological Association.

Ettema, J.S., & Glasser, T.L. (1989). *Custodians of conscience*. New York: Columbia University Press.

Foot, P. (2001). *Natural goodness*. Oxford: Oxford University Press.

Flanagan, O., Sarkissian, H., & Wong, D. (2008). What is the nature of morality? A response to Casebeer, Railton and Ruse. In *Moral psychology (Vol. 1: The evolution of morality: adaptations and innateness)* (W. Sinnott-Armstrong, Ed.), 45–52. Cambridge, MA: MIT Press.

Frimer, J.A., & Walker, L.J. (2009). Reconciling the self and morality: An empirical model of moral centrality development. *Developmental Psychology 45* (6), 1669–1681.

Gardner, H., Csikszentmihalyi, M., & Damon, W. (2001). *Good work: When excellence and ethics meet*. New York: Basic Books.

Habermas, J. (1996). *Between facts and norms: Contributions to a discourse theory of law and democracy*. (Trans. W. Rehg). Cambridge, MA: MIT Press.

Hardy, S.A., & Carlo, G. (2005). Identity as a source of moral motivation. *Human Development 84* (4), 232–256.

Huff, C.W., Barnard, L., & Frey, W. (2008a). Good computing: A pedagogically focused model of virtue in the practice of computing (part 1). *Journal of Information, Communication and Ethics in Society 6* (3), 246–278.

Huff, C.W., Barnard, L., & Frey, W. (2008b). Good computing: A pedagogically focused model of virtue in the practice of computing (part 2). *Journal of Information, Communication and Ethics in Society* 6 (4), 284–316.

Hursthouse, R. (1995). Applying virtue ethics. In *Virtues and reasons: Philippa Foot and moral theory* (R. Hursthouse, G. Lawrence, & W. Quinn, Eds.), 57–75. Oxford: Clarendon Press.

Hursthouse, R. (1999). *On virtue ethics.* Oxford: Oxford University Press.

Hursthouse, R. (2012). Human nature and Aristotelian virtue ethics. *Royal Institute of Philosophy Supplement 70*, 169–188.

Klaidman, S., & Beauchamp, T.L. (1987). *The virtuous journalist.* New York: Oxford University Press.

Kohlberg, L. (1984). The psychology of moral development. New York: Harper & Row.

Lapsley, D.K. (2008). Moral self-identity as the aim of education. In *Handbook of moral and character education* (L.P. Nucci & D. Narvaez, Eds.), 30–52. New York: Routledge.

Little, B.R. (1983). Personal projects: A rationale and method for investigation. *Environment and Behavior 15*, 273–309.

MacIntyre, A. (1990). Moral dilemmas. *Philosophy and Phenomenological Research 50*, Suppl., 367–382.

Maslow, A. (1971). *The farther reaches of human nature.* New York: Viking Press.

McGregor, I., & Little, B.R. (1998). Personal projects, happiness, and meaning: On doing well and being yourself. *Journal of Personality and Social Psychology 74* (2), 494–512.

Nussbaum, M.C. (1995). Aristotle on human nature and the foundations of ethics. In *World, mind and ethics: Essays on the ethical philosophy of Bernard Williams* (J.E.J. Altham & R. Harrison, Eds.), 86–131. Cambridge: Cambridge University Press.

Osswald, S., Greitemeyer, T., Fischer, P., & Frey, D. (2010). Moral prototypes and moral behavior: Specific effects on emotional precursors of moral behavior and on moral behavior by the activation of moral prototypes. *European Journal of Social Psychology 40*, 1078–1094.

Pappas, G.F. (2008). *John Dewey's ethics: Democracy as experience.* Bloomington: Indiana University Press.

Plaisance, P.L. (2013). Virtue ethics and digital "flourishing": An application of Philippa Foot to life online. *Journal of Mass Media Ethics 28* (2), 91–102.

Putnam, H. (1981). *Reason, truth, and history.* New York: Cambridge University Press.

Quinn, A. (2007). Moral virtues for journalists. *Journal of Media Ethics 22* (2 & 3), 168–186.

Roberts, B.W., Walton, K., & Viechtbauer, W. (2006). Patterns of mean-level change in personality traits across the course of life: A meta-analysis of longitudinal studies. *Psychological Bulletin 132*, 1–25.

Schwartz, S.H. (1992). Universals in the content and structure of values: Theoretical advances and empirical tests in 20 countries. *Advances in Experimental Psychology 25*, 1–65.

Schwartz, S.H., & Bilsky, W. (1990). Toward a theory of the universal content and structure of values: Extensions and cross-cultural replications. *Journal of Personality and Social Psychology 58* (5), 878–891.

Schwartz, S.H., & Boehnke, K. (2004). Evaluating the structure of human values with confirmatory factor analysis. *Journal of Research in Personality 38*, 230–255.

Walker, L.J., & Hennig, K.H. (2004). Differing conceptions of moral exemplarity: Just, brave, and caring. *Journal of Personality and Social Psychology 86* (4), 629–647.

Wilkins, L., & Coleman, R. (2005). The moral media: How journalists reason about ethics. Mahwah, NJ: Lawrence Erlbaum Associates.

The Life Story Interview

INTRODUCTION

This is an interview about the *story of your life*. As a social scientist, I am interested in hearing your story, including parts of the past as you remember them and the future as you imagine it. The story is selective; it does not include everything that has ever happened to you. Instead, I will ask you to focus on a few key things in your life—a few key scenes, characters, and ideas. There are no right or wrong answers to my questions. Instead, your task is simply to tell me about some of the most important things that have happened in your life and how you imagine your life developing in the future. We will likely skip several of the questions listed, since they are not relevant to the focus of my research. I will try to keep the overall time as close to an hour as possible.

Please know that my purpose in doing this interview is not to figure out what is wrong with you or to do some kind of deep clinical analysis! Nor should you think of this interview as a "therapy session" of some kind. The interview is for research purposes only, and its main goal is simply to hear your story. As social scientists, my colleagues and I collect people's life stories in order to understand the different ways in which people in our society and in others live their lives and the different ways in which they understand who they are. Everything you say is voluntary, anonymous, and confidential.

I think you will enjoy the interview. Do you have any questions?

Adapted from: Dan P. McAdams, The Foley Center for the Study of Lives, Northwestern University. Revised February 2008.

A. LIFE CHAPTERS

Please begin by thinking about your life as if it were a book or novel. Imagine that the book has a table of contents containing the titles of the main chapters in the story. To begin here, please describe very briefly what the main chapters in the book might be. Please give each chapter a title, tell me just a little bit about what each chapter is about, and say a word or two about how we get from one chapter to the next. As a storyteller here, what you want to do is to give me an overall plot summary of your story, going chapter by chapter. You may have as many chapters as you want, but I would suggest having between about 2 and 7 of them. We will want to spend no more than about 20 minutes on this first section of the interview, so please keep your descriptions of the chapters relatively brief.

[*Note to interviewer: The interviewer should feel free to ask questions of clarification and elaboration throughout the interview, but especially in this first part. This first section of the interview should run between 15 and 30 minutes.*]

B. KEY SCENES IN THE LIFE STORY

Now that you have described the overall plot outline for your life, I would like you to focus in on a few key scenes that stand out in the story. A key scene would be an event or specific incident that took place at a particular time and place. Consider a key scene to be a moment in your life story that stands out for a particular reason—perhaps because it was especially good or bad, particularly vivid, important, or memorable. For each of the eight key events we will consider, I ask that you describe in detail what happened, when and where it happened, who was involved, and what you were thinking and feeling in the event. In addition, I ask that you tell me why you think this particular scene is *important* or significant in your life. What does the scene say about you as a person? Please be specific.

1 **High point.** Please describe a scene, episode, or moment in your life that stands out as an especially positive experience. This might be *the* high point scene of your entire life, or else an especially happy, joyous, exciting, or wonderful moment in the story. Please describe this high point scene in detail. What happened, when and where, who was involved, and what were you thinking and feeling? Also, please say a word or two about why you think this particular moment was so good and what the scene may say about who you are as a person.

2 **Low point.** The second scene is the opposite of the first. Thinking back over your entire life, please identify a scene that stands out as a low point, if not *the* low point in your life story.

Even though this event is unpleasant, I would appreciate your providing as much detail as you can about it. What happened in the event, where and when, who was involved, and what were you thinking and feeling? Also, please say a word or two about why you think this particular moment was so bad and what the scene may say about you or your life. [*Interviewer note: If the participants balks at doing this, tell him or her that the event does not really have to be the lowest point in the story but merely a very bad experience of some kind.*]

3 **Turning point.** In looking back over your life, it may be possible to identify certain key moments that stand out as turning points—episodes that marked an important change in you or your life story. Please identify a particular episode in your life story that you now see as a turning point in your life. If you cannot identify a key turning point that stands out clearly, please describe some event in your life wherein you went through an important change of some kind. Again, for this event please describe what happened, where and when, who was involved, and what you were thinking and feeling. Also, please say a word or two about what you think this event says about you as a person or about your life.

4 **Positive childhood memory.** The fourth scene is an early memory—from childhood or your teen-aged years—that stands out as especially *positive* in some way. This would be a very positive, happy memory from your early years. Please describe this good memory in detail. What happened, where and when, who was involved, and what were you thinking and feeling? Also, what does this memory say about you or about your life?

5 **Negative childhood memory.** The fifth scene is an early memory—from childhood or your teen-aged years—that stands out as especially *negative* in some way. This would be a very negative, unhappy memory from your early years, perhaps entailing sadness, fear, or some other very negative emotional experience. Please describe this bad memory in detail. What happened, where and when, who was involved, and what were you thinking and feeling? Also, what does this memory say about you or your life?

6 **Vivid adult memory.** Moving ahead to your adult years, please identify one scene that you have not already described in this section (in other words, do not repeat your high point, low point, or turning point scene) that stands out as especially vivid or meaningful. This would be an especially memorable, vivid, or important scene, positive or negative, from your adult years. Please describe this scene in detail, tell what happened, when and where, who was involved, and what you were thinking and feeling. Also, what does this memory say about you or your life?

7 **Wisdom event.** Please describe an event in your life in which you displayed *wisdom*. The episode might be one in which you acted or interacted in an especially wise way or provided wise counsel or advice, made a wise decision, or otherwise behaved in a particularly wise manner. What happened, where and when, who was involved, and what were you thinking and feeling? Also, what does this memory say about you and your life?

8 **Religious, spiritual, or mystical experience.** Whether they are religious or not, many people report that they have had experiences in their lives where they felt a sense of the transcendent or sacred, a sense of God or some almighty or ultimate force, or a feeling of oneness with nature, the world, or the universe. Thinking back on your entire life, please identify an episode or moment in which you felt something like this. This might be an experience that occurred within the context of your own religious tradition, if you have one, or it may be a spiritual or mystical experience of any kind. Please describe this transcendent experience in detail. What happened, where and when, who was involved, and what were you thinking and feeling? Also, what does this memory say about you or your life?

Now, we're going to talk about the future.

C. FUTURE SCRIPT

1 **The next chapter.** Your life story includes key chapters and scenes from your past, as you have described them, and it also includes how you see or imagine your future. Please describe what you see to be the next chapter in your life. What is going to come next in your life story?

2 **Dreams, hopes, and plans for the future.** Please describe your plans, dreams, or hopes for the future. What do you hope to accomplish in the future in your life story?

3 **Life project.** Do you have a project in life? A life project is something that you have been working on and plan to work on in the future chapters of your life story. The project might involve your family or your work life, or it might be a hobby, avocation, or pastime. Please describe any project that you are currently working on or plan to work on in the future. Tell me what the project is, how you got involved in the project or will get involved in the project, how the project might develop, and why you think this project is important for you and/or for other people.

D. CHALLENGES

This next section considers the various challenges, struggles, and problems you have encountered in your life. I will begin with a general challenge, and then I will focus in on three particular areas or issues where many people experience challenges, problems, or crises.

1. **Life challenge.** Looking back over your entire life, please identify and describe what you now consider to be the greatest single challenge you have faced in your life. What is or was the challenge or problem? How did the challenge or problem develop? How did you address or deal with this challenge or problem? What is the significance of this challenge or problem in your own life story?

2. **Health.** Looking back over your entire life, please identify and describe a scene or period in your life, including the present time, wherein you or a close family member confronted a major *health* problem, challenge, or crisis. Please describe in detail what the health problem is or was and how it developed. If relevant, please discuss any experience you had with the health-care system regarding this crisis or problem. In addition, please talk about how you coped with the problem and what impact this health crisis, problem, or challenge has had on you and your overall life story.

3. **Loss.** As people get older, they invariably suffer losses of one kind or another. By loss I am referring here to the loss of important people in your life, perhaps through death or separation. These are *interpersonal* losses—the loss of a person. Looking back over your entire life, please identify and describe the greatest interpersonal loss you have experienced. This could be a loss you experienced at any time in your life, going back to childhood and up to the present day. Please describe this loss and the process of the loss. How have you coped with the loss? What effect has this loss had on you and your life story?

4. **Failure, regret.** Everybody experiences failure and regrets in life, even for the happiest and luckiest lives. Looking back over your entire life, please identify and describe the greatest failure or regret you have experienced. The failure or regret can occur in any area of your life—work, family, friendships, or any other area. Please describe the failure or regret and the way in which the failure or regret came to be. How have you coped with this failure or regret? What effect has this failure or regret had on you and your life story?

E. PERSONAL IDEOLOGY

Now, I would like to ask a few questions about your fundamental beliefs and values and about questions of meaning and morality in your life. Please give some thought to each of these questions.

1 **Religious/ethical values.** Consider for a moment the religious or spiritual aspects of your life. Please describe in a nutshell your religious beliefs and values, if indeed these are important to you. Whether you are religious or not, please describe your overall ethical or moral approach to life.

2 **Political/social values.** How do you approach political or social issues? Do you have a particular political point of view? Are there particular social issues or causes about which you feel strongly? Please explain.

3 **Change, development of religious and political views.** Please tell the story of how your religious, moral, and/or political views and values have developed over time. Have they changed in any important ways? Please explain.

4 **Single value.** What is the most important value in human living? Please explain.

5 **Other.** What else can you tell me that would help me understand your most fundamental beliefs and values about life and the world? What else can you tell me that would help me understand your overall philosophy of life?

F. LIFE THEME

Looking back over your entire life story with all its chapters, scenes, and challenges, and extending back into the past and ahead into the future, do you discern a central theme, message, or idea that runs throughout the story? What is the major theme in your life story? Please explain.

G. REFLECTION

Thank you for this interview. I have just one more question for you. Many of the stories you have told me are about experiences that stand out from the day-to-day. For example, we talked about a high point, a turning point, a scene about your health, etc. Given that most people don't share their life stories in this way on a regular basis, I'm wondering if you might reflect for one last moment about what this interview, here today, has been like for you. What were your thoughts and feelings during the interview? How do you think this interview has affected you? Do you have any other comments about the interview process?

Moral Agency in Media: A Study of Professional Exemplars

Thank you for your willingness to participate in this research project. This survey aims to provide a fuller, more detailed picture of the range of factors that influence the abilities of media practitioners to excel in their work. I hope you find the exercise engaging and worthwhile. As a reminder, the project's intent is to examine patterns and relationships among various factors, and no names are attached to any data. All information is to be treated with strict confidentiality. This survey has five parts. I encourage you to fill out each at your leisure and to take your time. There are no hidden "right" answers to any of the questions; most of the items presented here are well-established and tested among social psychologists and have been used with people in other professions.

I'd like to start out by getting a little information about you.

How many years have you been a professional journalist? _____

How many news organizations have you worked for in your career? _____

How long have you worked for your current news organization? ____ years

Your current job title is:

_____ News anchor

_____ Reporter (please list your primary beat and years on that beat)

_____

_____ Copy editor/slot editor/assignment editor

_____ Graphic artist

_____ Photographer/videographer

_____ Section editor (please list your section, i.e., metro, sports, etc.)

_____

_____ Producer

_____ National/wire editor

_____ News director
_____ Night editor/copy desk chief
_____ Managing editor/program director
_____ Executive editor
_____ Other (please specify): _____
What is the title of your immediate supervisor? _____
How many years have you been in your current position? _____

PART ONE: PERSONAL TRAITS

Here are a number of characteristics that may or may not apply to you. For example, do you agree that you are someone who likes to spend time with others? Using the scale below, please write a number next to each statement to indicate the extent to which you agree or disagree with that statement.

1	2	3	4	5
Disagree strongly	Disagree a little	Neither agree nor disagree	Agree a little	Agree strongly

I see myself as someone who . . .

_____ 1. Is talkative
_____ 2. Tends to find fault with others
_____ 3. Does a thorough job
_____ 4. Is depressed and blue
_____ 5. Is original, comes up with new ideas
_____ 6. Is reserved
_____ 7. Is helpful and unselfish with others
_____ 8. Can be somewhat careless
_____ 9. Is relaxed, handles stress well
_____ 10. Is curious about many different things
_____ 11. Is full of energy
_____ 12. Starts quarrels with others
_____ 13. Is a reliable worker
_____ 14. Can be tense

_____ 15. Is ingenious, a deep thinker
_____ 16. Generates a lot of enthusiasm
_____ 17. Has a forgiving nature
_____ 18. Tends to be disorganized
_____ 19. Worries a lot
_____ 20. Has an active imagination
_____ 21. Tends to be quiet
_____ 22. Is generally trusting
_____ 23. Tends to be lazy
_____ 24. Is emotionally stable, not easily upset
_____ 25. Is inventive
_____ 26. Has an assertive personality
_____ 27. Can be cold and aloof
_____ 28. Perseveres until the task is finished
_____ 29. Can be moody

_____ 30. Values artistic, aesthetic experiences

_____ 31. Is sometimes shy and inhibited

_____ 32. Is considerate and kind to almost everyone

_____ 33. Does things efficiently

_____ 34. Remains calm in tense situations

_____ 35. Prefers work that is routine

_____ 36. Is outgoing, sociable

_____ 37. Is sometimes rude to others

_____ 38. Makes plans and follows through with them

_____ 39. Gets nervous easily

_____ 40. Likes to reflect, play with ideas

_____ 41. Has few artistic interests

_____ 42. Likes to cooperate with others

_____ 43. Is easily distracted

_____ 44. Is sophisticated in art, music, or literature

PART TWO: WORKPLACE CLIMATE

The following statements explore your perceptions of the organization for which you work. Please respond to them in terms of how it really is in your organization, not how you would prefer it to be. Indicate whether you agree with the statements by using the scale below.

To what extent are the following statements true about your organization?

Completely false	Mostly false	Somewhat false	Somewhat true	Mostly true	Completely true
0	1	2	3	4	5

_____ 1. In this organization, people are mostly out for themselves.

_____ 2. The major responsibility for people in this organization is to consider efficiency first.

_____ 3. In this organization, people are expected to follow their own personal and moral beliefs.

_____ 4. People are expected to do anything to further the organization's interests.

_____ 5. In this organization, people look out for each other's good.

_____ 6. There is no room for one's own personal morals or ethics in this organization.

_____ 7. It is very important to follow strictly the organization's rules and procedures here.

_____ 8. Work is considered sub-standard only when it hurts the organization's interests.

_____ 9. Each person in this organization decides for himself what is right and wrong.

_____ 10. In this organization, people protect their own interest above other considerations.

_____ 11. The most important consideration in this organization is each person's sense of right and wrong.

_____ 12. The most important concern is the good of all the people in the organization.

_____ 13. The first consideration is whether a decision violates any law.

_____ 14. People are expected to comply with the law and professional standards over and above other considerations.

_____ 15. Everyone is expected to stick by company rules and procedures.

_____ 16. In this organization, our major concern is always what is best for the other person.

_____ 17. People are concerned with the organization's interests—to the exclusion of all else.

_____ 18. Successful people in this organization go by the book.

_____ 19. The most efficient way is always the right way in this organization.

_____ 20. In this organization, people are expected to strictly follow legal or professional standards.

_____ 21. Our major consideration is what is best for everyone in the organization.

_____ 22. In this organization, people are guided by their own personal ethics.

_____ 23. Successful people in this organization strictly obey company policies.

_____ 24. In this organization, the law or ethical code of their profession is the major consideration.

_____ 25. In this organization, each person is expected, above all, to work efficiently.

_____ 26. It is expected that you will always do what is right for the customer and public.

_____ 27. People in this organization view team spirit as important.

_____ 28. People in this organization have a strong sense of responsibility to the outside community.

_____ 29. Decisions here are primarily views in terms of contribution to profit.

_____ 30. People in this organization are actively concerned about the customers', and the public's, interest.

_____ 31. People are very concerned about what is generally best for employees in the organization.

_____ 32. What is best for each individual is a primary concern in this organization.

_____ 33. People in this organization are very concerned about what is best for themselves.

_____ 34. The effect of decisions on the customer and the public are a primary concern in this organization.

_____ 35. It is expected that each individual is cared for when making decisions here.

_____ 36. Efficient solutions to problems are always sought here.

PART THREE: ETHICAL IDEOLOGIES

For the following, please read each statement carefully. Then indicate the extent to which you agree or disagree with the statement by placing in front of the statement the number corresponding to your feelings, where:

1 = Completely disagree	4 = Slightly disagree	7 = Moderately agree
2 = Largely disagree	5 = Neither agree nor disagree	8 = Largely agree
3 = Moderately disagree	6 = Slightly agree	9 = Completely agree

_____ 1. A person should make certain that their actions never intentionally harm another even to a small degree.

_____ 2. Risks to another should never be tolerated, irrespective of how small the risks might be.

_____ 3. The existence of potential harm to others is always wrong, irrespective of the benefits to be gained.

_____ 4. One should never psychologically or physically harm another person.

_____ 5. One should not perform an action which might in any way threaten the dignity and welfare of another individual.

_____ 6. If an action could harm an innocent other, then it should not be done.

_____ 7. Deciding whether or not to perform an act by balancing the positive consequences of the act against the negative consequences of the act is immoral.

_____ 8. The dignity and welfare of people should be the most important concern in any society.

_____ 9. It is never necessary to sacrifice the welfare of others.

_____ 10. Moral actions are those which closely match ideals of the most "perfect" action.

_____ 11. There are no ethical principles that are so important that they should be a part of any code of ethics.

_____ 12. What is ethical varies from one situation and society to another.

_____ 13. Moral standards should be seen as being individualistic; what one person considers to be moral may be judged to be immoral by another person.

_____ 14. Different types of moralities cannot be compared as to "rightness."

_____ 15. Questions of what is ethical for everyone can never be resolved since what is moral or immoral is up to the individual.

_____ 16. Moral standards are simply *personal* rules which indicate how a person should behave, and are not to be applied in making judgments of others.

_____ 17. Ethical considerations in interpersonal relations are so complex that individuals should be allowed to formulate their own individual codes.

_____ 18. Rigidly codifying an ethical position that prevents certain types of actions could stand in the way of better human relations and adjustment.

_____ 19. No rule concerning lying can be formulated; whether a lie is permissible or not permissible totally depends on the situation.

_____ 20. Whether a lie is judged to be moral or immoral depends upon circumstances surrounding the action.

PART FOUR: DEFINING ISSUES TEST

[Redacted for proprietary purposes]

PART FIVE: DEMOGRAPHIC DATA

Finally, we have a few more questions about you and your background. These items will be combined anonymously with the responses from other participants and will be used to see if there are patterns that relate to professional training, roles, experience or other demographic factors.

How old were you on your last birthday? _____
What is your highest level of formal completed education?

_____ High school/GED
_____ College courses, no degree
_____ Associate degree
_____ Bachelor's degree
_____ Master's degree
_____ Ph.D./J.D./M.D.

Do you have a degree in journalism or mass communication?
_____ Yes _____ No

If you do not have a journalism or mass communication degree, have you taken any college-level journalism courses? _____ Yes _____ No

Did you take a course that focused on media ethics as part of your college education? _____ Yes _____ No

Have you attended any professional workshops or training sessions in journalism? _____ Yes _____ No

How long have you lived in your current community? _____

Gender: _____ Male _____ Female

Income:

_____ Less than $20,000
_____ $20,001 to $35,000
_____ $35,001 to $50,000
_____ $50,001 to $65,000
_____ $65,001 to $80,000
_____ $80,001 to $95,000
_____ $95,001 to $110,000
_____ $110,001 or more
_____ Prefer not to answer

Racial/ethnic heritage:

_____ White, not of Hispanic/Latino origin
_____ Asian or Pacific Islander
_____ Black, not of Hispanic/Latino origin
_____ Biracial/multiracial
_____ Hispanic/Latino
_____ Other (please specify): _____
_____ Prefer not to answer

In terms of my stance on social issues, I consider myself to be (circle one):

| Conservative | | | | | | | Liberal | |
| 1 | 2 | 3 | 4 | 5 | 6 | 7 | 8 | 9 |

In terms of my stance on fiscal issues, I consider myself to be (circle one):

| Conservative | | | | | | | Liberal | |
| 1 | 2 | 3 | 4 | 5 | 6 | 7 | 8 | 9 |

In terms of my stance on foreign policy, I consider myself to be (circle one):

| Conservative | | | | | | | Liberal | |
| 1 | 2 | 3 | 4 | 5 | 6 | 7 | 8 | 9 |

Overall, I consider my political orientation to be (circle one):

Conservative   Liberal

1   2   3   4   5   6   7   8   9

Thank you for taking your time to complete this survey. If you would like a summary of the results when the study is completed, please provide your e-mail address. Your e-mail address and all of the other information in this survey will be kept in strict confidence as required by the Human Subjects Committee of Colorado State University. If you have any questions about this survey, please feel free to contact me at patrick.plaisance@colostate.edu or (970) 491-6484.

Your e-mail address where we could send a summary of results:

_____

INDEX

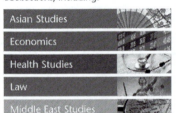

Made in the USA
Lexington, KY
05 May 2016